Technology, Tradition and Survival

In memory of Donald Hill

Technology Tradition and Survival

Aspects of Material Culture in the Middle East and Central Asia

Editors

RICHARD TAPPER
KEITH MCLACHLAN

Published with the assistance of the Islamic Educational, Scientific
and Cultural Organization (ISESCO), the British Institute for
Persian Studies (BIPS) and the Centre of Near and
Middle Eastern Studies (CNMES) at SOAS

LONDON AND NEW YORK

First published 2003 by Routledge

2 Park Square, Milton Park, Abingdon, Oxfordsire OX14 4RN
52 Vanderbilt Avenue, New York, NY 10017
Routledge is an imprint of the Taylor & Francis Group, an informa business

First issued in paperback 2018

Transferred to Digital Printing 2008

British Library Cataloguing in Publication Data

Technology, tradition and survival: aspects of material culture in the Middle East
and Central asia.—(History and society in the Islamic world)
1. Material culture—Middle East 2. Material culture—Asia, Central 3.
Technology—Middle East 4. Technology—Asia, Central 5. Middle East—
Social life and customs 6. Asia, Central—Social life and customs
I. tapper, Richard II. McLachlan, K.S. (Keith Stanley), 1937—
303.4'83'0956

ISBN 978-0-7146-4927-6 (hbk)
ISBN 978-0-7146-4487-5 (pbk)

Library of Congress Cataloging-in-Publication Data

Technology, tradition and survival: aspects of material culture in the Middle East
and central Asia/editors—Richard Tapper, Keith McLachlan.
p. cm.—(Cass series—history and society in the Islamic world, ISSN 1466– 9390)
Includes bibliographical references and index.
ISBN 0-7146-4927-9 (Print Edition) (cloth)—ISBN 0-7146-4487-0 (pbk.)
1. Civilization, Islamic—congrsses. 2. Civilization, Western—Islamic
influences—Congresses. 3. Islam and science—Congresses. 4. Islamic
countries—Social life and customs—Congresses. I. Tapper, Richard. II.
McLachlan, K.S. (Keith Stanley) III. Series.
DS36. T433 2003
303.48'3'0917671–dc21
2003048999

Contents

Figures

Plates

Contributors

Mahmoud Abdullahzadeh is Director of the Department of International Studies and Culture at the Cultural Research Bureau, Iran, and Editor of the Iranian *Journal of Political Economy*. He teaches politics and has published in both Persian and English.

Peter Andrews, a qualified architect, is a research fellow at the University of Bamberg. Since 1966 he has, with the help of his wife Mügül, done extensive fieldwork on the material culture of nomads in Morocco, Turkey, Iran, Qatar and Mongolia, besides having worked in India and Pakistan. His publications include the two-volume monograph *Felt Tents and Pavilions: The Nomadic Tradition and its Interaction with Princely Tentage* (1999) and the edited books *Nomad Tent Types of the Middle East* (4 volumes, 1997 continuing), and *Ethnic Groups in the Republic of Turkey* (2nd edn 2002), and he is at present completing a monograph on the Central Asian tents of the twentieth century.

Elisabeth Beazley is a retired architect. She worked for several seasons in Iran on digs run by Professor David Stronach for the British Institute of Persian Studies, and became increasingly interested in the mud-brick vernacular buildings on the Plateau, many of which she surveyed. This led to the joint publication with Michael Harverson of *Living with the Desert: Working Buildings of the Iranian Plateau* (1982). Other books include *Design and Detail of the Space between Buildings* (1960); *Designed to Live In* (1962); *Madocks and the Wonder of Wales* (1967); *Designed for Recreation* (1969); *The Shell Guide to North Wales* (with Lionel Brett, 1971); and the *Companion Guides to North and South Wales* (with Peter Howell, 1975 and 1977).

Roderic Dutton is Director of the Centre for Overseas Research and Development at the University of Durham. He has directed and co-directed long-term series of rural research and action research projects in Oman and Jordan in addition to working/research years spent in Libya and Tunisia. His publications include the monograph *Changing Rural Systems in Oman: The Khabura Project* (1999) and the edited (and co-edited) volumes *The Scientific Results of the Royal Geographical Society's Oman Wahiba Sands Project 1985–1987* (1988), *Prosopis spp.: Aspects of their Value, Research and Development* (1993), *Arid Land Resources and their Management: Jordan's Desert Margin* (1999), and *Population Dynamics, Socioeconomic Change and Land Colonization in Northern Jordan, with special reference to the Badia Programme Research and Development Project area* (1999).

Rifaat Ebied is Foundation Professor of Semitic Studies in the University of Sydney, Australia, and a Fellow of the Australian Academy of the Humanities. He has published extensively in the field of Semitic Studies in general and Arabic, Islamic and Syriac Studies in particular. His publications include numerous books and articles of edited Arabic and Syriac medieval texts as well as various entries in the new edition of *The Encyclopaedia of Islam*.

Klaus Ferdinand is Professor Emeritus and former head of Department of Ethnography and Social Anthropology, Aarhus University, and the Ethnographical Collections at the Moesgård Museum, Denmark. Since the early 1950s he has done fieldwork in Afghanistan, Qatar and Iran, working on nomadic cultures, especially Pashtuns, and among the Hazaras in Afghanistan, and making extensive collections for Danish Ethnographic Museums. In 1985–87 he was ethnographic consultant to the new Bahrain National Museum. He has promoted or initiated research projects on Contemporary Islam and on Islam in Denmark, as well as the Carlsberg Foundation's Nomad Research Project. He has published extensively on material culture (tents, windmills and watermills, etc.), on Afghanistan and on the museumization of the Bedouin; his books include the monograph *The Bedouins of Qatar* (1993), and the edited *Contributions to Islamic Studies: Iran, Afghanistan and Pakistan* (1987 with Christel Braae) and *Islam: State and Society* (1988 with Mehdi Mozaffari).

Michael Harverson is a retired schoolteacher, whose career started at Isfahan in Iran. He is President and Editor of the International Molinological Society. He has engaged in fieldwork on traditional windmills and watermills in Iran, Afghanistan and Morocco, and co-authored, with Elisabeth Beazley, *Living with the Desert: Working Buildings of the Iranian Plateau* (1982). He has published reports on the watermills of Iran (1993) and on those of the Atlas Mountains (1995), also *Mills of the Muslim World* (2000). He has contributed to *Encyclopaedia Iranica* and *The Encydopedia of Vernacular Architecture of the World* (1997).

Donald Hill (1922–94) was the leading historian of medieval Arab technology. Originally an engineer by training and profession, he worked over many years in various Arab countries. He acquired a PhD in Arabic history, and translated a number of important Arab treatises on technological matters, as well as *The Termination of Hostilities in the Early Arab Conquests, A.D. 634–656* (1971), *Islamic Technology: An Illustrated History* (1986), *Islamic Science and Engineering* (1993), *A History of Engineering in Classical and Mediaeval Times* (1984) and the posthumous collection by David A. King, *Studies in Medieval Islamic Technology* (1998).

Ghada Karmi is an expert on medieval Arabic/Islamic medicine, in which she holds a doctorate from London University. She practised as a physician in Britain for many years. She has taught the history of Arabic medicine and science at two Middle Eastern Universities in Syria and Jordan and was for six years a Wellcome Research Fellow at the Wellcome Institute for the History of Medicine in London. Her publications include an edition of Al-Qamari's *Kitab al-Tanwir: An Early Arabic Dictionary* (1991) and many articles on Arabic medicine.

J.Derek Latham is Professor Emeritus of Arabic and Islamic Studies, Edinburgh University, and Honorary Research Fellow in Middle Eastern Studies, Manchester University. He has served both on the British Academy's Mediaeval Latin Dictionary Committee and on its Fontes Historiae Africanae Committee (Chairman, 1971–79); has been co-editor of, and contributed to, *The Cambridge History of Arabic Literature* (1983–90); has, since 1957 contributed to *Encyclopaedia of Islam* (articles mainly relating to Muslim Spain, the Maghrib and Islamic law); and has, since 1984, been etymological consultant (Arabic, etc.) to the Oxford English Dictionaries. Founder member of the British Society for Middle Eastern Studies (President, 1985–87), he edited and contributed to its *Bulletin* (now *Journal*) from 1974 to 1989. His publications include *From Muslim Spain to Barbary: Studies in the History of the Muslim West* (1986).

Keith McLachlan is Emeritus Professor of London University and taught at the School of Oriental and African Studies. Among his principal research interests are agriculture and rural change in traditional societies with particular reference to the Middle East, where he has been engaged in research for over 45 years. His publications include *The Neglected Garden: The Politics and Ecology of Agriculture in Iran* (1988) and *Kuwait: Society of the Affluent Elite— Reality and Illusion* (2000) (in Arabic with A.A.al-Moosa).

Susan Roaf is Professor of Architecture and Co-director of the Oxford Centre for Sustainable Development at Oxford Brookes University. During ten years in Iran and Iraq she studied aspects of traditional technologies, including nomadic tents, windcatchers, ice-houses, landscape and water wheels. She has taught in Baghdad and Naples Universities; in Oxford, since 1990, she has developed the MSc in Energy Efficient Building. In 1995 she built her own Ecohouse in Oxford, with the first UK photovoltaic roof. Her research interests include building sustainability, ecotourism, water conservation, climate change, ventilation and passive buildings. Her numerous publications include *The Ecohouse Design Guide* (2001).

Richard Tapper is Professor of Anthropology in the University of London and teaches at the School of Oriental and African Studies. He has done extensive field research in Iran, Afghanistan and Turkey. His publications include the monographs *Pasture and Politics: Economics, Conflict and Ritual among Shahsevan Nomads of Northwestern Iran* (1979), *Frontier Nomads of Iran: A Political and Social History of the Shahsevan* (1997), and edited books on *Islam in Modern Turkey* (1991), *Culinary Cultures of the Middle East* (1994 with Sami Zubaida), *The New Iranian Cinema* (2002) and *The Nomadic Peoples of Iran* (2002 with Jon Thompson).

Jon Thompson is Director of the Beattie Carpet Archive in the Department of Eastern Art at the Ashmolean Museum, Oxford. He is involved in research and teaching in the field of carpets and textiles and has a special interest in the development of weaving technology. His publications include *Carpets: From the Tents, Cottages and Workshops of Asia* (1983 and 1988), *Silk, Carpets and the Silk Road* (1988) and *The Nomadic Peoples of Iran*, edited with Richard Tapper (2002).

Preface

The present volume arises from the papers given and discussions held during two international conferences on 'Material Cultures of the Middle East and Central Asia', held at the School of Oriental and African Studies (SOAS), London University, in the mid-1990s. The conferences were sponsored by The Islamic Educational, Scientific and Cultural Organization (ISESCO), Rabat, Morocco, and the Centre of Near and Middle Eastern Studies (CNMES) at SOAS.

The two conferences were designed to underline the skills in material culture in the Islamic Middle East and Central Asia with special reference to the innovation and diffusion of technology in energy, architecture, navigation and hydrology. Nomadic pastoralist, cultivator and urban systems were also reviewed. Overall, the meetings gave a new assessment of the roles of the Arabic, Persian and Turkic linguistic/cultural areas together with the Central Asian, Afghan and Caucasian regions as centres for innovation and diffusion of technologies in the Islamic period.

Studies of the material culture of these peoples augmented parallel debates in SOAS on culinary practices and the meanings of dress in society, the former published as Sami Zubaida and Richard Tapper (eds), *Culinary Cultures of the Middle East* (London: I.B. Tauris, 1994) and the latter as Nancy Lindisfarne and Bruce Ingham (eds), *Languages of Dress in the Middle East* (London: Curzon, 1997).

Transliteration into English has been standardized to a consistent system wherever possible, but the preferences of individual authors have been accepted in a number of cases of regional place and personal names.

The editors of this volume have a long list of debts to more colleagues and friends than can be catalogued here, for their assistance over the four years of the study. Particular thanks are due to His Excellency Dr Abdelaziz Othman Al-Twijerie and Dr Mohamed Chtatou of ISESCO for their generous financial sponsorship and moral support for this venture. George Joffé acted as an invaluable intermediary in communications with ISESCO. Lynne Townley and Diana Gur of CNMES gave unstinting administrative and secretarial backing. Our principal acknowledgement is, however, to the authors of the papers that make up this book, who have been patient and constructive in assisting the editors to complete their work. The editing was substantially completed in 1999, after which the production of the book was delayed by unforeseen circumstances.

Acknowledgements

Chapter 5. Illustrations taken from Donald Hill, *Islamic Science and Engineering* (Edinburgh: Edinburgh University Press, 1993).

Chapter 6. Figure 6.1 from Klaus Ferdinand, 'The Horizontal Windmills of Western Afghanistan', *Folk* 5, 1963, p. 77, drawn by Jens Aarup Jensen and reproduced with the permission of the author. Plate 4 by Richard Hewer.

Chapter 7. All illustrations taken from Elisabeth Beazley, 'The Pigeon Towers of Isfahan', *Iran* IV, 1966 and 'Some Vernacular Buildings of the Iranian Plateau', *Iran* XV, 1977 apart from Plate 19 taken from Elisabeth Beazley and Michael Harverson (eds), *Living With the Desert* (Warmister: Aris & Phillips Ltd, 1982).

Chapter 8. All illustrations from Aydin Germen (ed.), *Islamic Architecture and Planning, A Symposium Organised by the College of Architecture and Planning* (Dammam, Saudi Arabia: King Faisal University, 1983).

Chapter 9. Plates 25 and 26 reproduced with the permission of the Lattimore Institute, Brown University and the Verbieststicting, University of Leuven respectively.

Chapter 10. All illustrations reproduced with the permission of the Ethnographic Department, Moesgaard Museum, Denmark.

Chapter 11. Plate 38 reproduced with the permission of Patty-Jo Watson and Plates 47 and 48 reproduced with the permission of Cary Wolinsky, Stock Boston.

The Publisher has attempted to contact all appropriate copyright holders in respect of material used in this book. In certain cases this has not been possible and the Publisher apologises to any such copyright holders for this omission.

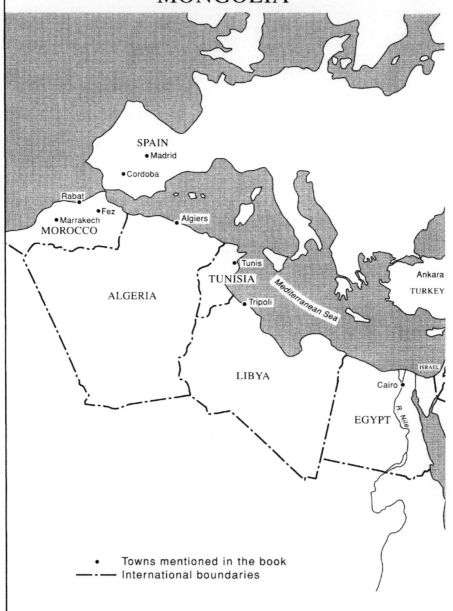

NORTH AFRICA, THE MIDDLE EAST AND CENTRAL ASIA with inset of MONGOLIA

SPAIN
• Madrid

• Cordoba

Rabat
•Fez

• Marrakech

MOROCCO

Algiers

ALGERIA

Tunis

TUNISIA

Tripoli

Mediterranean Sea

Ankara

TURKEY

ISRAEL

Cairo •

LIBYA

EGYPT

R. Nile

• Towns mentioned in the book
—·— International boundaries

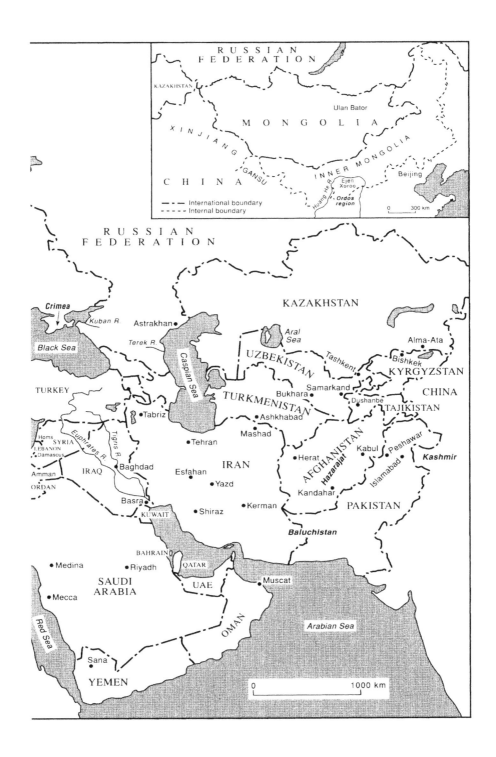

Inset map (top):

RUSSIAN FEDERATION

KAZAKHSTAN

Ulan Bator

XINJIANG

MONGOLIA

INNER MONGOLIA

GANSU

CHINA

Huang He R.

Ejen Xoroo

Ordos region

Beijing

—·—·— International boundary
········· Internal boundary

0   300 km

Main map:

RUSSIAN FEDERATION

KAZAKHSTAN

Crimea

Kuban R.

Astrakhan

Aral Sea

Terek R.

Alma-Ata

Black Sea

Caspian Sea

UZBEKISTAN

Tashkent

Bishkek

KYRGYZSTAN

TURKMENISTAN

Bukhara

Samarkand

Dushanbe

CHINA

TURKEY

Ashkhabad

TAJIKISTAN

Tabriz

Mashad

AFGHANISTAN

Homs

SYRIA

Euphrates R.

Tigris R.

Tehran

Herat

Hazarajat

Kabul

Peshawar

LEBANON

Damascus

IRAN

Kashmir

Baghdad

Esfahan

Islamabad

Amman

IRAQ

Yazd

Kandahar

ORDAN

Basra

Kerman

PAKISTAN

KUWAIT

Shiraz

Baluchistan

BAHRAIN

Medina

Riyadh

QATAR

SAUDI ARABIA

UAE

Muscat

Mecca

Red Sea

OMAN

Arabian Sea

Sana

YEMEN

0   1000 km

Introduction

Keith McLachlan and Richard Tapper

As we leave a century in which, it can be said, technology has advanced further and faster than in the whole of previous human history, and as we enter a new millennium in which these very technological advances bring the possibility of global ecological disasters and irreversible decline, there is much to reflect on, if we stop and take the time to do so. Not least, as the world inevitably moves in technological directions pioneered, and still largely steered, by the industrialized Western countries, it is time to reflect on alternative technologies that have existed in the past and sometimes, however precariously, survive. It is too easy to assume that preindustrial technologies have no place in an industrializing world, and to ignore not only the centuries over which they have often evolved and adapted to local conditions but the central role they have commonly played in the history of Western technology.

In the Middle East and Central Asia, as elsewhere in the world, political rhetoric increasingly speaks the easy language of ideological polarization: between East and West, left and right, religion and secularism... It is sad, but perhaps inevitable, that these polarizations tend to affect aspects of material culture and technology which have no inherent connection with ideology. The modern, the new, and the Western— apparent synonyms—beckon the rest of the world as desirable values, while valid and sustainable local techniques and products, simply because they are traditional, become tainted and rejected by former users, and despised or ignored by the West itself.[1]

Despite recent pioneering work by scholars such as the late Donald Hill (dedicatee of this volume) few in the industrialized West are aware of the traditional technologies of the Middle East and Central Asia. There is still little appreciation, for example, of the sophisticated science achieved in the centres of Islamic civilization over the centuries since the death of the Prophet Muhammad. There is a real danger, as erratic twentieth-century processes of modernization threaten to sweep away all vestiges of traditional culture, including physical remains and folk memories, that valuable and sustainable skills and technologies are being rapidly and wastefully discarded for short-term commercial purposes.

This book seeks to promote a wider knowledge of these technologies and material cultures. Each contributor addresses one or more of three related themes. First, many of them celebrate the history, originality, variety and sophistication of traditional science, technology and material culture in these regions. Second, Ebied, Latham and Hill also point to the influence of Islamic and Middle Eastern science and technology on the history of Europe and West. Third, Harverson, Beazley, Roaf, McLachlan and Dutton stress the threat posed by modern Western technologies to the survival of traditional technologies which have continuing value according to twenty-first-century standards of sustainability and appropriateness to local cultural, social and ecological conditions, and argue that there is a clear need for conservation of some artefacts that are under current threat of extinction. In addition, individual chapters focus on a range of specific aspects of technology and material culture: Ebied, Latham and Karmi on science and medicine; Hill, Dutton and Harverson on water technologies; Roaf, Beazley and Harverson on fixed forms of vernacular architecture; and Andrews and Ferdinand on the mobile tents of the nomads; Thompson on looms and weaving; McLachlan and Abdullahzadeh on bazaars.

The study of material culture and traditional technologies

Let us review, briefly, both what we understand by 'material culture', and the chequered history of the academic study of this subject.

Broadly, we consider two different kinds of material culture: on the one hand, the *technology* (including tools, skills and associated knowledge and traditions) involved in the process of *production* of material goods; and, on the other, the *products* themselves as commodities or valuables, both in *consumption* and use (tradition, purpose, meaning, value), and (where appropriate) in *circulation* (distribution, exchange, marketing); noting that such products—and technologies—may consist of fixed infrastructures and buildings, which cannot be circulated physically, although possession of them may well change as a result of purchase or the use of force.

Such material culture is the prime focus of study for both archaeology and museum studies. For the former, the material record constitutes the main form of evidence available for reconstructing the societies and the (non-material) cultures of the past. Material objects also fill the museums of the world, and it is the business of museum studies to classify and display them according to accepted categories and criteria of provenance, cultural areas and complexes, as well as of use, meaning and value. Reconstructions and categories, however, depend on—and also influence—current social theories as to how human societies work, and how and why they differ. Social theory is the concern of anthropologists, sociologists and historians, working with other kinds of methods and materials: contemporary ethnographic fieldwork, and written documents. That said, many specialists in material culture are less interested in the social aspects of objects they study than in what they consider to be either their function or their aesthetic value, or in objects as evidence for some historical scheme of provenance.

For many anthropologists, it is a commonplace that the study of material culture has only recently re-emerged as theoretically interesting. Students are taught that, around the turn of the last century, there were two dominant and competing theories of the distribution of world cultures. On the one hand, the Diffusionists studied how techniques, objects and ideas spread from some original source of invention (the 'horizontal' view); on the other, the Evolutionists proposed schemes of stages in human (pre-)history (the 'vertical' view), from the simple (=early) to the complex (=late, modern). Both 'schools' encompassed various forms and elaborations, but most focused on the evidence of material culture and technology, with the common (but not universally accepted) assumption that material and technological changes were the basis for changes in society (social relations, beliefs and customs, and so on).[2]

The usual story is that these rival schools both failed when their assumption that society was determined by productive technology was discredited by the so-called 'revolution' in empirical, language-based ethnography and the accompanying Functionalist and Structuralist coup, led in Britain during the 1920s to 1940s by Bronislaw Malinowski and A.R.Radcliffe-Brown. A new orthodoxy was propounded, that a material object on its own is no reliable indication of the culture (thoughts, beliefs and social organization) of its producers and consumers; that, since the cultures of pre-historical peoples cannot be known, it is fruitless to speculate about them; that effort should concentrate on discovering how present-day, observable societies work, and developing theories of culture or social structure that explain this functioning. For these so-called 'structural-functionalists', technology and material culture were only interesting as contexts of social relations or as channels or media of exchange. The collection, description, cataloguing and inventory of material culture might be exact and scholarly, but structural-functionalists considered them to be antiquarian pursuits, best left to the backwaters of museum studies and archaeology. For a time, museum studies of material culture did indeed stagnate theoretically, at least in Britain, though archaeology developed in new directions, particularly towards the sciences, with rapidly improving techniques for dating and analysing materials.

Some have questioned whether this account of the changing relationship between anthropology and the study of material culture is accurate, and have produced abundant evidence to show that the latter has always seemed out of fashion and is regularly being 'revived'.[3] In any case, in the 1960s and 1970s, as anthropologists became increasingly dissatisfied with structural-functionalism, a serious rapprochement with studies of material culture began. A variety of new fashions in anthropological theory, many of them inspired by the 'structuralism' of Lévi-Strauss, competed for attention. Prominent for a while, particularly in the 1970s, was a renewed materialist evolutionism in the form of neo-Marxism, though a focus on techniques and material factors in production, and in technology-driven change, was rather late to follow the interest in relations, forces and modes of production.[4]

Developments in other quarters brought a new focus of interest on historical and comparative studies of consumption, much of it inspired by Mauss's classic study of *The Gift,* and Braudel's histories of social life.[5] Aspects of consumption—exchange, value, symbolism: things as sign-bearers, hence as keys to 'culture'— became central issues for structuralist semiotics, the sociology of art and taste, studies of folklore and popular culture, and the new fields of cultural and media studies, while there were simultaneous advances in cognitive studies of the processes of representation and objectification. There were renewed calls for multi-disciplinary approaches to material culture in archaeology, geography and history.[6]

At the same time, a new respect developed for indigenous technologies such as vernacular architecture. With the repeated failure of post-war programmes of 'modernization' and development based on Euro-American theories and technologies, and the growth in popularity of ecologically aware Green political movements, in the 1970s there was increased (but still minority) pressure for the preservation, encouragement and development of 'intermediate', 'alternative', and 'appropriate' technologies, particularly for poorer developing countries. As Western technology and expertise lost their mystique, so Western academics began to lose their privileged position as expert knowers and interpreters of the meaning of things produced by others.

By the 1980s, there was renewed interest in things for themselves (not just as signs or symbols of something else), and studies of goods, commodities and consumption proliferated.[7] Material culture has been at the centre of theories addressing the processes of 'globalization' that characterized the world as the century neared its end and that have been linked with unprecedented 'deterritorialization' (transnational migration for work and pleasure) and the communications revolution, by which not only things but images of things are now available, virtually if not in reality, almost universally and almost instantaneously. There has been an explosion of intellectual activity (in print, in conferences, in electronic media) in anthropology, cultural studies and media studies, devoted to analysing material culture in the context of globalization.[8]

Technological change in the Middle East and Central Asia

For several decades, and notably since the oil boom of the early 1970s, the Middle East has been among the areas of the world most affected by processes of deterritorialization and globalization. The oil-rich countries in particular have rapidly cast aside traditional technologies and adopted new ones, sometimes without any consideration of long-term sustainability or aesthetics or of the social and cultural implications for either traditional producers or local consumers.

Western media accounts of this change often focus on visually striking images of advanced technology in age-old contexts: Cadillacs or Toyotas in the desert, the Bedouin with a hawk on one hand and a satellite telephone in the other, the Mojahed with his rocket launcher. Such images—whatever other misleading stereotypes they perpetuate—disguise the dilemmas that usually accompany technological change. Is mechanization necessarily improvement? Can traditional techniques not be adapted with the aid of contemporary skills, rather than being abandoned wholesale? Should 'obsolete' traditional material culture be preserved, and if so, in what form? If there is a choice between traditional and modern technologies, whose interests have priority: the national, the local, the consumer, the producer?

Some of these dilemmas can be illustrated by examining two cases of technological change, not discussed in detail elsewhere in this book: one is the *qanat* irrigation system, an example of an indigenous infrastructural technology; the other is felt-making, a craft practised with a variety of traditional tools, skills and processes.

The case of the *qanat*

Adaptation of new technologies to old is often possible and desirable for a variety of reasons. But in some cases, the old technology itself proves superior, from many points of view, to the new. There is a risk that the thrusting of rapid technological change on developing societies by the industrialized nations will lead to premature obsolescence and discarding of indigenous technologies which could still, both now and in the future, be deployed with advantage. The modernization of the Japanese equivalent of the *qanat*, the *mambo*,[9] is a case in point, where even a society at the cutting edge of advanced technology sees the improvement of traditional irrigation systems as useful. This Japanese view of continuity is one that could have interesting implications for the Middle East.

The *qanat* illustrates the virtues of traditional technology. Known as *kariz* in Afghanistan, *khattara* in Morocco and *falaj* in the Arabian peninsula, the *qanat* is a narrow-gauge underground canal leading water from a perforation of the upper water table (mother well) at a slight gradient to a point of use, possibly at a great distance from the water source. It generally has a long life cycle. Once completed, given adequate maintenance, it will keep flowing continuously, day and night, and, except in a few cases, throughout the four seasons. It needs no motive power other than that provided by gravity.

The benefits offered by *qanats* in the arid and semi-arid countries of the Middle East are considerable. They carry water from areas of availability to areas of need. They can run for long distances underground, and in consequence evaporation losses are kept extremely low. Seepage through the beds of the qanats is similar to that in most water channels. Few *qanat* water courses are fully lined, except where they traverse soft sands, where *qanat* makers, the *moqannis,* would use baked clay hoops as linings.[10] The *qanat* is a benign influence on the water table. Its withdrawal rate is normally closely adjusted to water flow with the phreatic aquifer, and is thus different from the extraction of water by motor pumps in wells that cause worsening depletion of the aquifer. Similarly, pollution of aquifers by *qanats* through salt and brackish water intrusion is very unusual. In wells, on the contrary, these problems affected many areas in and adjacent to the central deserts of Iran after the introduction of the diesel pump: Khorasan was particularly affected by increasing brackishness of underground water in the 1960s and 1970s. Provided that *qanats* are protected by the application of traditional practices and by legislation to protect their source or *harim* against other extraction, they can remain safe against any threat to their supply, short of natural catastrophes such as roof fall, earthquake, flooding or regional desiccation and prolonged drought, as, for example, occurred in the Qazvin area during the 1963 earthquake.

In the modern period, when oil revenues appear to be increasingly fluctuating and unreliable, *qanats* have two particularly valuable characteristics. First, they are indigenous in all senses: survey, construction and maintenance, together with supply of equipment and personnel, can all be done with local and mainly rural resources. Secondly, they have neither foreign dependency nor foreign currency costs in either initial construction or maintenance. These were, however, their only advantages, set against 11 negative features, identified in an assessment of factors for and against their use prepared for the Iranian Plan Organization in 1949 by Overseas Consultants Inc.[11] The antipathetic views of OCI—based in the United States and biased towards modern technology—tended to reinforce approaches to *qanats* by official planning authorities in Iran throughout the modern period.

Fickle alterations in government policies do not instantly affect water provision from *qanats,* though the encouragement of pumped wells in the catchment of *qanats* can have a dramatically adverse impact if sustained over an extended period of time. In so far as governments can protect or expose the water sources of *qanats,* the option remains for the authorities to conserve the output of existing *qanats.* The choice is also available for states to construct new units. In the 1980s the Iranian government favoured both the digging of new *qanats* and the rehabilitation of those that had become silted up. This suggests that the balance of argument in official circles on the issue of the abandonment of the *qanats* can be shifted to a more conservation-conscious stance.

It is estimated that the number of *qanats* in Iran has fluctuated over recent decades. In 1950 the Irrigation Agency estimated that there were 32–40,000 still in operation throughout the country. Paul English suggested that there were some 21,000 *qanats* in use in Iran in 1960, while the official agricultural census gave a total of 46,300 functioning in 1973. After the 1979 revolution, when there was some government emphasis on preserving indigenous irrigation and farming structures, there were thought to be as many as 40,000 *qanats* in use. Construction of new *qanats* and the reconstruction of old ones persisted through the 1980s.[12]

Favourable treatment for established farming systems and local solutions to technological problems, such as the *qanat,* can overcome some of the inherent constraints on its use as a source of irrigation water. Initial capital costs for *qanats* remain generally only slightly higher than for a mechanized well system, if account is taken of the fact that the cost of new wells is the loss of nearby old *qanats.* Water flow from *qanats* is maintained for 24 hours every day of the year. In many ways, water engineers tend to look on the water that runs through the system during the winter, when irrigation is not being used, as wasted.[13] A more convincing view is that in winter most unutilized water infiltrates back into the water table.

Traditional techniques are to hand for improving the flow from the mother well by extending the head of the tunnel deeper into the water table and/or establishing a new mother well—a process known in Iran as *pishkar-kani.* Supplies can also be increased by taking water from new short *qanats* into the existing canal. Meanwhile, underground tunnelling, it must be admitted, is a slow business. It is estimated that the average period needed to build a *qanat* is between two and seven years, though, as indicated by the modernization of the *mambo* in Japan, new construction techniques can be introduced to shorten this stage of development of *qanats.*

The greatest difficulty in the use of the *qanat* as an instrument of mass water provision remains its inflexibility. Yet therein lies an advantage, since the greatest single advantage of the village *qanat* is the fact that its water cannot easily be diverted for use elsewhere. The geographical inflexibility of the *qanat* in this sense is a considerable virtue. It is a reality, in the arid zone of the Middle East and Central Asia, that competition for water between agriculture and urban consumers is intensifying. In most cases, the purchasing power of municipal and industrial users is far greater than that of the farmers, so that water resources are being transferred increasingly out of agriculture.[14] In this situation, the non-portability of *qanat* water will be a critical advantage, since the system will remain operating as a set of small-scale, local and rural-dedicated supplies, safe from urban encroachments. The difference between the long-lived and symbiotic nature of the *qanat* and the short-term water-depleting character of the diesel set under these conditions, could determine whether many villages survive for an extended future or not.[15]

In this kind of context, therefore, the *qanat* in its various forms can still play a useful role in sustaining cropping in villages in the irrigated lands of the Middle East. To the present time, however, no balanced and rational policy of this kind towards the role of the *qanats* has emerged. The *qanat,* like so many other kinds of traditional technologies, has an uncertain future; there are hopeful signs that its sustainability may be increasingly recognized; but at worst, it is at great risk of extinction.

Felt-making in Iran, Afghanistan and Turkey

During the twentieth century, many traditional tools, skills and processes were gradually ousted by mechanization. Whose interests are served by such technological change? A brief comparative study of felt-making reveals the importance of social factors, not least the gender dimension, in the processes of production.

The craft of felt-making has a long history in much of the Middle East and Central Asia.[16] In the twentieth century, felt as a textile was used for a wide variety of purposes in different cultural contexts. These include articles of clothing, such as hats (from the fez and dervish caps in Turkey, to the Qashqai *börk* and other tribal hats in Iran); shoes, particularly in colder areas; and coats and cloaks, including the famous *kapanak* of Turkish and Kurdish shepherds. Felts are also used for animal covers—particularly to pad a riding or pack animal's back under the saddle; and as floor rugs and wall hangings, where they are more or less functional or ceremonial. Perhaps most important of all, some nomadic peoples have felt mats as the main covering for their dwellings (see Andrews' chapter in this volume).

As varied as the uses to which felt is put are the processes by which it is made. During ethnographic research in Iran, Afghanistan and Turkey, Richard Tapper observed felt being made in three different contexts, each of which, as it happened, represented a different technical process and a different social mode of felt production.

Among Shahsevan nomads in north-western Iran, studied between 1963 and 1966, felt mats were one of the main components of the dwellings, both the *alachigh* (a distinctive variety of the Central Asian round, frame-based tent) and the *küma* (a barrel-vaulted tent). Felt was also widely used as backing for the more valuable flat-woven rugs, to prevent wear: such felts were often dyed orange; while tent felts were ideally natural white (at least on the outside) and undecorated, except for the felts located around the doorway, and the door itself, where some effort and imagination were put into appropriate coloured (usually brown) designs. Felt-making was an all-male activity, carried out with the aid of village-based, specialist wool-carders and felt-cutters, and with men and boys of the camp recruited, on a reciprocal cooperative basis, for the labour of the actual fulling of the felts: this was done energetically by a team of three to six men stomping the rolled up felts up and down a specially prepared ground. Women's role in felt-making was confined to cooking a meal for the work team.[17]

Tapper revisited the Shahsevan briefly in 1993 and 1995, and found that almost all felt-making had been mechanized by the late 1980s. A number of former specialist carders, who used to tour the nomad camps with their bows to process the wool, had bought machines for this, as well as for fulling, and had set up ateliers in the local market town, Khiou (Meshkinshahr), literally hanging up their bows on the walls of the atelier. At the same time, the Nomadic Affairs Organization was selling the nomads canvas tents, which were considerably cheaper and more durable than the traditional *alachigh*. There were as many Shahsevan nomads as before (5–6,000 families), but now about half had taken advantage of these canvas tents; most camps were a combination of some of each. Those who could afford to do so still maintained and renewed their felt-covered *alachighs,* for reasons of comfort as well as nostalgia, but they were more or less forced to take their wool to the town workshops for processing. Although machine-made felt was cheaper, most Shahsevan considered it to be inferior in quality. Such a sentiment is of course common when a new, labour-saving, mechanized technology is introduced: the older product (whether felt, or stone-milled bread-flour for example) is usually considered to have been of finer quality, though not enough so, it appears in this case, to justify rejection of the new technology.

Durrani nomads of northern Afghanistan, studied in 1971/2, did little or no weaving, often contracting out to specialists the weaving of the goat-hair cloth which formed their tents (see Ferdinand's chapter in this volume). But they did make large numbers of felts, exclusively as floor-coverings, many of them forming central elements in a bride's trousseau. There were two main kinds of felt: the large *nitsey,* plain black but with cowrie-shells sown decoratively along the edges, displayed on top of camel loads, particularly for weddings (or on migration, though an alternative would be a bought knotted carpet); and the smaller *kras,* including two types, one plain grey, the other black, both often with simple coloured designs. A bride's trousseau or 'house' *(da nawe kor)* should include two *nitsey* and several *kras.* Most of the work of felt-making (the back-breaking labour of beating the wool to separate the fibres, laying the wool out and then rolling it with forearms) was done by women of the camp, again on a reciprocal cooperative basis, with men's contribution confined to the final heavy work of washing, stretching and beating the finished felts. Nomad men knew of the professional carder and his bow from local towns; but they had never considered employing them: felt-making was women's labour, after all, and that cost them nothing.[18]

As for Turkey, there is a fair amount of writing about traditional felt-making,[19] a specialized craft which appears to be declining fast. Yalvaç, a provincial town in south-western Turkey visited on numerous occasions between 1979 and 1984, was reputed for its decorated felt rugs, which were on sale in the local markets. People —villagers rather than townspeople—bought them as cheap substitutes for knotted carpets. There were a number of craftsmen in town, working in small ateliers, and all at that time using powered machines for carding and fulling.

The three different social modes of felt-production among Shahsevan nomads (men), Durrani nomads (women) and provincial Turks (male specialists) correspond to a certain extent with three different purposes of the product (respectively: tent-covers, prestige goods, ordinary floor-coverings) and three different processes (bow-teasing plus foot-stomping; hand-teasing and arm-rolling; electrical machinery). Such correlations could be pursued further into the culture and social organization of the respective producers and consumers. This case of traditional skills and processes shows how technological change through mechanization, which might bring radical improvements in productive efficiency, may be resisted by those who control the production process if they see no economic advantage, or by consumers who do not see an improvement in the quality of the product. Cultural aesthetics and economics both have a role in determining whether new technologies are welcomed.

Science and medicine

The book begins appropriately with Rifaat Ebied's review of 'Arab and Islamic contributions to European civilization'. Professor Ebied notes that the Arabs inherited a scientific tradition from the ancient world, but the burden of his chapter is how this was nurtured, augmented and passed on to others. He takes two main routes to tell this tale: first, how the Arab Islamic legacy bore on Europe in higher education, and second, how the Copts of Egypt in particular contributed to Christian civilization. The great scientific institutions that are now taken for granted in the West— universities, hospitals and observatories—were either invented by the Arabs, as in the first case, elaborated by them in concept as with the second, or much developed as in the third. Professor Ebied finds that the West, which, after all, was a great beneficiary of the legacy of learning that Arab, Persian and Turkic civilizations handed down to them, has forgotten this debt.

Among the great gifts of the ancient world to its successors were medicine and the culinary arts. Derek Latham, giving his chapter an additional dedication to the late Haskell Isaacs, MD, uses his own knowledge of Middle Eastern languages, archival sources and medicine to examine 'TB and its treatment in Mediaeval Islam', and shows how physicians worked with a system which was as valid and effective as possible and conceivable at the time. Ghada Karmi throws light on the nature of *al-Tibb al-Nabawi,* the Prophet's Medicine, a system of medical therapeutics which, based on Arab and Islamic ideas, was at its height in the classical Arabic period. That Dr Karmi can write of the system that 'traces of it still survive to our very own day' and that 'it may even enjoy a revival at the present time', offers some comfort that traditional practices can be maintained among the population at large into the contemporary age. Her second contribution shows how medieval Islamic medical texts are valuable sources of information on early Arabic cuisine, which played an integral part in the therapies of the time.

Vernacular architecture—fixed and mobile

This volume is dedicated to the memory of Donald R.Hill, who worked for many years on aspects of building construction in the Islamic Middle East. Dr Hill's chapter, written shortly before his death, deals with science and technology in medieval architecture. He makes the point that, until recent times, Muslim architects had a broad range of skills. He begins with the building of the original city of Baghdad on the instructions of Caliph al-Mansur in the eighth century and goes on to sing the praises of the great ninth-century engineer al-Karaji, who laid down the scientific principles on which hydraulic works should be undertaken. In the same way, he elaborates on the sciences developed by the surveyors of the eleventh century, such as al-Biruni, culminating with a review of the great medieval Muslim dam builders. He also discusses the evolution of the pointed arch and the migration to Europe of Islamic architectural features such as the ogival arch. In all, he gives a fine *tour d'horizon* of the importance of contributions by Muslim architects. He reminds the reader of the excitement of the technological and material innovations that stirred invention and development in the early Islamic period.[20]

The urgency of the problem of conservation or rescue of traditional technologies is acute. War and strife have depleted physical assets such as buildings and other works in places as far apart as Bosnia and Afghanistan. Where land is lost as a result of invasions, the future of monuments and buildings must also be uncertain. Quite apart from man-made disasters, the process of weathering on mud-brick, from which many traditional Middle Eastern buildings are made, is considerable. The comparatively recent abandonment of watermills and windmills, as noted by Michael Harverson, as well as that of the *qanat* in Iran,[21] has exposed whole sectors of traditional technology to a great deal of destruction by natural erosion. Harverson indicates just how acute the problem for the *qanats* is. In the case of traditional wind and watermills, the damage is almost irreversible and few examples even of the legendary vertical windmills of Neh (south-eastern Iran) are left for posterity to marvel at. Elisabeth Beazley demonstrates, in her chapter on ice-houses and pigeon towers on the Iranian plateau, that abandonment and deterioration of these buildings is rapidly underway, as traditional mud-brick materials erode and collapse under the impact of weathering and neglect. Susan Roaf draws similar conclusions on the wind-grabbers *(badgir),* but also finds some consolation in the adoption of wind-grabber technology in the Arabian peninsula.

Nomadic and tribal groups are a powerful component of the history of the Middle East and Central Asia. They are vital, if at times reluctant, parts of a number of contemporary nation-states. Tribalism is ill-regarded by the rulers of modern countries for a variety of reasons,[22] not least that they appear to conflict with notions of modernity and the claims of a centralized state. For all its drawbacks, however, it could be argued that its sustainable social security systems and its proven survival value make tribalism 'no anachronism in the last decades of the twentieth century'.[23] It is also a truism that nomadic land-use takes advantage of lands that, in physical and ecological senses, are marginal areas of dubious use for arable farming; Eckart Ehlers has pointed out that, in Iran, the trespass of the plough onto marginal tribal and village grazing lands is leading to extensive soil erosion of an alarming scale and geographical ambit.[24]

The nomadic tradition, for all its emphasis on a minimum of light, transportable materials, has over time produced exciting artefacts, not least in the form of their mobile architecture—the nomad tents. Peter Andrews makes an important contribution to the history of the Central Asian tent-forms still found in many parts of the Middle East. He discusses evidence for the morphology of early Mongol felt-tents, suggesting that many features of the contemporary Mongol 'yurt' have survived from the fifteenth century and earlier, though the roof-strut is a more recent development. Klaus Ferdinand describes in detail the dwellings—from the very different, Middle Eastern tradition of 'black tents'—and other aspects of the material culture of different groups of nomads in Qatar, with particular focus on items and processes of 'modernization'; which he contrasts with those that he found among Pashtun and Taimani Aimaq nomads of Afghanistan.

One feature of nomadic material cultures that Ferdinand describes is that of textile production, so important for tent fabrics (whether felt or cloth), clothing, and storage items. Looms and weaving are the central theme of Jon Thompson's chapter, in which he surveys the different techniques used in the region, pointing to recent adaptations of computer technology in Iran to assist both designers and weavers. Against those who romantically lament this ultra-modernization of technology, Thompson points to the advantages experienced by the weavers themselves, suggesting that perhaps their interests have at least equal priority to those of consumers of what is, after all, a luxury product.

Cities and bazaars

Among the largest-scale elements of material culture are the old cities of the Islamic world. These too, with their living quarters and commercial *suq*/bazaars, are rapidly deteriorating or, in the case of Kuwait, disappearing as modernization progresses. In this volume, three contributors discuss aspects of Islamic urban culture and their implications for their material structures. Keith McLachlan examines the conditions under which commercial survival of the bazaar is possible. Susan Roaf proposes an agenda for sustainable buildings for the future. Mahmoud Abdullahzadeh points to the centrality of the bazaar in the religious, social and cultural as well as economic life of the Muslim world, but sees its survival in Iran—both physical and commercial—as due to its historically important political role there.

An immediate example of the problems of the decline of the *medina,* and some of the answers to them, is the walled city of Tripoli (Libya).[25] The Tripoli *medina* is one of the classical sites of the Mediterranean. The basic street plan was laid down in the Roman period, when the walls were constructed on the landward sides against incursions from the interior of Tripolitania. The high walls survived many invasions, each conqueror restoring the damage done. In the eighth century the Muslim rulers built a wall on the sea facing side of the city. Three great gates gave access to the town, Bab Zanota on the west, Bab Hawara on the south-east and Bab Al-Bahr in the north wall. The castle, Al-Saraya Al-Hamra, occupies a site known to be pre-Roman in the eastern quadrant of the city, and still dominates the skyline of Tripoli.

The old city itself was made up of a series of separate quarters, two major parts of which were Jewish.[26] Narrow streets criss-cross the old city, and off them run blind alleys. Individual houses in the old city still display their great cloistered courtyards and ornate tile, wood and plaster work. There are also several grand serais or *funduqs,* where merchants lodged their goods and their animals around large courtyards. Generally less decorated than private houses, they none the less played an important role in the life of the city when the large traders organized and managed trans-Saharan caravans. Pottery, metalwork, traditional clothing and jewellery were made in the various *suqs*. Some of the *suqs* still trade under vaulted brick ceilings, though very few goods are now manufactured *in situ*.

Sadly, there was an exodus of the traditional residents from the old city after independence in 1951.[27] Families moved to occupy houses and apartments vacated by the departing Italians in the new city, to take advantage of better sanitation, water supply and other facilities. By the mid-1970s the situation of the *medina* had deteriorated so badly that the majority of residents in the old city were foreign immigrant workers. Neglect of the fragile buildings enabled damp to enter their fabric, and many tumbled to ruin. The Libyan authorities determined at that time to halt the rot, and established a group to undertake restoration of key buildings and to write up the history of the city. In addition to the establishment of a research workshop and library in the old city, the main mosques, synagogues and consular houses have been restored in excellent taste. Unfortunately, however, small-scale restorations have done little to save the less prominent private buildings or to bring back real life to the *medina*. Tripoli is thus a stark warning of what happens when traditional economy and values are allowed to be overwhelmed.

Material culture and the confrontation with the oil economy

The problem of the protection of traditional material culture in the Middle East is most acute in the oil-exporting states, though, given the recent emergence of the Muslim states of the Caspian basin such as Kazakhstan and Azerbaijan as new oil-producers, the difficulty is an increasing one in the region as a whole.

Oil revenues began to flow into the region comparatively recently, starting in 1950 but in most Arab countries from 1970. For many small-scale oil exporters, the impact of this new industry will soon pass away. While oil or natural gas are in demand, the oil-exporting economies will be moderately prosperous and exhibit 'economic development' of a cosmetic kind sustained by oil revenues.[28] The longer-term future is less secure. Meanwhile these states undergo pressures that might be designed to strip away all vestiges of traditional material culture.[29]

A number of fierce pressures are at work on society in an early developing oil state.[30] There is a shortage of skills adequate to support both the pre-oil sectors and new demands. Since the modern sector pays high salary rates, traditional activities and their associated skills lose their economic attractiveness. Natural resources such as land and water, especially near major towns and cities, are less valued for farming than for other uses such as residential occupation or industry.[31]

In addition to these and other understandable difficulties which plague developing countries as a whole, the oil exporters, large and small, find that the possession of large reserves of oil and natural gas has brought additional difficulties and may not even have solved the question of shortages of capital.[32] Indeed, the oil-rich states have other damaging characteristics, all of which put traditional material cultures at risk. In oil economies, wage rates tend to rise rapidly. Government salaries for nationals are politically sensitive. They are constantly improved, both to ensure the political goodwill of the population and to help distribute oil income. The oil sector, and any other profitable economic area where managerial or technical skills are in demand, set the pace for wage rises elsewhere in the economy. Therefore wages tend constantly to be pushed upwards, which makes labour costs relatively high *vis-à-vis* other developing countries.[33]

The concentration of population in urban areas, so typical of oil-exporting economies in the Arabian peninsula, Iraq, Iran and North Africa, draws people away from agricultural employment.[34] Food output drops sharply. The population looks increasingly for urban employment with government departments and public-funded organizations. At the same time, large segments of the workforce are imported from abroad.[35] Initially this movement is in response to the very rapid rate of development, which outstrips local labour resources both in quality and quantity. Very soon, however, the indigenous population, enjoying a privileged income provided by the state, comes to rely on immigrants to undertake all the more menial occupations. The trading and property-owning part of the native population also depends on the immigrants to provide a domestic market.[36] The economic and social costs of maintaining foreign immigrant labour are very high. The system of local masters and foreign workers diminishes the likelihood of a hard-working, independent local population. Local pre-oil economic activities, especially farming, animal herding and traditional handicraft industries, wither away.[37] The fate of the oil exporters is to become import-dependent. The main use of revenues is to import goods, services and labour. The more new industries are set up and new constructions completed, the greater the dependence on imports to supply and maintain them.

The sudden and temporary nature of oil wealth causes economic difficulties.[38] Economic development based on transient wealth has proved difficult, as Roderick Dutton demonstrates in the case of the problems associated with the decline of traditional rural technologies, with special reference to Oman. Dutton has lived and researched in the Arabian peninsula for many years. He has seen in recent decades a rapid wilting of the technologies of irrigation and cultivation, as rural communities have become caught up in the economic upheaval associated with growing oil revenues. As personal incomes have risen, so many characteristics of the rentier society have engulfed the Sultanate of Oman: drift of population from the countryside, declining employment in agriculture and dependence on imported technology in home, field and office. The rents from oil have in effect permitted the creation of a leisured nation in Oman and other states, and the principal preoccupation of the government is to ensure that the rents continue. Dutton's chapter is a plea for more protection of agricultural life, so that the traditional material culture of rural Oman can be kept in use against the day when imported goods are less readily or cheaply at the disposal of the country.

Sensible economic planning would obviously take account of the needs of the nation in the era after oil. The stark contrasts between considerable wealth in the present and the poor prospects of living well in the near future have, unfortunately, rarely manifested themselves in cautious use of non-hydrocarbon resources, traditional technologies and the established skills of the labour force. In Kuwait, for example, elaboration of the domestic economic structure has been ignored in favour of protection and diversification of future sources of foreign exchange rent income, whether from oil or from external investments. The facts of life in Kuwait show that the majority of Kuwaitis opt for consumption in the form of leisure. If a classical social model must be applied to Kuwait and similar oil-based countries of the region, it seems wise though mischievous to suggest that the most fitting social commentary is appropriately found in Thorstein Veblen.[39] The implications of a desire for leisure amongst the populations of oil-exporting states is that traditional skills, once lost, are lost for ever.

Conclusion

In concluding this introduction, it is worth drawing attention to some of the problems that beset the contemporary study of material culture.

One problem is the dual tendency of academic studies towards dichotomy and hierarchy. The concept of 'material culture' is itself based on a dichotomy between material (things) and non-material (ideas, customs, rituals, relationships), resonating strongly with a ranking of 'High Culture' (art, music, literature) above popular culture (folklore). Several of the academic approaches to the interpretation of material cultures, mentioned earlier, employ dichotomies, explicit or hinted: between instrumental and expressive/symbolic aspects of things, or between the practical and the discursive, between objects in exchange (with a focus on their purpose and function) and objects as signifiers. Perhaps the most widely employed of all—by analysts and users alike—is that between the 'traditional' and the 'modern', two labels with powerful ideological and hierarchical implications.

Secondly, while a variety of 'globalizing' processes (variously labelled modernization, Westernization, commoditization; Americanization, Coca-colonization) have undoubtedly been a major force for cultural homogenization in the world for some time, it is clear that they work in no simple way. To put it briefly, the fact that a thing is now found globally (or trans-culturally) does not mean that it serves the same purposes or has the same cultural meanings in any two places. An apparently uniform item (Coca-Cola, wrist-watches, automobiles, computers, public space, the veil) has myriad meanings according to context—and even according to the individual user. Globalization has been countered by differentiating processes of localization and political and cultural fragmentation, of which the most extreme manifestations have been the bloody 'ethnic' conflicts of the 1980s and 1990s. At several levels, in all parts of the world, there have been political attempts to 'invent tradition'.[40] While the world is still divided most prominently into nation-states, the commonest and most powerful of these movements has been the nationalization of culture, which thereby becomes part of national ideology.

The consequence is that, at the beginning of the twenty-first century as never before, culture (whether material or otherwise) is a political matter. One aspect of the study of material culture which should be sensitive to this, but rarely is, is the apparently simple matter of categorization and labelling. A technical-functional label (e.g. windmill, carpet, medicine) is normally unproblematic, but difficulties may arise when ethnic (e.g. Arab, Baluch, Armenian), regional (e.g. Mediterranean, Caucasian), national or other categories are appended: is the item only found in that ethnic, local or national context, or is it thought to originate there? Is the category accepted (or disputed) by the makers or users of the item themselves, or is it merely a Western academic or commercial classification? National categories, in particular, may reflect (or indeed bring about) a national government's appropriation of an item that is exclusive to a particular, possibly oppressed, minority. Wide use of any such categories is, to say the least, politically problematic.

Indeed, the very use, by many scholars and experts in the technology and material culture of the Middle East and Central Asia, of the term 'Islamic', bears closer examination than it usually receives. The particular application of this label to cities of these regions has been the subject of some discussion in recent years (see McLachlan's chapter in this volume), and has drawn attention to the need to be more careful in such labelling.

Islam obviously embraces a far wider geography than these regions. This book is nevertheless a celebration of the material culture of the heartlands of Islam—the Arab, Persian and Turkish historical-linguistic zones. Thus, Central Asia, including Afghanistan, is looked at in association with the Arabian peninsula and Iran. Many topics, however, have immediate reference both to the greater Middle East with North Africa and to the Islamic world at large.

Notes

1. We are not referring here to recent prophecies of a 21st-century world *Kulturkampf,* such as that of Samuel Huntington, 'The clash of civilizations?' *Foreign Affairs* 72 (3), 1993; cf. Roy Mottahedeh, 'The clash of civilizations: an Islamicist's critique', *Harvard Middle Eastern and Islamic Review* 2 (2), 1995, pp. 1–26.
2. For a useful, brief but unfortunately not widely available survey, see Daniel Miller, 'Things ain't what they used to be,' *Royal Anthr. Inst. News (RAIN)* 59, 1983, pp. 5–7. See also Barrie Reynolds, 'The relevance of material culture to anthropology', *JASO* 14 (2), 1983, pp. 209–17.

3. See the interesting debate on this theme, following Ulla Johansen's article, 'Materielle oder materialisierte Kultur?' *Zeitschrift für Ethnologie* 117, 1992, pp. 1–15; Christian F.Feest et al., 'Diskussion', *Zeitschrift für Ethnologie* 118, 1993, pp. 141–197. Richard Tapper is indebted to Peter Andrews and Professor Johansen for drawing this debate to his attention.

4. See Jean-Pierre Digard, 'La technologie en anthropologie: fin de parcours ou nouveau souffle?' *L'Homme* 19 (1), 1979, pp. 73–104. Digard is the author of a significant monograph on material culture: *Techniques des Nomades Baxtyâri d'Iran* (Paris: Maison des Sciences de l'Homme/Cambridge University Press, 1981). Other significant anthropological studies of nomad material cultures in the Middle East have continued to be published in Denmark thanks to the Carlsberg Foundation Nomads Research Project (see Ferdinand's chapter below).

5. Marcel Mauss, *The Gift*, tr. Ian Cunnison (London: Cohen and West, 1954; orig. 1925); Fernand Braudel, e.g. *The Structures of Everyday Life* (London: Collins, 1981; orig. 1975); see also Pierre Bourdieu, *Distinction* (Cambridge, MA: Harvard University Press, 1984; orig. 1979); Jack Goody, *Cooking, Cuisine and Class* (Cambridge University Press, 1982) and other studies.

6. E.g. Nikki Keddie, 'Material culture and geography: towards a holistic comparative history of the Middle East', *Comparative Studies in Society and History* 26 (4), 1984, pp. 709–35. Cf. Christian Bromberger, 'Technologie et analyse sémantique des objets: pour une sémio-technologie,' *L'Homme* 19 (1), 1979, pp. 105–140.

7. Key texts include Jean Baudrillard, *La Société de Consommation, ses Mythes, ses Structures* (Paris: Denoel, 1970); Mary Douglas and Baron Isherwood, *The World of Goods* (London: Allen Lane, 1979); Arjun Appadurai (ed.), *The Social Life of Things* (Cambridge: Cambridge University Press, 1986) (including Brian Spooner's 'Weavers and dealers; the authenticity of an oriental carpet'); Daniel Miller, *Material Culture and Mass Consumption* (Oxford: Blackwell, 1987). Several museums displayed the new approaches to the public, for example the ground-breaking 'Collections Passion' exhibition in Neuchâtel, Switzerland; cf. Pierre Centlivres, 'Des "instructions" aux collections: la production ethnographie de l'image de l'Orient', *Collections Passion* (Neuchâtel: Musée d'Ethnographie, 1982), pp. 33–61.

8. A key text is Arjun Appadurai, 'Disjunction and difference in the global cultural economy', *Public Culture* 2 (2), 1990, pp. 1–24. For recent reviews of the state of studies of material culture, see B.Pfaffenburger, 'Social anthropology of technology', *Ann. Review of Anthropology* 21, 1992; Barrie Reynolds and Margaret A.Stott (eds), *Material Anthropology: Contemporary Approaches to Material Culture* (London, New York, Lanham, 1987). A number of lively, recently founded journals are devoted to this field: *Material Culture* (London), RES (Cambridge, MA), *Techniques et Cultures* (Paris).

9. S.Okazaki, '*Qanats* and *mambos*: brothers of irrigation technology', *Chiri* 30 (6), 1985, pp. 76–83.

10. Paul Ward English, *City and Village in Iran* (Madison: Wisconsin University, Press, 1966), p. 139.

11. Overseas Consultants Inc. *Report,* Vol. III, New York, 1949, pp. 149–58; cf. the later report by Henri Goblot, *Les Qanats: Une Technique d'Acquisition de l'Eau* (Paris: Mouton, 1979).

12. J.Murray, *Iran Today* (Tehran: Plan Organisation, 1950), pp. 72–3; *English City and Village,* pp. 135–60; K.S.McLachlan, 'Farm outlook', *MEED Special Report: Iran* 34/8 (London: Emap, 1990), pp. xiv–xviii.

13. A.M.Alamouti, 'Ground water resources of Iran', in *Hydrology and Water Resources Development* (Ankara: Cento, 1966), p. 427.

14. The need for water transfer from agriculture to municipal and industrial use has been described by J.A.Allan as a logical step in the water-short arid zones of the world. While there is a great deal of economic logic in moving water from low value-added to high value-added activities (see J.A.Allan, 'Fortunately there are substitutes for water otherwise our hydropolitical futures would be impossible' in *Priorities for Water Resources Allocation and Management,* London: ODA, 1993, p. 19), the long-term food supply and social costs of agricultural and rural decline arising from such a policy are incalculable.

15. K.S.McLachlan, 'Xavier De Planhol's Persian gardens: the rise and fall of traditional Persian agrarian culture,' in D.Balland (ed.) *Mélanges Xavier de Planhol* (Paris/Tehran: IFRI, 1996).

16. See e.g. Veronica Gervers, 'Felt in Eurasia,' in Anthony N.Landreau (ed.) *Yörük: The Nomadic Weaving Tradition of the Middle East* (Pittsburgh: Carnegie Institute Museum of Art, 1978); M.E.Burkett, *The Art of the Felt Maker* (Kendall, Abbot Hall Art Gallery, 1979).

17. See further, Peter A.Andrews, 'Alachïkh and küme: the felt tents of Azarbaijan', in Rainer Graefe and Peter Andrews, *Geschichte des Konstruierens III* (Konzepte SFB 230, Heft 28; Stuttgart: Kurz, 1987) pp. 49–135.

18. Information on Durrani women's felt-making comes largely from the fieldnotes of Nancy Lindisfarne-Tapper, with whom Richard Tapper did joint research among the Durrani in 1971–2; see Nancy Tapper, *Bartered Brides: Politics, Gender and Marriage in an Afghan Tribal Society* (Cambridge: Cambridge University Press, 1991).

19. See Burkett, *The Art of the Felt Maker.* Marlene Lange has recently researched felt-making in Turkey, see e.g. 'Felt craft in Turkey', *International Felt Makers News* 33, 1993, pp. 13–22 (translated by Anne Bain from *Basler Zeitung* 36, 5 September 1992); Stephanie Bunn, who kindly sent a copy of this paper, has herself done extensive research on felt-making in Central Asia.

20. See also A.M.Watson, *Agricultural Innovation in the Early Islamic World* (Cambridge: Cambridge University Press, 1983), pp. 1–6.

21. McLachlan, 'Xavier De Planhol's Persian gardens'.

22. See, for example, J.Black-Michaud, *Sheep and Land: The Economics of Power in a Tribal Society* (Cambridge: Cambridge University Press, 1986), pp. 84–6.

23. Richard Tapper, 'Introduction', in Richard Tapper (ed.), *The Conflict of Tribe and State in Iran and Afghanistan* (London: Croom Helm, 1983), p. 75.

24. Address to the British Institute of Persian Studies, London, November 1995.

25. A.McLachlan and K.S.McLachlan, *North Africa Handbook* (Bath:Trade & Travel, 1995), pp. 615–19.

26. Hara is the name designating the Jewish quarters of Tripoli.

27. See K.S.McLachlan, 'Tripoli and Tripolitania: conflict and cohesion during the period of the Barbary corsairs', in *Settlement and Conflict in the Mediterranean World,* Transactions of the Institute of British Geographers 3 (3), 1978, pp. 285–94 and 'Tripoli—city, oasis and hinterland: reflections on the old city 1551 to the present,' in *Libyan Studies,* Ninth Annual Report of the British Institute for Libyan Studies, London, 1978, pp. 53–4.

28. For a discussion of the problems of development in oil-exporting countries see E.Penrose, *Iraq: International Relations and National Development* (London: Benn, 1978), pp. 452–96, and K.S.McLachlan, 'Saudi Arabia: political and economic evolution', in I.Netton (ed.) *Arabia and the Gulf: from Traditional Society to Modern States* (London: Croom Helm, 1986), pp. 27–50.

29. J.Bulloch, *The Gulf: A Portrait of Kuwait, Qatar, Bahrain and the UAE* (London: Century, 1984), pp. 185–99.

30. Cf. P.Lienhardt, *Disorientations: A Society in Flux, Kuwait in the 1950s* (Reading: Ithaca, 1993).

31. J.A.Allan and A.Warren (eds), *Deserts: The Encroaching Wilderness* (London: Mitchell Beazley, 1993), pp. 164–5.

32. A.McLachlan and K.S.McLachlan, *Oil and Economic Development in the Gulf* (London: Murray, 1989), pp. 30–41.

33. H.Katouzian, *The Political Economy of Modern Iran 1926–1979* (London: Macmillan, 1981), p. 284.

34. N.C.Grill, *Urbanisation in the Arabian Peninsula* (Occasional Paper No. 25, Durham: Centre for Middle Eastern & Islamic Studies, 1984), pp. 62–81.

35. Ismail Serageldin et al., *Manpower and International Labor Migration in the Middle East and North Africa* (New York: Oxford University Press for the World Bank, 1983) pp. 3–5.

36. S.Y.Alessa, *The Manpower Problem in Kuwait* (London: KPI, 1981), pp. 31–33, and A.A.Al-Moosa and K.S.McLachlan, *Immigrant Labour in Kuwait* (London: Croom Helm, 1985), pp. 91–5.

37. F.H.Y.Abdul Al-Razzak, *Marine Resources of Kuwait* (London: KPI, 1984), p. 194. Dr Al-Razzak's book discusses the decline in the Kuwaiti fishing industry.

38. F.Halliday, *Iran: Dictatorship and Development* (Harmondsworth: Penguin, 1979), pp. 138–72.

39. Thorstein Veblen, *The Theory of the Leisure Class* (New York and London: Macmillan, 1899).

40. Eric Hobsbawm and Terence Ranger (eds), *The Invention of Tradition* (Cambridge University Press, 1983). Cf. Sami Zubaida, 'National, communal and global dimensions in Middle Eastern food cultures', in Sami Zubaida and Richard Tapper (eds), *Culinary Cultures of the Middle East* (London, New York: I.B.Tauris, 1994).

Chapter 1
Arab and Islamic Contributions to European Civilization
Rifaat Y.Ebied

It has been established beyond a shadow of doubt that the Arabs were the inheritors of the scientific tradition of late antiquity. They preserved it, elaborated it, adorned it with valuable additions, and finally passed it on to Europe. The story of how this came about is not simple, but, although much research needs to be done before the fine details are understood and verified, the broad outlines are clear and well attested.

The purpose of this chapter is to outline the major elements in the massive contributions made by the Arabs, both Muslims and Christians, to European civilization. The chapter falls into two parts: (i) the influence of the Arab-Islamic legacy on Europe in the various fields of knowledge, with particular emphasis on the Islamic origins of the system of higher education, that is, the creation of the university as an institution; (ii) the contribution of the Copts (Egyptian Christians) to Christian civilization in its formative centuries in such fields as monastic rule (which was instrumental in the preservation of world culture), missionary enterprises (which reached as far as the British Isles on the fringe of medieval Europe), liturgical vocal music, and ecclesiastical art and architecture.

The Arab-Islamic legacy: astronomy, medicine, higher education

Three important types of institution were part of the legacy of the Middle Ages to the modern world: hospitals, observatories and universities. Of these, it has long been accepted that the first two were innovations produced by the Arabian civilization of Islam. Although the Greeks invented a number of astronomical instruments, the observatory as a permanently organized and specialized institution came into existence under the auspices of the Caliphs, the successors of the Arabian Prophet Muhammad. The first permanent observatory of which we have record was that founded by the Caliph Ma'mun (reigned AD 813–833) in his capital city of Baghdad in about the year 830. Astronomy, together with alchemy, was thus the first science to preoccupy the Muslims and to be most fruitfully elaborated by them. It is noteworthy that it was also typical of the interests of the Greek scholars of late antiquity, particularly those in Alexandria.

Arab interest in the study of mathematics and astronomy was always lively, because of their obvious practical advantages. Mathematics was useful for commercial purposes, such as computation of the rather complicated Islamic laws of inheritance and as a basis for measuring distances. Astronomy was useful for determining the times of prayer and adjusting the calendar. The Arabs combined theoretical knowledge with technical skill, and excelled at the construction of precision instruments for astronomical use. The numerous Arabic astronomical works, particularly those produced in Spain, had an immense influence on Europe. Suffice it to say that today, for example, the very appellations of the constellations still bear the names given them by Muslim astronomers: Acrab (from *'aqrab,* 'scorpion'); Altair (from *al-ta'ir,* 'the flyer'), Deneb (from *dhanab,* 'tail'), and words such as zenith and nadir, all still in use today, recall the works of the Muslim scholars of al-Andalus (Spain).

The most important of the Arabs' many contributions to medicine in the Middle Ages was the foundation and running of numerous hospitals. If they did not actually *invent* the hospital as an institution, they devoted such attention to the organization, financing and upkeep of hospitals that many of their features are still familiar characteristics in their present-day successors. The Arabs' interest in medicine goes back to the very earliest times. The Prophet himself stated that 'there was a remedy for every illness', and was aware that some diseases were contagious. Muslim and Christian physicians made many significant additions to the body of medical knowledge which they inherited from the Greeks. Ibn al-Nafis (thirteenth century), for example, discovered the lesser circulation of the blood hundreds of years before Sir William Harvey (d. 1657) who became famous throughout Europe after the publication in 1628 of his book *On the Movement of the Heart and Blood in Animals*.[1]

The great contribution of the Arabs was to put the study of medicine on a scientific footing and to eliminate superstition and harmful folk-practices. Elaborate codes were formulated to regulate the professional conduct of doctors, and certain ethical qualities were obligatory. As the eleventh-century erudite Muslim jurist and historian Ibn Hazm (d. 1064), put it: 'A doctor should be kind, understanding, friendly, good, able to endure insults and adverse criticism; he must keep his hair short, and his fingernails too; he must wear clean, white clothes, and behave with dignity.'

There is also much circumstantial evidence to show that the third great medieval institution, the university, was to a large extent an invention of the civilization of Islam. There has, however, long been a reluctance among Western historians to admit that resemblances between Muslim and Christian centres of higher education in the Middle Ages were anything more than a series of coincidences, even though there has never been any dispute that a large proportion of European university textbooks used in the Middle Ages were translated from Arabic. Among the authors of scientific, medical and philosophical textbooks, Muslim scholars such as Avicenna, Averroes, Albategnius, Alfarabi, Avempace, Avenzoar, Albucasis, Arzachel and Alpetragius loomed very large. If there were no other evidence than this for the educational influence of the civilization of Islam on European Christendom, these names might be thought sufficient to suggest the strong possibility that the European universities which used such textbooks, in spite of the hostility between Islam and Christendom, must themselves have had very important original links with the civilization which produced such works.

In fact more evidence is accumulating which shows that it is within the borders of medieval Islam that the origins of the medieval European university must be sought. To begin with, there is the undisputed fact that Muslim centres of higher learning were functioning well over a century before the earliest ones to be founded in Europe. The mosque-college of al-Qarawiyyin in Fez (Morocco) was founded in AD 859, that of Cordova in the first half of the tenth century, the mosque-college of al-Azhar in Cairo in AD 972, and the House of Wisdom in the same city in the eleventh century, to mention only a few. In Europe the appearance of the first centres of higher learning was much later—the Universities of Bologna, Paris, Montpellier and Oxford were certainly not in existence earlier than the twelfth century, and in any case are junior to the Oriental universities.

When these early universities appeared in Christian Europe, they displayed many features in common with their Islamic counterparts. The student bodies were generally organized in 'nations'—that is, they were grouped for purposes of accommodation according to their place of origin. In the University of al-Azhar in Cairo there was separate accommodation for students from Morocco, from Upper Egypt, from Iraq, and so on; at the University of Paris the student body included the 'English nation', the 'Flemish nation', and others. Traces of this geographical organization of students remains in the names of some of the Oxford colleges, such as Lincoln, Worcester and Hertford.

Another feature of resemblance was the donning by university teachers of a distinctive form of dress, the gown, for lectures and other official functions. The wearing of loose gowns of a very similar style to those used in Christian Europe was an early practice in the great medieval centres of Islamic learning. However, I do not mean to imply by this that the Arabs were pioneers in this respect since, as is known, the early Christian Fathers had a similar practice in wearing a distinctive Episcopal garment, and similarly there is the well-known biblical tradition of wearing priestly garments.

Early academic terminology in Christian Europe also shows an interesting resemblance, in that the original European term for a university, *studium generale,* looks very much like a translation of the Arabic academic term *majlis 'amm,* which means a 'general gathering (for study)'. The meaning of the Arabic phrase, *majlis 'amm,* is identical with the definition of *studium generale* given by H.Rashdall in his monumental work, *The Universities of Europe in the Middle Ages,* as 'a place where students from all parts are received'. Similar definitions are given by Wieruszowski and more recently by Cobban.[2]

However, it must be admitted that research with regard to this interesting point is very much at an early stage, since the earliest manuscript we have hitherto come across which contains this Arabic phrase dates from the seventeenth century, and naturally it could be argued that the Arabic phrase is a translation of the Latin rather than the other way round. But the possibility of tracing earlier Arabic documents containing this phrase cannot be ruled out. The most likely home for such documents is Spain.

A further, attractive point of resemblance, was the widespread practice of imparting free instruction, without exacting payment from pupils. Again, the tradition of the wandering scholar was known in the lands of Islam long before it became a feature of scholastic life in Christendom. Muslim students did not assume that any one professor had a complete command of a whole field of study, and migrating from one centre of learning to another became an accepted feature of an academic career early on in the lands of Islam. Young men undertook vast journeys from Spain to Mecca, or from Morocco to Baghdad, leaving their homes practically without any money at all to sit at the feet of a chosen master.

It may well have been these continual migrations of scholars from one city to another which gave rise to the introduction of one of the most characteristic features of the organization of Islamic higher education—the *ijazah* (licence to teach). The *ijazah* was a written diploma granted by a professor to his student when the latter had successfully concluded a course of study, and conferred upon him the right to teach others the subject or subjects he had been studying. Such licences to teach were being issued as early as the ninth century. For scholars who travelled in search of learning from one academic centre to another (and such centres might be as far apart as Cordova and Baghdad), these licences to teach were important as academic passports and certificates of competence in particular fields.[3]

When we come to examine the history of the development of the Christian universities, we find that the earliest form of degree which they granted was none other than a *licentia docendi,* a 'licence to teach'.

The medieval Islamic universities enjoyed more *Lehrfreiheit* (freedom of teaching) and *Lernfreiheit* (freedom to study/ uncontrolled study) to use the terminology of the German academic ideal, than the early Christian universities, and it is therefore not surprising that each individual professor issued his own 'licences to teach', while in Europe this right was jealously reserved to the rector or head of the university. Apart from this difference of issuing authority, however, the *ijazah* and the *licentia docendi* were identical instruments of academic life.

These resemblances between the academic arrangements of Islam and those of Christian Europe are remarkable enough, but when we recall in addition the role played by medieval Spain in contacts between Islam and Christendom, their significance increases still further.

Islamic Spain was one of the great centres of medieval learning and culture, and after the capture of Toledo by the Christians in 1085 it became the chief channel through which the products of Islamic scholarship reached Christian Europe. In Toledo, Archbishop Raymond (d. 1251) founded a school of translation in order to make Arabic works available in Latin.

Christian scholars came to Spain to study the 'Arab Sciences'; they included such celebrated Englishmen as Adelard of Bath and Michael Scot. Muslim savants in Spain played a significant role in educating these individuals, and 'the testimony of scholars in the Middle Ages abundantly justifies the thesis that Islamic learning provided them with much material for their studies'.[4] The treasures of Arabic philosophical, scientific and medical literature were given a Latin dress suitable for their use by Christian university teachers and students. It would hardly be surprising, therefore, if, along with such basic things as textbooks, Christian scholars brought back with them from Spain features of university organization as well. How might this strong probability be shown to be a certainty? In other words, how can what has been hitherto dismissed as a mere series of coincidences be shown to be in fact a series of cultural borrowings?

One of the most eminent orientalists England has produced in the twentieth century, the late Professor Alfred Guillaume,[5] proposed (in the first edition of *The Legacy of Islam*,[6] that the proof of the connection between Islamic and Western universities might be found if a satisfactory explanation could be produced of the medieval term *baccalareus* or *baccalaureus*, the original form of the English 'bachelor' in its sense of the holder of a first university degree. In this connection he pointed out that the etymology of this word given in the *Oxford English Dictionary* can hardly be taken seriously: in a desperate attempt to save the Latin origin of the term it suggests an ultimate origin from *vacca*, cow.

Guillaume's dry observation that the etymology of this word given in the *Oxford English Dictionary* 'can hardly be said to explain [this term] satisfactorily' is echoed by many European authorities, including standard encyclopaedias and major reference works and dictionaries, in the sense that they confine themselves to recording that the word is medieval Latin and do not venture beyond this. The Spanish *Enciclopedia Universal Ilustrada Europeo-Americana*[7] proposes the otherwise discounted suggestion that the origin of the term is to be sought in the compound *vacca* (=berry)+*laureus* (= laurel); this is repeated in *Enciclopedia del Idioma* vol. 7.[8]

Guillaume went on to point out that *baccalareus* may well have been a distorted Latin transliteration of some Arabic academic phrase such as *bi-haqq al-riwaya*, i.e. 'with the right to teach on the authority of another', bearing in mind that many distorted Arabic words were taken into Latin and the European vernaculars in the Middle Ages, of which a considerable number are still in current use. They include such familiar words as 'cheque' (from Arabic *sakk*), 'tariff' (from Arabic *ta'rif*), 'admiral' (from Arabic *amir al-bahr*), and many more. Guillaume admitted, however, that he had never actually come across this phrase *bi-haqq al-riwaya* in any Arabic document, and his proposed etymology has up to now remained only an interesting speculation.

In recent investigations, however, into various surviving examples of medieval and later *ijazat*, my colleague the late Dr M.J.L.Young of the University of Leeds and I have shown not only that a phrase virtually identical to that suggested by Guillaume was actually used in Arabic academic documents, but that it was used in precisely the sense required for his suggested etymology. Our study of this term and its implications for the history of the medieval universities has appeared recently in *The Islamic Quarterly* (London) with full documentation.[9]

We now come to the point of greatest significance, the fact that the earliest *ijazah* (in a manuscript preserved in Cambridge University Library) in which the phrase *bi-haqq al-riwaya* has so far been found is dated AD 1147, while the first occurrence of the term *baccalareus* in Europe, in the sense of the holder of the lowest university degree, does not occur before 1231, the year in which a system of degrees was established at the University of Paris by the bull *Parens scientiarum* of Pope Gregory IX.

The phraseology used in these *ijazat* suggests that Guillaume's proposal may well indicate the true origin of the puzzling noun *baccalareus* in the Arabic adverbial phrase *bi-haqq al-riwaya*. It is worthy of note that Rashdall, while stating that the etymology of the word is doubtful, thought it likely that it was first used as a slang term; this is precisely the way in which scholars might have used the Arabic *bi-haqq al-riwaya* colloquially, for want of an immediately convenient Latin equivalent, in the same way that European merchants adopted Arabic terms such as 'tare' (from *tarh*), 'mohatra' (from *mukhatara*), 'arsenal' (from *dar al-sina'a*), and the already mentioned 'cheque' and 'tariff', without troubling to think of suitable European renderings of these useful words.

The intermediate stages by which *bi-haqq al-riwaya* could have been transformed into *baccalareus* cannot be determined with absolute certainty, but I suggest that the following considerations may illustrate the manner of this progression. In the first syllable of *baccalareus* the change from *bi-haqq* to *bacc* with loss of *'h'* can be paralleled in other Arabic borrowings into medieval Latin. The unassimilated 'l' in the second syllable of the word can be paralleled in many Latin borrowings from Arabic in literary sources; if, however, in accordance with Rashdall's suggestion,[10] *baccalareus* arose from a colloquial usage, we would have to assume the likelihood of Spain being the area in which it was first used, and that the assimilation of the *lam* of the article to a following 'sun' letter did not occur in the spoken Arabic of Spain. In regard to *riwaya*, metathesis may well have occurred. Thus the following progression could be envisaged: *bi-haqq al-riwaya>b-haqq lurea>baccalure* (?a)*>baccalareus*.

Thus it seems likely that our university term 'Bachelor' derives from a phrase used in Islamic university diplomas, and, taken with the other significant features of resemblance mentioned above, strongly implies that European universities were modelled on those of Islam.

The contribution of the Copts

In the second part of this chapter, I present a brief survey of the immense contribution of the Copts to Christian civilization, confining myself to one or two major areas.

The Copts have occasionally been described as a schismatic Eastern Christian minority, a lonely community in the land of their ancestors. Their place in the general history of Christianity and their importance in human annals have long been forgotten. This is partly because they themselves had chosen to live in complete oblivion after the tragedy of the Council of Chalcedon in AD 451, which caused the irreparable cleavage of Christendom into two hostile camps, Eastern and Western, or monophysite and diophysite.

However, since the rediscovery of the Copts and their Christianity, interest has been intensified in the attempt to explore the religious traditions and values of this most ancient, primitive form of the faith. Scholars of all creeds were stunned as the pages of Coptic history began to unfold and reveal the massive contributions of the Copts to Christian civilization all over the world in its formative centuries. But before I briefly outline the major elements of these contributions, let me define the term 'Copt' and the origins of that community.

Ever since I arrived in Europe and later on in Australia, I have been repeatedly asked these questions: 'Who are the Copts? To what race or races do they belong? Are they really the descendants of the ancient race of Egypt, or a mixture of the several nations that governed Egypt or made it their home?'

The term is simply equivalent to the word 'Egyptian', and the Copts.) therefore, have the right to call themselves the direct descendants of the ancient Egyptians, or, as they are sometimes labelled, 'the modern sons of the Pharaohs'. 'Copt' is derived from the Greek *Aigyptos,* which in turn is a corruption of the ancient Egyptian *Hak-ka-Ptah,* i.e. the house of the temple of Ptah, a most highly revered deity in Egyptian mythology. With the removal of the prefix and suffix, the stem 'gypt' remains and is transformed into

'Copt' in European languages. When the Muslims came in the seventh century, Egypt became known as Dar al-Qibt, home of the Copts, who were the Christian Egyptians to distinguish them from the native citizens.

From the dawn of the Christian faith the Copts played a very significant role in the development of organized Christianity. They established two momentous universal movements which had the greatest impact on Europe: first, the monastic rule, or monasticism, which must be regarded as truly and purely the gift of Egypt to Christendom. With its introduction to Europe, it was destined to become the sole custodian of culture and Christian civilization in the Dark Ages. The planting of the Coptic cenobitic rule in Europe and other continents of the Old World was achieved largely by the efforts of some of the great names, and it continued to influence European monasticism beyond the Middle Ages. In fact the contribution of the Copts in this field persisted until the modern age.

The second movement through which the Copts left their mark in Europe and elsewhere was a huge missionary enterprise into Africa and Europe, reaching Ethiopia in the south and the British Isles in the north, long before the advent of St Patrick or St Augustine of Canterbury in AD 597. This endeavour was a historically significant by-product of the monastic movement. The eminent historian Stanley Lane-Poole says:

> We do not know how much we in the British Isles owe to these remote hermits. It is more than probable that to them we are indebted for the first preaching of the gospel in England, where, till the coming of Augustine, the Egyptian monastic rule prevailed. But more important is the belief that Irish Christianity, the great civilizing agent of the early Middle Ages among the northern nations, was the child of the Egyptian Church... Every one knows that the handicraft of the Irish monks in the ninth and tenth centuries far excelled anything that could be found elsewhere in Europe; and if the Byzantine-looking decoration of their splendid gold and silver work, and their unrivalled illuminations, can be traced to the influence of Egyptian missionaries, we have more to thank the Copts for than has been imagined.[11]

The contributions of the Copts extended to other fields, including liturgical vocal music. It is not inconceivable that the Coptic missionaries who crossed over to Europe at the dawn of our era could have carried with them the essence of the native Coptic chanting.

In the realm of architecture, it can be assumed that the origins of the basilical style in the Christian world may be traced to ancient Egypt, with Coptic craftsmanship being the bridge between the ancient temple and the modern cathedral. After all, the Copts were accustomed to transforming the ancient heathen temples into Christian churches.

This chapter was intended as a brief survey of the significant contributions made by the Arabs, both Muslims and Christians, to world culture, and in particular to European civilization in the various spheres of knowledge. The study of Islamic and Coptic civilization has been relatively neglected by European scholars, and few European universities make adequate provision for teaching and research in the fields of Arabic, Christian Arabic and Islamic studies. For example, of over one hundred universities in Britain, only a dozen or so make any provision at all for teaching Arabic, and of these institutions only a handful have departments exclusively devoted to Arabic studies. The situation is not much different in Australia; indeed it may even be worse insofar as, of over forty universities and other tertiary institutions, only four make any provision at all for teaching Arabic, and of these only one, the University of Sydney, has a department devoted to Arabic studies. It is therefore likely that further research in these fields will strengthen our understanding of many hitherto obscure problems, including the important connection between medieval

Islamic and Christian institutions of higher learning, and will confirm that in the organization of these institutions the Arabs were not only the predecessors of Europe, but also its exemplars.

Notes

1. William Harvey, *An Anatomical Disputation Concerning the Movement of the Heart and Blood in Living Creatures,* (trans. etc.) Gweneth Whitteridge (Oxford: Blackwell, 1976).
2. Hastings Rashdall, *The Universities of Europe in the Middle Ages* (new edn, Oxford: Blackwell, 1942), I, p. 6; Helene Wieruszowski, *The Medieval University: Masters, Students, Learning* (Princeton, NJ: von Nostrand, 1966); Alan B.Cobban, *The Medieval Universities: their Development and Organization* (London: Methuen, 1975).
3. For the use of the *ijazah* in the Islamic educational system, see Jan Just Witkam, 'The human element between text and reader: the *ijazah* in Arabic manuscripts', in *The Codicology of Islamic Manuscripts: Proceedings of the Second Conference of al-Furqan Islamic Heritage Foundation 1993* (London, 1995), pp. 123–36; George Makdisi, *The Rise of Colleges, Institutions of Learning in Islam and the West* (Edinburgh: Edinburgh University Press, 1981).
4. Alfred Guillaume, 'Philosophy and theology', in Sir Thomas Arnold and Alfred Guillaume (eds), *The Legacy of Islam* (Oxford: Oxford University Press, 1931), p. 243.
5. Guillaume (b. 8 November 1888) held many distinguished posts, including the Chair of Arabic and headship of the Department of Near and Middle East at SOAS from 1947–55; thereafter Professor Emeritus until his death in November 1965. He was also Member of the Arab Academy of Damascus (1949) and of the Arab Academy of Baghdad (1950).
6. *The Legacy of Islam*, p. 245, note 4.
7. Vol. 7 (Madrid: Espasa-Calpe, 1910), *s.v.* Bacalario, p. 51.
8. Ed. Martín Alonso, Vol. 1 (Madrid: Aguilar, 1958), *s.v.* Bacalario, p. 607.
9. R.Y.Ebied and M.J.L.Young, 'New light on the origin of the term "Baccalaureate"', *Islamic Quarterly* 18 (1/2), 1975, pp. 3–7.
10. Rashdall, *Universities of Europe*, pp. 207–8.
11. Stanley Lane-Poole, *Cairo—Sketches of its History, Monuments and Social Life* (London: J.S.Virtue, 1898), pp. 203–4.

Chapter 2
TB and its Treatment in Medieval Islam (Dedicated to the memory of H.D.Isaacs MD)
J.Derek Latham

Early in the tenth century of the Christian era, Ishâq b. 'Imrân, a Muslim physician from 'Abbâsid Baghdad versed in the principles and practice of scientific medicine, trained a Jewish pupil, Ishâq b. Sulaymân (*c.* 855–950). In due course Ishâq (later known to Europe as Isaac Judaeus and, later, Isaac Israeli) became physician in Qayrawân (Kairouan, Tunisia) to the Aghlabid Ziyâdat-Allâh (903–9) and then to the Fâtimid 'Ubaydallâh al-Mahdî (909–34), under whose patronage he wrote some notable medical works. Of these, his *Book on Fevers* won wide esteem. Translated from Arabic into Latin and Castilian, it was used in Europe as a standard textbook until the seventeenth century, and Charles Singer, the well-known historian of science, describes it as 'one of the best medical works available in the Middle Ages'.[1] The work comprises five parts, of which the third treats of 'hectic fever', or what is in effect pulmonary tuberculosis. This chapter examines Ishâq's approach to the disease in readily intelligible terms, and shows that the treatment available in medieval Islam was basically as sound as it could be prior to the advent of antibiotics and modern surgical procedures.

Fevers in early medicine

By way of introduction to the subject of 'hectic fever', some observations on fevers in general seem appropriate. In medicine the word 'fever' was, and indeed remains, a term of wide application, since it denotes not only an increase in body temperature above the normal, but also any one of a variety of diseases of which such an abnormal increase is a prominent symptom. In many cases, the abnormal increase in temperature is regarded as only *symptomatic* of and therefore *secondary* to the disordered bodily state with which it is found in association. For example, injuries to the nervous system and unpleasant sensations in nervous subjects and children may occasion a rise in temperature. However, there is a wide range of diseases in which fever is the predominant feature and factor and which result from the formation, in the system, of a toxin upon which all the symptoms depend. These diseases are designated *primary* or *specific* fevers, which we now know to be due to micro-organisms whose toxic products lead to increased wasting of the tissues and other pathological phenomena. Three examples of such maladies are typhoid fever (enteric fever), scarlet fever and yellow fever.

Although there are certain diseases, such as myxoedema and Bright's disease (disorders of the thyroid gland and kidneys, respectively), which are afebrile, i.e. not characterized by a fever in the sense of an abnormal rise of temperature, such an abnormal rise is, as we all know, one of the commonest accompaniments of disease in general. A number of diseases have a characteristic course of temperature, which, since the advent of the clinical thermometer,[2] can be charted quite accurately and readily identified from the picture presented on the chart. Thus, enteric fever, pneumonia, measles, advanced pulmonary tuberculosis and malaria are usually quite recognizable by a physician inspecting the relevant temperature charts. It is also a fact that in some diseases a high temperature is less ominous than in others. Thus, in pneumonia, for example, a temperature of 105° (40.5° C) is more the rule than the exception, while in rheumatic fever or diphtheria a temperature of even 104° (40° C) would give cause for concern.

Given the background that I have just outlined, it is scarcely surprising that a place for fevers should have been found in the Hippocratic and Galenic scheme of ancient medicine and, after that, in the scientific medical system of the medieval Muslim world, the natural heir to that scheme. It is no less surprising that the picture that presented itself to physicians of both eras should have been one of some complexity. There was, of course, no clinical thermometer to chart the course of a temperature; the only pyrometric device available to a clinician was his own hand, and consequently palpation, or examination by touch, was the only pyrometric procedure. As for pathogenic bacteria, how could anything be known before the invention of the microscope? Nevertheless, the physicians of late antiquity *did* attempt to provide solutions to the problems with which febrile diseases confronted them. That there was not just one febrile condition to which the term 'fever' could be applied *exclusively,* but rather a variety of disorders characterized by fevers of varying intensity and duration was a clearly discernible fact of scientific clinical experience, leading to attempts to identify and classify febrile conditions for the purposes of differential diagnosis. In some cases identification and classification presented no particular difficulty. Such was the case with malaria, for instance: characteristic patterns of frequency and duration readily lent themselves to categorization under the heads of quotidian, tertian, quartan, and so on.

In the wake of identification and classification there followed attempts at explanation. In the case of medieval Islam, such attempts were largely bedevilled by the legacy of Greek medical thought which revolved around the teachings of Galen. For the medical world of medieval Islam, Galen was by far the most significant of all the Greek physicians.[3] Accordingly, it inherited all his unsound concepts of physiology and pathology, thus providing practitioners with a system of false reasoning on which to base aetiology. And so it is that in medieval Arabic medical works fevers are to be found, time and again, both classified and identified according to Galenic teaching.[4]

Be that as it may, it must not be assumed that, in the matter of fevers, no advance on Galen was attempted or achieved in the medieval Muslim world. In the field of medicine generally, Galenic teaching did not pass entirely without challenge. In particular, the celebrated clinician al-Râzî (865–925) had his doubts about aspects of Galenic medicine that could be seen to be inconsistent with his own experience,[5] and, as is clear from A.Z.Iskandar's thorough examination of al-Râzî's views on fevers, a measure of progress was made.[6] His identification and classification of fevers was as exhaustive as was possible within the framework of contemporary medical knowledge. An acute awareness of the need to distinguish with accuracy one fever from another within a range of different kinds is the hallmark of his thinking, of which the point of departure is his insistence that a fever is either a disease *per se* or a symptom. In other words, *primary,* or *specific,* fevers were to be differentiated from *secondary,* or *symptomatic,* fevers.

'Hectic fever'

Among primary fevers that are diseases *per se,* al-Râzî includes, in a list of such prepared for the purposes of differential diagnosis, that fever which the Greeks termed *hektikos,* i.e. 'habitual' in the sense of its being integrated into the bodily constitution. The fever so described was that accompanying the morbid condition commonly termed consumption, which, as most laymen know, is a wasting disease—in Greek *phthisis*—or decline of the body arising from tuberculous disease, or, more succinctly, TB.[7]

For its first acquaintance with this disease in any scientific sense, Western Europe is undoubtedly indebted to the world of medieval Islam. The acquaintance dates from the eleventh century of the Christian era, and derives from the Latin version of an Arabic treatise on fevers, entitled *Kitâb al-Hummayât* (Book of Fevers), by a physician and philosopher some ten years older than al-Râzî. Known to the Latin West as Isaac Judaeus, and to the Arab world into which he was born as Ishâq b.Sulaymân al-Isrâ'îlî,[8] Isaac, as we shall call him from now on, had spent the first part of his career as an oculist in Cairo—he came of an Egyptian Jewish family—and then moved to Kairouan (Tunisia), the capital of the Aghlabid dynasty of Ifrîqiyâ. There, around the beginning of the tenth century, he avidly assimilated from his Muslim teacher, Ishâq b.'Imrân, the principles and practice of Greco-oriental medicine as taught in 'Abbâsid Baghdad. For Ishâq b.'Imrân had trained and practised in Baghdad before being enticed to Kairouan by the Aghlabid Ziyâdat-Allâh III b. 'Abd Allâh to serve him as court physician. In due course, Isaac succeeded him in that office and, even after the overthrow of Ziyâdat-Allâh by the Fâtimid 'Ubaydallâh al-Mahdî (reg. 909–34), continued his career as court physician. Under the Fâtimid's patronage he wrote many of the medical works that were to earn him a place in the history of medicine. Of these none was more famous than his *Kitâb al-Hummayât*.[9]

The Latin version of this treatise on fevers we owe to Constantinus Africanus (Constantine the African),[10] who was born a Muslim in Tunis in 1010 or 1015 and died a Christian monk at Monte Cassino in Italy in 1087. That Constantine's work generally infused new life into the medical school of Salerno, and, beyond that, influenced and fertilized the development of European medicine, is a virtual certainty. At all events, it was he who was responsible for introducing Isaac's *Hummayât* to Europe.

In all, the treatise comprises five *maqâlât,* or discourses, on the following topics: (1) the nature of fevers; (2) ephemeral fever; (3) hectic fever; (4) acute fevers; (5) putrid fevers. The importance attached to hectic fever is clear from the fact that he isolates it from other fevers and devotes one out of his five discourses exclusively to that one topic. Why he should have done so is not hard to understand, if we take account of the fact that it is primarily pulmonary tuberculosis that he is dealing with. This is abundantly clear from all that he has to say in the body of his discourse.

If we look at the manner in which the disease is contracted and bear in mind the seriousness of the condition, Isaac's preoccupation with it will readily be grasped. In almost all cases, direct inhalation of the tubercle bacillus—*Mycobacterium tuberculosis,* a microorganism identified by Koch only a little over one hundred years ago (1882)—is the mode of infection. The victim will have inhaled either bacilli-laden dust or droplets expelled in coughing by an infected person. Outside the human body, the bacillus succumbs neither to drying nor to freezing, and under ordinary circumstances *only direct sunlight* will destroy it. Dried in the dust and blown about in *places not directly exposed to the sun's rays,* each bacillus of the several thousand million coughed up daily by a person with advancing tuberculosis is a serious menace to public health. Given the Mediterranean and Middle Eastern urban environment, pulmonary tuberculosis must have been rife in medieval Muslim cities, with their shaded, narrow streets and dark corners, not to mention the unhealthy domestic conditions in which women and children spent the greater part of their time. That it was well known in the palaces in which Isaac practised his medicine we can be sure; we have only to read between the lines of his discourse. This, of course, need not surprise. No matter what their status in life, inhabitants of hot countries tend to take cover from the heat in dark and ill-ventilated places where the bacillus, present in the sputa of infected persons, thrives. In particular, the almost windowless rooms of urban dwellings that served as women's quarters in pre-modern Islam were ideal breeding grounds for the bacillus.

Isaac's description of TB

The value of Isaac's discourse does not lie in any new concepts of physiology and pathology, for, in this respect, he is wholly dependent on his ancient predecessors; it lies, rather, in the care that he has taken to select and assemble from the corpus of Galenic medicine all that could be usefully said of pulmonary tuberculosis *as a progressive disease* at the time of his writing. What is important is that he sees and handles the subject as a unity and avoids the classificatory fragmentation that led both Galen and, eventually, Ibn Sînâ (Avicenna) to deal with 'the pulmonary ulcers' of advanced pulmonary tuberculosis in isolation from the general tuberculous condition. The signs and symptoms of a progressive disease are accurately described, and he clearly recognizes the important relationship between loss of weight and persistent low-grade pyrexia. Although he does not say so in so many words, he sees that relationship as diagnostically significant. Indeed he actually opens his discourse on the fever generated by tuberculosis with an introductory comment on the whole subject of 'decline' *(dhubûl)*:

> Before beginning to treat of this particular fever [sc. 'hectic fever' commonly known as consumption *(sill)*] we must first examine decline, and be fully conversant with its quiddity and form, its causes and categories, and such kinds of decline as are accompanied by fever and those which are not. We shall next go on to discuss fever following decline and deal with the causes that occasion it.[11]

This is a sound observation, for loss of weight is still considered one of the early signs of TB. Despite the fact that Isaac entitles his discourse on tuberculosis 'Hectic Fever *(Hummâ aqtîqûs)* commonly known as Consumption *(sill)*', he mainly speaks of the disease as *dhubûl,* for which 'decline' is perhaps the best and most convenient rendering of the term in English. He also uses the expression *hummâ al-diqq,* which may be rendered 'phthisic fever'. The French physician and Arabist H.-P.-J. Renaud noted that in Morocco, as elsewhere, *dubûl [sic]* was synonymous with *merd as-sell (=marad al-sill),* 'nom que porte toujours la maladie consomptive par excellence, la phtisie pulmonaire'.[12]

For evidence of Isaac's dependence on Galen, however, we need look no further than his description of a patient in advanced stages of the disease. In parts, Galen's own words from *Peri diaphorôn pyretôn* are reproduced in translation almost verbatim: 'you will find...the eyes sunken as if engulfed and containing a dry, white rheum'—words patently echoing Galen's *ophthalmous koilous ametrôs theasê kathaper en bothrois tisin egkeimenous...kai mên kai lêmai kat'autous emphainontai xêrai.*[13] Again, in Isaac's 'the pulse will be weak, small, hard and coarse', we clearly perceive Galen's *ho de sphygmos iskhnos kai sklêros kai amydros kai pyknos.*[14] Throughout his description of the facies of a consumptive in the last stages of his disease, Isaac echoes Galen. He writes:

> the orbital bones and temples alike lose all their flesh; depressions are formed in the temples; eyelids and eyebrows move heavily because of their dryness and lack of moisture; and the skin on the forehead stretches, and becomes dehydrated and parched. When [patients in this condition] lie down, they close their eyes as if in involuntary sleep brought on by such [outward signs as we describe], but really caused by debility and dissolution of their faculties. If you palpate them you will find their bodies parched, dehydrated and cold by virtue of the fact that there is neither heat nor moisture to get through to the skin. If you keep your hand firmly and long enough on the body for it to transmit your own heat and moisture to the point touched by your hand, you will notice the heat creep slowly beneath it. Moreover, if you uncover the abdomen, you will find that it appears to be devoid of viscera. If you then palpate it, you will find it to be like a flat board and of a dry leathery texture. Also, if you pinch the skin of the abdomen and pull it away, it will stretch as you pull and remain in an

upright position for the simple reason that it contains no moisture to keep it malleable and enable it to regain its normal position. From signs such as these the patients presenting them can be taken to be moribund.[15]

It is interesting to note that much of what is said here could have been written in the twentieth century. Thus, in *Hutchison's Clinical Methods* we read:

If a fold of healthy skin is pinched up, it immediately flattens itself out again when released. Sometimes, however, it only does so very slowly, remaining for a considerable time in a creased condition. This may be of little or no significance in old persons with loose inelastic skins, but may be an important sign of dehydration.[16]

Echoing Hippocrates, Isaac writes of the urine passed by a patient suffering from advanced TB:

this will be oily and contain matter presenting the appearance of laminae *(safâ'ih)*... When the process [of dissolution and liquefaction of the organs] is complete, the urine becomes so oily that if you pour it into a vessel you will hear it emit a sound like that of oil and quite unlike that of water.[17]

Al-Râzî was not prepared to take the word of the ancients on this point. Noting that he had never observed any such phenomenon in the urine of phthisic patients, he was quite prepared to say it could never happen.[18] But was he right? The description we are offered of the urine is that which certainly could have been observed in a consumptive at the stage of amyloid degeneration, or 'waxy disease', as it was termed. In this condition—rarely, if ever, seen today by Western doctors—the fibrous tissues degenerate into a substance somewhat resembling wax. The cause is toxaemia, and one of the signs is profuse albuminuria (albumen in the urine). Be that as it may, it is not uncommon for there to be amyloid or lardaceous changes in the kidneys of patients suffering from chronic tuberculosis.

The extent of Isaac's knowledge of the nature of pulmonary tuberculosis is not always easily perceived. On the contrary, vital aspects of it are obscured by his almost obsessive preoccupation with aetiology, of which, as noted earlier, he could not have the slightest inkling. Regrettably, he spends so much time and expends so many words on what, given his unquestioning acceptance of his ancient predecessors' physiological concepts, could never amount to anything but a carefully constructed edifice of scientific absurdity. For all that he scrupulously endeavours, with philosophical precision, to ensure that his reader will understand his reasoning process, he nevertheless tends either to underemphasize or to mention casually or to leave to inference signs and symptoms of which we can be certain he was aware, and to which a modern writer of medical textbooks would give prominence.

And so it is that he omits to spell out for us the part played by drenching night sweats, say; we are left to deduce his knowledge of it from what he has to say of heat and dehydration and the measures he proposes to conserve the body's moisture.[19] He makes no attempt to impress upon us the part played by the troublesome cough, or tussis, that is among the early symptoms of the disease and which assumes ominous significance when accompanied by continued loss of weight. He evidently takes it for granted that his reader is familiar with tussis, haemoptysis (expectoration of blood) and tuberculous enteritis: for, when we come to that part of his discourse in which he takes up the question of treatment, his prescriptions provide for the management of such symptoms.[20] He shows himself very much alive to the constitutional disturbances experienced by the victims of phthisis and to the gravity of tuberculous enteritis, followed at the ulcerative stage by the ominous passage of blood in the stools.[21] Yet, despite the fact that Isaac offers no *systematic* account of what is in fact toxaemic disturbance of digestive functions with all that follows in the way of dyspepsia, vomiting, diarrhoea, and so on and so forth, we can discern that his whole approach to phthisis is refreshingly different from that of Galen or Ibn Sînâ, in that, as already noted, he sees and handles his subject as a unity and avoids the kind of classificatory fragmentation that led both of these luminaries of medicine to deal with the 'pulmonary ulcers' of 'consumption' in isolation from the general tuberculous condition.

That Isaac should have failed to glean anything at all about the aetiology of pulmonary TB is perfectly intelligible for the reasons already noted. On the other hand, he could perhaps have been expected to show some awareness of the infectious nature of the disease, since infection, or the 'transmissibility' *(i'dâ')* of diseases is discussed, albeit imprecisely, by writers of Arabic medical works from the ninth century onwards.[22] (Isaac, it will be recalled, died around the middle of that century.) Add to which, in the following century 'consumption' *(sill)* was certainly classified by 'Alî b. al-'Abbâs al-Majûsî (Haly Abbas to the West; d. 994) as one of the transmissible diseases *(amrâd mu'diya)*,[23] i.e. an illness that could be transmitted to one sitting close to a patient and inhaling during conversation what was described as 'an evil vapour' emanating from the patient's body (nowadays the medical profession speaks of 'droplet infection').

Isaac's treatment of TB

Isaac's approach to the treatment of pulmonary tuberculosis is where he is to be seen at his best. It is in the sphere of therapeutics that it becomes abundantly clear that, at the practical clinical level, he is far more conversant with the condition with which he is dealing than his physiological speculations may lead one to suppose. He stresses the importance of physical and mental rest (mainly by indicating the dangers of mental and physical stress and strain);[24] a regular and disciplined routine along with supervision (a theme that runs throughout the treatise);[25] fresh air and good ventilation together with the use of clothing that is light and cool;[26] diet and exercise appropriate to the patient's needs and degree of tolerance,[27] and so on.

To diet and hydrotherapy he attaches particular importance.[28] To take hydrotherapy first, it is important to realise that, even though Isaac, labouring under certain misconceptions inherited from Galen and the ancients (who found that frequent baths prevented scabies but failed to recognize that it was mere cleanliness that was the key to success), overrates the therapeutic value of the bath, hydrotherapy is not to be dismissed out of hand: it has its part to play in skin hygiene, and, it must be said, a properly regulated daily bath of the right kind could have marked beneficial effects on patients.[29]

As for diet, Isaac's advice is hard to fault: food must not only be wholesome and nourishing, it must also be readily digestible, and, if necessary, fed to the patient in smallish amounts so as to avoid overloading his stomach and throwing an unacceptable burden on a disordered digestive system.[30] Paying strict attention to bowel movements and bearing in mind the threat posed by diarrhoea and dehydration from that and other causes, such as sweating and overheating, he advises what he terms 'rinsed bread' *(khubz maghsûl)*[31]—that is to say, gluten-free bread (even today gluten-free bread is prescribed for patients suffering from faulty intestinal absorption of essential foods such as fat, vitamins, etc.; this malabsorption syndrome is a characteristic of coeliac disease, sprue and other maladies)—a copious fluid intake, and, where called for, the inclusion in the diet of some astringent such as the juice of the pomegranate (all parts of which are so).[32]

Milk is rightly seen as an important element of diet.[33] Isaac, it should be noted, prefers the milk of asses or goats; he observes that human milk is the finest nutrient, followed by that of asses, but that most people find both kinds repugnant with the result that, for them, goat's milk must be substituted. In this connection it is worth noting that in recent years the value of mare's milk—which is probably not far different from ass's milk—in the treatment of tuberculosis has been put to the test. In 1969 the assistant medical director

Plate 1 Pul-i-Kashgan bridge, Iran (from Aurel Stein, *Old Routes of Western Iran,* London: Macmillan, 1940, plate 80, p. 266).

Plate 2 Windmills at Khaf: viewed from the north. Notice the winnowing slits near the ground below each of the main wind slits.

Plate 3 Mill roofscape in Nishtafun, 1977; dome, barrel vault and domes.

Plate 4 Afghan windmills (IslamQala) viewed from the south. Notice curved and stepped walls (Richard Hewer, 1971).

Plate 5 Vitruvian millwheel at Pol-e-Shahrestan, outside Isfahan (1962).

Plate 6 Band-e Gerger at Shushtar, mills in foreground (1992).

Plate 7 Drop-tower at Esteban (1992).

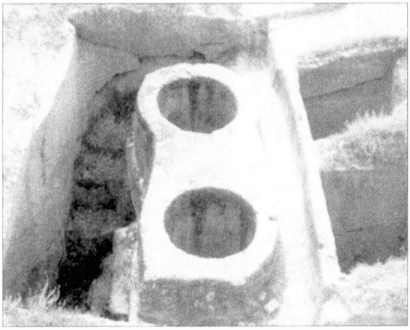

Plate 8 Paired drop-towers at Shushtar (1992).

Plate 9 A new millstone for an Afghan mill in Band-e Amir (1977). It is still wedged on the poplar trunk to which the ox in the foreground was harnessed when the stone was trundled here from the quarry. A team of men had urged on the ox and controlled and braked the stone, weighing about one ton, by means of the longer end of the axle.

Plate 10 Wind-wheel at Nishtafun, showing pattern of construction and materials (1977).

Plate 11 Reed mat sails at Chahar Farsakh, near Neh. Notice the crooked spokes, the jointed wind-shaft (unusual) and the ramshackle rigging (1977).

Plate 12 Stones and grinding place at Fin (1992).

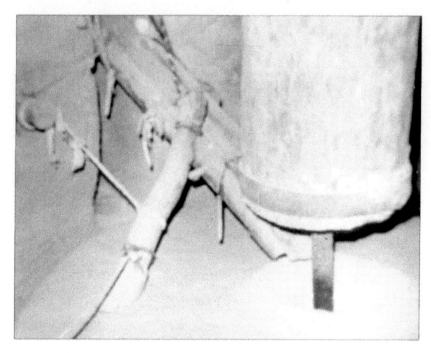

Plate 13 The shoe feeding grain to the stones. Notice the suspension of the feeder channel from the grain hopper, and the vibrator stick responding to the uneven upper surface of the revolving runner stone (1992).

Plate 14 Horizontal millwheel at Esteban (1992).

Plate 15 The western of the two surviving towers of the Hazar Jarib, believed to date from the reign of Shah Abbas (1587–1629). Photograph 1963.

Plate 16 The eastern tower of the Hazar Jarib (1963).

of a TB sanatorium at Ettenheim in Germany reported that, after a total of 135 litres (about 250 pints) per patient, at a litre a day, almost half the patients showed improvement according to X-rays. In 13 per cent of patients with open cavities in the lungs, the cavities closed. In a further 31 per cent there was a significant reduction in the size of the cavities—and almost all patients put on weight. The suggestion was that this comparatively sweet milk with a very high proportion of lactose—in this respect it resembles human milk—brings about changes in the intestinal environment which favour the growth of certain bacteria. It was suspected that these acid-loving bacteria—together with the high content of trace elements and vitamins in mare's milk—stimulate the body into producing more white blood cells, thus increasing the power of resistance against TB.[34] Mare's milk, incidentally, contains four times as much vitamin C as cow's milk, and twice as much as that in human milk. Nothing of all this was, of course, known either to Galen or to Isaac: all that they would have known was that the treatment was beneficial.

One of the most engaging and revealing portions of Isaac's discourse has to do with the general management of the phthisic patient. As one reads it, one is put immediately in mind of the Hippocratic idea of the effect of the environment on health, as propounded in Hippocrates' treatise on Air, Earth and Locality. What is engaging about it is that it evokes a setting that is quite Alhambresque, and what is revealing is that the recommendations it sets forth are unmistakably those, not of a practitioner writing for the public at large, but of a court physician ministering to Aghlabid and Fâtimid royal households. Parts of it are worth quoting:

> When it is winter and not too cold, ways of regulating the air are not called for. Should the weather be unduly cold, however, moderately warm outer garments should be worn to prevent the intensity of the cold from gripping the external surface of the body... If it is summer, some means of cooling and moistening the air should be devised. This may be achieved by seeing that the places in which the patient is seated by day are spacious, roomy apartments with a northern exposure and similarly oriented doors. To the front of them there should be slatted ventilating-windows... The ventilating-windows should be draped with coarse canvas soaked in fresh water against an inner layer of closely woven stiff material similarly soaked, followed by a layer of soaked soft linen stuffs. In the ventilating-windows there should be vessels of newly turned pottery made of a highly scented clay... and filled with fresh, clear filtered water. The patient's position...should be in front of the opening to the ventilating-window on bedding of linen or Tabaristani papyrus... Playing fountains should be installed in front of the patient so that he may listen to the gentle fall of water; for the splash of water, if light and gentle, will induce sleep... Soft, freshly washed linen clothing perfumed with sandal should be worn... At the end of the day the patient should go up to quarters with a northern exposure that are freely ventilated, sprinkled with fresh water, carpeted with aromatic plants and all kinds of odoriferous mats. Alternatively, use may be made of a kiosk or pavilion pitched out in the open and draped with linen cloths.[35]

From this passage it will be readily seen how a phthisic patient might benefit from exposure to the fresh air, though that may well not have been the main consideration but only incidental to the cooling of a feverish patient.

If we may revert to Isaac's dietary advice, it will be noted that great emphasis is laid on nutrition, careful guidance being offered on such matters as the size and frequency of meals as well as on the content, as the following passage well illustrates:

> Since patients in the condition in question [sc. just strong enough to be put on solid food] will be such that, although in need of nourishment, they are too weak to be able to digest it fully because the

stomach is too weak, even though the nourishment is in itself quite moderate, you will have to feed them little by little several times a day. They should, then, be fed three times a day until, when they can take food normally on a stomach that is strong enough to digest it properly, they can bring down feeding to only twice a day, and we can gradually increase the amount. The amount of food offered at the first meal should, however, be such that it is easily ingested by the stomach and can be fully and truly digested before the next food is taken… Since the second meal will be attended by factors aiding ingestion and true digestion, such as rest and sleep taken by the consumer as well as a long interval of time following [ingestion], this second meal should have more strength and durability to it and take longer to digest.[36]

The nature of foods prescribed for patients able to cope with solids includes a range of wholesome and easily digested meats obtainable from fowl and game-birds. Thus, in suitable circumstances the patient may have 'a supper consisting of well-made bread of flour base taken with francolin, grouse, chicken or capon together with their wings or the wings of country-bred free-ranging fowl *(al-dajâj al-râ'iya fî al-qurâ)'*.[37] For very weak patients, however, a bouillon of sucking-kid's meat with apple juice is recommended. Isaac's detailed instructions run as follows:

Take the lean from a kid's neck, ribs and shoulders, and cut into small pieces. Place in a pot and boil slowly in a little water with a pinch of salt. Stir all the while. Once the water with which it has been moistened has been absorbed, add a second lot to soften the meat. When the meat has expressed its juice and begun to shrink, strain and add half the quantity of apple juice; then add to the whole preparation a fragrant, aromatic syrup in an amount equivalent to one-tenth of the total volume, and give to the patient to drink. This preparation… will greatly strengthen patients who have lost their appetite and are debilitated as a result of marked physical deterioration.[38]

Be that as it may, Isaac warns that his patient may well have reached the terminal stages of his illness and be unable to take any more. And so, if his bouillon does not make any impression, and the doctor notes failing strength and lassitude, and if the patient's limbs seem to have dwindled and wasted even more than previously and he seems to have no blood in his veins, and if, moreover, the forearm has grown thin and wasted away, then, says he, 'discontinue treatment and take it for certain that your patient is moribund'.[39]

In his approach to the management of tuberculous patients Isaac accords precedence to nutrition and other measures aimed at constitutional regeneration. He writes: 'As far as you can, you should avoid the use of medicaments and resort to them only when compelled to do so. Even then, you should use only those which are mildest, easiest on Nature, and least drastic, having first assured yourself of their capacity to soothe.'[40] Consequently, in addressing himself to the matter of symptomatic treatment, he relies on a comparatively small range of carefully selected materia medica as he prescribes for patients requiring relief from the most troublesome and distressing afflictions arising from their tuberculous condition. His prescriptions include anti-tussives containing opium in its natural poppy-seed form for the relief of the irksome cough;[41] various throat lozenges, pastilles, and linctuses for similar and related conditions;[42] demulcents containing marshmallow, gum arabic and almonds, presumably for those with irritation of the throat and larynx arising from extension of the tuberculous infection to the trachea;[43] and, for diarrhoea in varying degrees of severity, compounds containing astringent juices, boles, chalk and other binding agents.[44]

What is surprising, perhaps, is that nowhere in Isaac's scheme of management do fresh fruit and vegetables receive the attention or emphasis they deserve. (Not all fruit and vegetables, of course, would be suitable for tuberculous patients, especially those in advanced stages of the disease and afflicted with enteritis and diarrhoea.) It may well be, of course, that fruit was normally eaten as liberally as in antiquity, and for that reason merits no special mention. Isaac does, of course, recommend various fruit juices, including blackcurrant, which is rich in vitamin C, although this fact would obviously have been unknown to him.

Conclusion

What verdict, we may ask in conclusion, should be passed on Isaac's influential discourse on 'hectic fever'? In answer, two points may be made. On the one hand, it must be conceded that the physiology, pathology, medicine and therapeutics of Hippocrates and Galen are the bricks of which it is built, as it were. On the other hand, they are utilized and cemented in a manner different from that employed by those from whom they have been taken, and the result is a handbook which, *as a clinical companion* in the subject to which it addresses itself, has no Hippocratic or Galenic counterpart.

Notes

1. *A Short History of Scientific Ideas to 1900* (Oxford: Clarendon, 1966; first publ. 1959), p. 148.
2. Thermometers of any kind were unknown until the time of Galileo (1564–1642).
3. See R.Walzer, '$\underline{Dj}$âlînûs', *EI²*, Vol. 2, pp. 402f.
4. His main teaching is contained in his *Peri Diaphorôn Pyretôn,* Vol. 7, pp. 273–405; to be found in C.G.Kühn (ed.), *Claudii Galeni Opera Omnia,* 20 vols (Leipzig, 1821–33).
5. His work *Kitâb al-Shukûk 'alâ Jâlînûs* (Doubts about Galen) is partly philosophical.
6. See, in particular, A.Z.Iskandar, 'A Study of ar-Râzî's Medical Writings with Selected Texts and Translations', DPhil thesis (in two parts), Oxford University, 1959. Cf. A.Z.Iskandar, *A Catalogue of Arabic Manuscripts on Medicine and Science in the Wellcome Historical Medical Library* (Publications of the Wellcome Historical Medical Library: Catalogue Series MS. 2 (1966), London, 1967), p. 32 and n. 5.
7. On Arabic terminology, see n. 11 below.
8. On whom, see A.Altmann in *EI²,* Vol. 4, p. 111b.
9. Isaac Judaeus, *Kitâb al-Hummayât li-Ishâq ibn Sulaymân al-Isrâ'îlî (al-Maqâla al-Thâlitha: Fî al-Sill). Isaac Judaeus: On Fevers (The Third Discourse: On Consumption)* Together with an Appendix containing a Facsimile of the Latin Version of this Discourse (Venice, 1576), (ed. and trans.) J.D.Latham and H.D.Isaacs (Arabic Technical and Scientific Texts Vol. 8, Cambridge: Middle East Centre, 1981). Isaac himself seems to have rated three of his medical works above all others: *K.al-Hummayât* (On Fevers), *K. al-Bawl* (On Urine), *K.al-Adwiya al-Mufrada wa-l-Aghdiya* (On Simples and Foods).
10. On whom see B.ben Yahia, in *EI²,* Vol. 2, pp. 59f.
11. Isaac, *Hummayat,* text, p. 1, tr. p. 1. NB, at some points I have slightly modified the English translation given in the published work.
12. H.-P.-J.Renaud, 'Trois études de la médecine arabe en occident, etc.', *Hespéris* 12, 1931, p. 222.
13. Isaac, text, p. 17. Cf. tr. p. 17; Galen, Vol. 7, p. 316. The white, dry rheum, or waste matter, in the canthi of the eyes results from dehydration: the normal secretion, deprived of moisture, inspissates (cf. Isaac, text, p. 17, tr. p. 18).
14. Isaac, text, p. 18. Cf. tr. p. 18; Galen, Vol. 7, p. 317.
15. Isaac, text, pp. 17f., tr. p. 18.
16. D.Hunter and R.R.Bomford, *Hutchison's Clinical Methods* (London: Cassell, 1956), p. 247.
17. Isaac, text, p. 18, tr. p. 19.
18. See A.Z.Iskandar, 'Rhazes' clinical experience. New material', *al-Machriq* 56, 1962, p. 233.

19. Isaac, *passim,* but see, e.g., text, p. 6f., tr. p. 7; text, pp. 1 1f., tr. p. 12f.; text, p. 21, tr. p. 21; text, p. 30, tr. p. 31 and n. 100 at p. 91; text, p. 33, tr. p. 33; text, pp. 38f., tr. pp. 38f; text, p. 48, tr. p. 49 and n. 147 at p. 99.

20. Isaac, text, pp. 63–80, tr. pp. 63–78.

21. On constitutional disturbances, see, in particular, Isaac, text, pp. 6ff., tr. pp. 7ff; text, p. 66, tr. p. 66. On enteritis and diarrhoea, see Isaac, text, p. 27, tr. p. 28; text, pp. 69–72, tr. pp. 69–71; n. 192 at p. 106, n. 197 at p. 107, n. 200 at pp. 107f.

22. See M.Ullmann, *Islamic Medicine* (Islamic Surveys 11, Edinburgh University Press, 1978), pp. 86–96.

23. Ullmann, *Islamic Medicine,* p. 88.

24. See, e.g., Isaac, text, pp. 6f., tr. p. 7; text, p. 38, tr. pp. 38f.; text, p. 69, tr. p. 69 and n. 21 at p. 82.

25. See, however, Isaac, text, pp. 33ff., tr. pp. 34ff.; text, pp. 40f., tr. pp. 40f.

26. Isaac, text, pp. 25f., tr. p. 26; text, pp. 29f., tr. pp. 29–31.

27. Isaac, text, pp. 44ff., tr. pp. 44ff.; text, pp. 36f., tr. p. 37.

28. See, in particular, Isaac, text, pp. 33–8, tr. pp. 34–8 (diet); text, pp. 38–42, tr. pp. 38–42; text, pp. 51–3, tr. pp. 51–3 (hydrotherapy).

29. See Isaac, n. 148 at p. 99.

30. Isaac, text, pp. 33–6, tr. pp. 33–6.

31. Isaac, text, p. 21, tr. p. 22. Cf. text, p. 25, tr. p. 26.

32. Isaac, text, p. 23, tr. p. 24; text, p. 65, tr. p. 65; text, p. 69, tr. p. 69; text, p. 75, tr. p. 74.

33. Isaac, text, p. 37, tr. p. 37; text, pp. 42f., tr. pp. 42–4; text, pp. 53f., tr. pp. 53–5. On cow's milk and buttermilk, see Isaac, text, p. 47, tr. p. 47; text, p. 67, tr. p. 67.

34. Medical report in the *Sunday Times,* 16 November 1969. A summary is given in Isaac, p. 95, n. 132.

35. Isaac, text, pp. 28–30, tr. p. 29–31.

36. Isaac, text, pp. 47f., tr. p. 48.

37. Isaac, text, pp. 43f., tr. p. 44. Cf. text, pp. 71, 72, tr., pp. 70, 71.

38. Isaac, text, pp. 68f., tr. p. 68.

39. Isaac, text, p. 69, tr. p. 69.

40. Isaac, text, p. 21, tr. p. 22.

41. Isaac, text, p. 73, tr. p. 72; text, p. 75, tr. p. 74.

42. See, e.g., Isaac, text, pp. 66ff., tr. pp. 66f.

43. See, e.g., Isaac, text, pp. 73–5, tr. pp. 73–5.

44. Isaac, text, pp. 69–71, tr. pp. 69f.

Chapter 3
Al-Tibb al-Nabawi: The Prophet's Medicine
Ghada Karmi

The medicine of the Prophet, *al-Tibb al-Nabawi,* was a system of medical therapeutics which flourished during the later classical Arabic period, that is from the thirteenth century onwards. It was so called because of its alleged derivation from the Hadith, the sayings and practice of the Prophet Muhammad. In that way, it represented a system of medicine different from that which was current throughout the Arabic/Islamic world of the early medieval period. This medicine had largely been derived from Greek theory and practice and was the accepted method for all teaching and treatment during the first centuries of Islam. Indeed, it continued to dominate medical practice in one form or another until the nineteenth century, and traces of it still survive to our own day.

The Prophet's Medicine, on the other hand, never attained such prominence and did not influence the medical elite or reach the teaching curricula. But it formed a distinct strand in the medical tradition of the Arabic and Islamic world, and as such deserves analysis and attention. It may even enjoy a revival at the present time, if the trend towards Islamism which is currently sweeping the Arab world and elsewhere continues. In its day, it probably represented the expression of a folk tradition which had always existed in the region and which vied with 'establishment medicine'. Thus, it was typically a mixture of elements, some of them magical and superstitious, orally transmitted, as well as a corpus of written works which presented the Prophet's Medicine as a legitimate science.

Graeco-Arabic medicine

The medicine of the classical Islamic age, known as Arabic medicine —not because everyone who originated or practised it was an Arab, but because of the language in which its texts were written—first became established in the Islamic world during the seventh century AD. It reached its zenith in the ninth, tenth and eleventh centuries, the age of Al-Razi, Ibn Sina and Ibn Rushd. At one time, its influence stretched from Spain to Samarkand. By way of Spain, it crossed into medieval Europe where, in Latin dress, it continued to influence medical ideas and medical education in Europe until the sixteenth century and beyond. Its origins were undoubtedly Greek, at first mediated through Syriac doctors and writers, which is hardly surprising in view of the inevitable contacts between the early Arab conquerors and the Syriac-speaking peoples of the Near East. The major cities here—Damascus, Antioch, Caesarea, Jerusalem and Alexandria—were all considerably hellenized by the time of the Arab conquests. All official business was conducted in Greek, those aspiring to high office had to learn Greek, and the intelligentsia used Greek as their everyday language. The hellenization process was greatly accelerated by the establishment of the Christian Church and this directly affected urban dwellers. Even so, many people in Syria still spoke and wrote in Syriac.

At the beginning of the eighth century, the Abbasid caliphs invited Syriac-speaking physicians from the school of Jundi-Shapur in Persia to Baghdad, and thus paved the way for the massive translation movement of medical works from Greek into Arabic via Syriac and later from the original Greek. This ensured the establishment of Greek medicine in its dominant position within the Arabic-speaking world thereafter.

The school of Jundi-Shapur, about which little is known but much has been written, was developed by the Persian emperor, Khosrou Anushirvan, in the middle of the sixth century. This emperor had a great interest in learning and attracted a large number of Greek scholars to his academy. By the time of the Arab conquest, Jundi-Shapur was said to have had a hospital and a flourishing academy, staffed by Syriac-speaking Christian doctors practising Greek medicine. Its fame was so great that the caliph invited its director and his colleagues to set up something similar in Baghdad. In this way, Greek influence through Syriac began to make itself felt in Arabic medical circles, and this in turn led to the subsequent flourishing of Greek medicine among the Arabs and the creation of an extensive Arabic medical literature based on Greek medicine. In a relatively short time, this Graeco-Arabic medicine was thoroughly adopted by the intelligentsia of the Islamic state and became established medical dogma.

What was this Graeco-Arabic medicine? Put at its simplest, it was the ancient theory of humours which had been handed down to Arabic doctors through Greek medical writings, but which they elaborated and developed to a considerable degree. In essence, this theory held that the body was composed of four *elements*—air, fire, earth and water—and four *humours*—blood, phlegm, yellow bile and black bile. The theory explained all health and disease in terms of the condition of the four basic body fluids: the humours. Each of the humours had two *qualities,* hot or cold, wet or dry. Thus, phlegm was cold and wet; blood, hot and wet; yellow bile, hot and dry; and black bile, cold and dry.

Every individual had a slight preponderance of one of the humours, which gave him or her their *temperament*—hence (in English): sanguine, phlegmatic, choleric, melancholic. Perfect health was defined as a state in which the humours were in balance, in equilibrium with each other. Disease resulted when one or more humours altered in quantity or quality relative to the others. Each resulting ailment was defined by relation to its causative humour, hence choleric, phlegmatic, sanguine or black diseases. Treatment was designed to remove the offending humour by various means, and/or to oppose its qualities. Hence, therapeutic herbs, drugs and also foods were characterized according to their humoral qualities. They could be heating or cooling, moistening or drying. The humoral classification of medicines and foods was extensively developed by the Arabic doctors, and they were given a score which measured their properties in degrees, such that treatment could be more appropriate and exact.

Of course, humoralism dominated medical thinking in Europe as well, and the widespread prevalence of humoral words and concepts in English as used today is testament to this. The extent to which the Arabs developed, innovated or improved on Greek medicine is a subject of much debate. The argument has traditionally been polarized between those who claim that the Arabs made original contributions and those who say they were mere transmitters of the Greek legacy.

This debate is not unique to medicine. It has been equally applied to Arabic science, philosophy, engineering, art and architecture. It is certainly true that Arabic doctors drew on a large Greek medical literature for the source of their medicine. The available evidence suggests that, in essence, the theoretical basis of Arabic medicine remained Greek, but certain special areas were developed by the Arabs to a much larger extent, for example, ophthalmology, surgery and pharmacology. Even so, it was Greek humoral theory which formed the framework and the limits of all Arabic medical thinking, observation and discovery. We know that the early Abbasid caliphs of Baghdad invited Indian physicians and scholars to their court, rewarded them generously and held them in high esteem. Nevertheless, Indian medicine and the Indian world-view never really caught on with the Arabs, and they remained committed to Greek medicine and Greek philosophy. At their hands, Greek medicine became highly organized and systematized to the ultimate degree. This feature is best exemplified in Ibn Sina's monumental work, *al-Qanun fi'l-Tibb,* which brought together the whole of Arabic medical theory and practice, and was the medical bible for generations of doctors and scholars.[1] Even today, it is a basic textbook for training in the so-called *Unani Tibb* of the Hamdard National Institute in Karachi, where doctors are taught traditional Arabic medicine.

Within the confines of humoralism, Graeco-Arabic medicine was a rational system, remarkably free of magic, superstition and religious influences. A good illustration of this last point is provided by the frequent prescriptions for wine found in Arabic medical books. Indeed, there was a well-established tradition for the use of wine in disease, presumably stemming from the Greeks. Dioscorides, the second-century Greek herbalist, for example, devoted a long section of his *Materia Medica* to the medicinal effects of wine.[2] Much later, the Arabic physician, al-Razi, wrote a separate tract on wine, called *al-Maqala fi'l-Sharab.*[3] Wine was even prescribed for headache brought on by drinking too much wine! The practice was evidently so well accepted that none of the medical books includes any references to the religious prohibition on the drinking of wine. Nowhere in these texts is there any compromise with religious dogma and, although most of the writers would have been familiar with the religious sayings on health, these never appear in their writings on medicine. In the same way, Maimonides, the prominent Jewish doctor who was also a rabbi, never, in any of his medical works, drew on Talmudic medicine, with which he would have been especially familiar. But despite this, there seems to have been a parallel interest in astrology and the occult. A quite separate literature existed on what may be termed astrological medicine. This was chiefly concerned with the effect of the planets on the human body, including birth, death, pregnancy and disease, the most favourable astrological times for various remedies and procedures, and predictions of health and disease. However, astrological medicine remained a sideline curiosity and never attained the status of Graeco-Arabic medicine.

The Prophet's Medicine

Into this secular medical milieu, a hostile and different medical alternative in the shape of the Prophet's Medicine, *al-Tibb al-Nabawi,* made its appearance sometime after 1100 AD. It presented itself through the writings of jurists, historians and religious scholars, not physicians. According to Hajji Khalifa, the seventeenth-century Arabic bibliographer, the earliest of these, by Abul-Hasan 'Ali al-Rida, goes back as far as the reign of the Abbasid caliph al-Ma'mun (reg. 833–842), but the book is no longer extant. Elgood asserts that another example, the book on *Tibb an-Nabi* by Abu Nu'aim Ahmad al-Isfahani, dates from either the eleventh or the twelfth century.[4] The bulk of Prophetic medicine literature, however, seems to have been written sometime later, after 1200 AD. Ibn al-Jawzi (d. 1200) included a special section on the Prophet's sayings relating to health in a larger book on the Quran and Hadith.[5] His student, Dia' al-Din Muhammad al-Maqdisi, who died in 1245, wrote a separate book on *al-Tibb al-Nabawi* which survives in manuscript form. The best known is the *al-Tibb al-Nabawi* of Ibn Qayyim al-Jawziyya, who died in Damascus in 1350. This formed a part of a large book called *Zad al-Mi'ad bi huda khayr al-'Ibad, and for this reason* was not included in Hajji Khalifa's listing of books on the Prophet's Medicine.[6] The section on the Prophet's Medicine was copied many times over in subsequent centuries, an indication of its popularity perhaps.[7] The historian 'Abd Allah Muhammad b. Ahmad al-Dhahabi (d. 1348) also wrote a book on the Prophet's Medicine which was a collection of Prophetic traditions taken from Bukhari's and other compilations of the Hadith. Roughly contemporary with al-Dhahabi was the writer of another book on the Prophet's Medicine, al-Surramarri (d. 1374). Later books include *K. al-Rahma fi'l-Tibb wal-Hikma* by Muhammad al-Sanawbari (d. 1412) and another by al-Azraq, a fifteenth-century writer. The famous Jalal al-

Din al-Suyuti (d. 1505) also wrote a book on the Prophet's Medicine.[8] Elgood cites a further four books on the same subject, including one written in Urdu of unknown date.

The Prophet's Medicine was in fact a collection of injunctions and anecdotes about health and the cure of disease, all purportedly going back to the Prophet Muhammad. They claimed to originate from the books of Prophetic traditions or *Hadith,* that is the accounts of what the Prophet said or did, or of his approval of what was said and done, collected in several volumes. The *Hadith* is supposed to guide Muslims in all matters moral, spiritual and practical. Inevitably, as in all oral histories, many traditions of dubious authenticity were incorporated into the *Hadith.* Some of these went on to form the substance of the Prophet's Medicine. It also included many pre-Islamic magical practices and beliefs which had persisted into the Islamic era and reappeared in religious guise, dignified with the Prophet's authority.

What little we know about medical conditions and their cure in pre-Islamic Arabia suggests that magic and superstition played a very large part.[9] For example, the story is told that when once there was an epidemic of fever (presumably malarial in origin) in the Arabian oasis of Khaybar, people visiting the place would bray at the gates like donkeys to protect themselves. The reason was that they believed the fever attacked only humans, and by imitating donkeys they hoped to make it think they were not human and so to avoid catching it. In another example, a man could repel an attack of insanity or an invasion of spirits by befouling himself with menstrual cloths and surrounding himself with dead men's bones. An illness could be expelled by transference to someone else. For example, in a fever, a thread is tied round the arm of the patient. Whoever undoes the thread will have the fever transferred to him, and the patient will recover. If someone is bitten by a snake, he can be cured if he holds pieces of women's jewellery in his hand and rattles them all night.

As for treatment, the commonest pre-Islamic operations seem to have been cupping and the cautery. These were used for a wide variety of conditions from scab and open wounds to mental illness and dropsy. It is noteworthy here that one of the traditions ascribed to the Prophet and cited in later books of the Prophet's medicine is the saying: 'There are only three treatments: honey, cupping and the cautery.' Another important remedy widely used was camel's urine. According to a pre-Islamic Arabian poet, it seems that mangy camels were themselves treated with human urine. Camel's milk was also used in medical treatment, as was the gall of wild beasts. Henna was prescribed for skin conditions, and a small number of other plants were also used medicinally. One of these was the 'black grain', *al-habba al-sawda',* which features in another so-called Prophetic recommendation for its use in fever. Magic and superstition were rife: for example, epilepsy was explained on the basis of demons entering the body of the patient. The plague was said to be caused by the bite of a *jinni.* Snakes could cause abortion. Magic spells were used against the effects of the evil eye or against snake and scorpion bites. It is interesting that many of these pre-Islamic beliefs and practices re-surfaced in later Islamic times in the guise of Prophetic medicine.

The Prophet's Medicine was drawn from three sources: pre-Islamic folk medicine, general injunctions in the *Hadith,* and Graeco-Arabic medicine. The claim of *al-Tibb al-Nabawi* to a religious origin does not reside in the Quran, which has nothing to say about medicine or healing, but rather in the *Hadith.* In fact, the different collections of *Hadith,* such as those by al-Bukhari, Muslim, al-Tirmidhi and so on, had their own medical sections which were collections of the medical teachings and recommendations ascribed to the Prophet.

Bukhari collected some 80 paragraphs on this subject. Three strands are to be found in them: first, theological, that is the meaning of disease, the significance of taking secular remedies for the pious and the like. An example of this strand is the famous saying: 'God has created no disease for which he has not also created a cure.' Or again: 'Science is of two kinds: the science of bodies and the science of religions.' In the Muslim view, disease was not a punishment for sin. On the contrary, disease is God-sent as a part of creation and man must pray to God for guidance in learning how to cure it. This idea is to be seen in the attitudes to the great plague epidemics which attacked Syria and Palestine in the mid-fourteenth century. Several contemporary writers who described the plague put it down to impurity of the air or to a simple fact of God's creation, but rarely to divine anger or retribution.[10] Prayer was of no avail in postponing death, for the exact span of each human life was predestined by God. The Quran says: 'To every people is a term appointed; when their term is reached, not an hour can they delay it nor an hour advance it.'[11]

Hadith literature also speaks of the obligations which Muslims had towards the sick; visiting and caring for them was a religious duty. Segregation of the sexes did not apply to sick people, for women could be permitted to nurse sick men. The second strand in Bukhari's collection on medicine may be described as a set of general injunctions on health. For example, the Prophet said: 'Travel! It keeps you healthy.' Contagion is the subject of other injunctions. In a plague epidemic, the Prophet advised that people avoid the place, but if they were already there when the disease started, they should not attempt to leave. He recommended swift flight away from those afflicted by leprosy. Or again, in a tradition about the causation of disease: 'All disease comes from the stomach, and dietary regimen is the principal treatment.'

This connection between the health of the stomach and the body's general health was an ancient and widespread belief among the Arabs until this very day. People nowadays still talk about their stomachs being 'dirty', that is, full of unhealthy matter, and feeling generally ill is quite often ascribed to this cause. In a reference to food and drink, the Quran says: 'eat and drink, but not to excess. God likes not excesses.'[12] The anecdote is recounted that a physician who was either a Jew or a Christian (he is described as being from among the 'people of the book'), on hearing these words from the Quran and the Prophet, exclaimed that the hundred medical books he'd written had been superseded. He embraced Islam forthwith, exclaiming, 'Your Book and your Prophet have left nothing for Galen!' (This refers to the first-century Greek physician whose writings and medical ideas dominated Arabic medicine.)

The third strand concerns drugs and remedies. Honey had a place of pre-eminence in all Prophetic treatments, a custom which persists in the Arabic-speaking world today. I even came across a man in Aleppo when I was working there who instilled honey into his ears in the hope of curing his deafness! Fever could be treated by pouring water over the patient. The 'black grain' mentioned above also features widely, as does the milk and urine of camels. Many of the remedies are clearly magical, in spite of the clear Islamic prohibition on sorcery, *sihr*. For example, amulets were made up for various diseases. One common practice involved the writing of Quranic verses on a piece of cloth. This was then soaked in water, which the patient drank. Al-Suyuti defended these practices, saying: 'The recitation of charms and the wearing of amulets are a form of refuge with God in order to secure health, just as is done in the case of medicines.'[13] The following story also illustrates the influence of magic on the Prophet's medicine. Al-Suyuti recounts that a man once disputed the Prophet's authority that cupping should never be performed on a Saturday, for it might lead to leprosy, and did so. He was instantly struck down with the disease. Whereupon he repented to the Prophet, who appeared to him in a dream and the man recovered.[14]

Many treatments recommended in the Prophet's Medicine include herbs and drugs taken from later Graeco-Arabic formularies. The link with Graeco-Arabic medicine, which the Prophet's Medicine otherwise refuted, is an interesting one. Many of the medical concepts, as well as remedies, are directly taken from humoral theory. For example, this passage from *al-Tibb al-Nabawi* of Ibn Jawziyya is couched in clear humoral terms:

If honey is drunk before breakfast, it dissolves phlegm, washes staleness out of the stomach, clarifies the viscid matter within it, expels the superfluities from it, warms it to a moderate degree...but it harms the bilious patient because it is hot and so is yellow bile and the honey may agitate the bile.[15]

Or in another passage, 'to protect against epidemics, evacuate the moist superfluities, reduce the diet and incline towards the drying regimen…during a plague, [recommend] rest to quieten the disturbance of the humours'.[16] Greek medical authorities are often cited in the text and much of the material is a bewildering mix of theology, superstition and humoralism.

Al-Jawziyya's book on the Prophet's Medicine is instructive to study. *Al-Tibb al-Nabawi* is divided into 277 chapters which deal with individual diseases, remedies, medico-legal matters, malpractice and the competence of doctors. There is a long section on the Evil Eye, and this author too defends the use of prayer, charms and incantations in the treatment of disease. Although he ascribes every major statement in the book to the Prophet, it is hard to believe that many of these so-called traditions were in fact authentic.

However, the really interesting feature of the book is its attempt to confirm the truth of the Prophet's injunctions on health by explaining them in terms of humoral medicine. For example, he interprets the Prophet's famous saying about how to behave during epidemics, referred to above—'do not enter a land which has an epidemic, but if inside, do not leave'—as follows: 'The body is never without an evil superfluity, which is excited by exercise because this mixes it with the good *chymos* and will bring out a major disease… leaving an epidemic will lead to movement',[17] and hence this will make the person susceptible to the plague, and the truth of the Prophet's advice can now be affirmed. Elsewhere, we have this in a chapter on dropsy.[18] The Prophet is reported as saying that drinking camel's urine and camel's milk would cure this ailment, and indeed, he says, patients who tried this remedy recovered. Al-Jawziyya then gives a tortuous justification of this practice in humoral terms, saying that urine has a diuretic action and hence would drain off the fluid in the body of the dropsical patient. He then presents a series of quotations from the works of al-Razi and al-Isra'ili on the merits and qualities of camel's milk, and he cites Ibn Sina (whom he calls 'the author of *al-Qanun*'), on the curative properties of this milk in treating dropsy.

There are numerous other examples in the book of this retrospective explanation and justification, whose aim is to demonstrate how right the Prophet was within the scientific framework of later times. To my mind, this is reminiscent of the activities of present-day devout Muslims who attempt to explain Quranic verses about the universe or the human body by recourse to modern science.

In summary, therefore, the Prophet's Medicine was a collection of injunctions on health, purportedly emanating from the Prophet Muhammad. They were culled from the books of Prophetic *Hadith* and dealt mainly with the sick and with healing. The result is a combination of inconsistent statements and prescriptions, representing a mixture of pre-Islamic medicine and magic, with an overlay of Greek humoralism. What proportion of the Prophet's Medicine could genuinely lay claim to being prophetic is not known, but it is likely that it was not very much. Its authenticity was called into question early on in Arabic circles: the fourteenth-century social historian, Ibn Khaldun, drew attention to its secular, bedouin origins. His comment is worth quoting in full:

Traditions concerned with the medicine of the Prophet are of the Bedouin type. It is in no way part of divine revelation. Such medical matters were merely part of Arab custom and happened to be mentioned in connection with the circumstances of the Prophet, like other things that were customary in his generation. They were not mentioned in order to imply that that particular way of practising medicine is stipulated by the religious law. Muhammad was sent to teach us the religious law. He was not sent to teach us medicine or any other worldly matter… None of the statements concerning medicine that occur in sound traditions should be considered to have the force of law. There is nothing to indicate that this is the case. The only thing is that if that type of medicine is used for the sake of a divine blessing and in true religious faith, it may be very useful. However, that would have nothing to do with humoral medicine but be the result of true faith.[19]

Ibn al-Khatib, an Andalusian writer who died in 1348, when discussing the plague epidemics, repudiated the validity of traditions in the Prophet's medicine as incompatible with the evidence of the senses.[20] But, as we shall see, such sentiments did not deter religious zealots from urging the faithful to adopt the Prophet's Medicine as the only true method of healing for Muslims.

Significance of the Prophet's Medicine

What was the significance of the Prophet's Medicine? Modern scholars are in no doubt that it represented a shift of authority from ancient Greek medicine, which was regarded as heathen, to the Prophet of Islam; that is, a shift from reason to religious belief, and 'the dethronement of Galenic medicine by Bedouin quackery'.[21]

Writers on the Prophet's Medicine made no secret of their hostility to the Greek system. Al-Surramarri, who was a fanatical proponent of the Prophet's Medicine, says that his book was there to demonstrate that Galenic medicine could only be validated by reference to the Prophet. Ullmann comments that the purpose of the Prophet's medicine was to reinforce orthodox belief over heathen Galenic medicine.[22] If this is correct, why should it have happened, given that hellenistic medicine had been in use throughout the Islamic world for several hundred years before the books on the Prophet's Medicine made their appearance, without any evidence of its rejection by the generality of people? And is there anything significant about the timing of its appearance? What precipitated the hostility to it and the shift towards orthodox belief? Was it part of a wider movement in an Islamic world which was beginning a process of political fragmentation and needed to reassert its identity by reference to indigenous—hence, religious— culture? Or was it something simpler: the expression of a lay medicine in the face of an established medical elite?

The short answer is, we do not know. We may, however, infer that the historical evidence we have about the medicine of the medieval Islamic world is chiefly the history of great men and great books. Little is known about the medicine which ordinary people used, and what access they had to doctors and to hospitals. We may suppose that urban dwellers had reasonable access, but the situation must have been very different in the countryside. Most, if not all, 'good' doctors practised in the major cities, a situation not very different from that in today's Arab world, and the country areas remained isolated. It is also likely that urban dwellers' access to medicine was not universally good but was linked to wealth and class. This situation may have been responsible for the appearance of a specific genre of Arabic medical book from the ninth century onwards, catering for people who had no access to a doctor, either because they lived outside major cities or because they could not afford the doctor's fees. Hence such titles as 'The poor man's medicine', or 'For him who has no physician to attend him'. Likewise also the numerous books of 'Traveller's medicine' which were intended to help those who were far from home and hence had no access to a doctor.

It may be conjectured that the people who needed such books also had an ongoing medical practice to which they resorted in time of need. And such practices are likely to be closer to folk medicine than to the educated literary medicine which was the preserve of the urban intelligentsia of the Islamic world. In this sense, the Prophet's Medicine was no more than a continuation of ancient folk practices, amended to conform to Islam, and yet another example of the self-help systems which did not require the services of a doctor. It would have been handed down as an evolving oral tradition which was not documented until the later centuries of Islam, appearing then as 'the Medicine of the Prophet'. Indeed, even today, traces of ancient Arabian folk and magical practices are still to be found in the Arab world, mixed with accretions from medieval humoral medicine.[23]

The Prophet's Medicine provides an insight into an alternative history and tradition which may help to throw as much light on the history of Islamic society as on the history of medicine. It deserves deeper and wider research and study.

Notes

1. Ibn Sina, *Al-Qanun fi'l-Tibb* (Cairo: Bulaq, 1887, and many other editions).
2. *The Greek Herbal of Dioscorides,* trans. J.Goodyer (1656), (ed.) R.T.Gunter (New York: Hafner, 1959), pp. 603–23.
3. Al-Razi, *Maqala fi'l-Sharab,* in M.Ullmann, *Die Medizin im Islam* (Leiden: Brill, 1970), p. 200.
4. C.Elgood, 'The medicine of the Prophet', *Medical History* 6, 1962, pp. 146–53.
5. Ullmann, *Die Medizin,* p. 185.
6. Ibn Qayyim al-Jawziyya, *Al-Tibb al-Nabawi,* (ed.) Muhammad b.Said Rajih (Beirut: Dar al-Kitab al-'Arabi, 1983); Elgood, 'The medicine', p. 148.
7. al-Jawziyya, *Al-Tibb al-Nabawi,* Introduction.
8. Ullmann, *Die Medizin,* pp. 186–7.
9. M.Ullmann, *Islamic Medicine* (Edinburgh: Edinburgh University Press, 1978), pp. 2–5.
10. M.Dols, *The Black Death in the Middle East* (Princeton, NJ: Princeton University Press, 1977), pp. 109–13.
11. Quran, S. 7, v.34.
12. Quran, S. 7, v.31.
13. C.Burghel, 'Secular and religious features of medieval Arabic medicine', in C.Leslie (ed.) *Asian Medical Systems* (Berkeley: University of California Press, 1976), pp. 54–61.
14. C.Burghel, 'Secular and religious features'.
15. al-Jawziyya, *Al-Tibb al-Nabawi,* p. 204.
16. al-Jawziyya, *Al-Tibb al-Nabawi,* p. 34.
17. al-Jawziyya, *Al- Tibb al-Nabawi.*
18. al-Jawziyya, *Al-Tibb al-Nabawi,* p. 36.
19. Ibn Khaldun, *The Muqaddimah. An Introduction to History,* (trans.) F. Rosenthal (Bollinger Series 43, 2nd edn, Princeton University Press, 1967), Vol. 3, pp. 150–1.
20. Ibn al-Khatib, quoted in Burghel, 'Secular and religious features', p. 56.
21. Burghel, 'Secular and religious features', p. 59.
22. Ullman, *Die Medizin,* p. 185; *Islamic Medicine,* p. 5.
23. G.Karmi, 'The colonisation of traditional Arabic medicine', in R.Porter (ed.) *Patients and Practitioners* (Cambridge University Press, 1985), pp. 315–39.

Chapter 4
Early Arabic Cuisine: The Evidence from Medieval Arabic Medical Texts
Ghada Karmi

Medieval Islamic society had a considerable interest in the culinary arts. Several books on cookery survive, spanning the period from the tenth century to the fourteenth, most notably those of Ibn Sayyar al-Warraq,[1] al-Baghdadi,[2] and later texts from Egypt and the Islamic west in Spain. These books provide a picture of what must have been a thriving interest in elaborate foods, sweets and drinks, many decorated and scented, and a fascinating range of spices, meats and vegetables.

What is less well known is that there was an alternative and perhaps unexpected tradition to the cuisine of the classical Islamic age. Medieval Arabic medical textbooks would seem to be an unlikely source for information on cookery. Yet, in the case of Arabic/Islamic culture, this was very much the case. The reason for this bears no relation to the hedonism which motivated many of the tracts on cookery, but resides rather in the fact that diet was regarded as an essential part of the theory and practice of medicine at that time. Medical textbooks of the classical period of Islam always contained sections on what the patient should eat and drink, especially during convalescence. A healthy regimen of foods and drinks was the key, not only to recovery from illness, but also for the preservation of health. Whole tracts were devoted to particular foods with medicinal properties, and no doctor's prescription would have been complete without a set of instructions on diet. Many famous physicians wrote exclusive books on dietetics, for example Hunayn ibn Ishaq, al-Razi and Ibn Sina. Al-Majusi devoted 15 chapters of his great medical encyclopaedia, *al-Kamil fi'l-Sina'a al-Tibbiyya,* to the subject.[3]

This tradition can be traced back to the ancient Greeks, from whom Arabic doctors derived much of the basis of their medical theory, as outlined briefly in the previous chapter. Hippocrates' 'Regimen in acute disease' dealt exclusively with the question of diet and its effects on the constitution, as well as the timing and frequency of meals.[4] Likewise, the first-century Greek physician, Galen, wrote ten books on dietetics. The bulk of Greek medical literature had been translated into Arabic early in the Islamic state, during the eighth and ninth Christian centuries, and the books of Hippocrates and Galen were well known to Arabic physicians. However, none of these Greek works provides us with the range and richness of detail of the Arabic books. It would be difficult indeed to piece together a picture of ancient Greek cuisine relying on Greek medical material only.

The Islamic physicians did not of course intend their medical writings to act as recipe books for the general public. In that sense, the data on the contemporary cuisine was, so to speak, a side effect of these works. But inadvertently, they act as an invaluable source of knowledge about the society of the time, in a historical period peculiarly devoid of sociological documentation. It has often been remarked that we lack a social history of Islam during the classical age. There is no Arabic history of ordinary people, and no Muslim Samuel Pepys or John Evelyns exist to illuminate the detail of everyday life. The medieval books on *Hisba,* or market regulation., may be regarded as an indirect and partial source of sociological information, but aside from the travellers' books of such men as Ibn Battuta and Ibn Jubayr, *The Arabian*

Nights is probably the closest source there is on Islamic society of the tenth and eleventh centuries. It is not widely known that medical books of the period represent another untapped source for sociological information and should be studied with that aim in view.

The theory of humours, according to which early Islamic physicians operated, has been described briefly in the previous chapter. Because foods were classified according to their qualities, such as hot and cold, and could also give rise to the production of humours (for example, cheese, aubergines and dried meat all engender the black bile), they had a place in the genesis and treatment of disease. But there was another reason for their association with health, and that was in the doctrine of the six *non-naturals*. These were regarded as fundamental to health and consisted of such things as sleep and waking, exercise, bodily evacuations and psychological states. They were important in the preservation of health—what we would now call preventive medicine—and foods and drinks were one of the non-naturals. Hence, medical practice required attention to diet in two main areas: the treatment of disease and the prevention of ill health.

Medical sources on foods and drinks

I concentrate on the works of a little-known tenth-century physician, Abu Mansur al-Hasan ibn Nuh al-Qamari, as a typical example of the kind of commonplace medical writing at the time. Al-Qamari formed the subject of an extensive study into medical writing of the early Islamic centuries which I carried out some years ago. The usual medical textbook during this period was the so-called *kunnash,* a compilation of medical theory and practice meant for use by practising doctors. Some of these *kunnashat* were very grand, for example the medical works of Ibn Sina, whose *Kitab al-Qanun* was a sort of super-*kunnash,* and they could be very large books. Many, however, were of manageable size and combined comprehensiveness with compactness. In time, they gave rise to a whole genre of epitomes and handbooks which were very popular not only among Arabic readers but also, in translated form, in medieval Europe. These books usually had the same form. They classified diseases from head to toe, starting with the brain and going down through the body to the feet. This strikes a modern reader as strange, since medical books of today arrange their material according to a mixture of criteria, such as anatomical site, function and cause.

Abu Mansur al-Qamari was a fourth/tenth-century physician of Persian origin whose chief claim to fame was the dubious assertion that he was one of Ibn Sina's teachers in medicine. Little is otherwise known of his life, but he has left us with two books, one a *kunnash* of medicine, called *Kitab al-Ghina wal-Muna,* and the second, a small medical dictionary called *Kitab al-Tanwir fi'l-Istilahat al-Tibbiyya.*[5] This latter work is, to the best of my knowledge, the earliest Arabic medical dictionary on record. A third work of his, *Kitab 'Ilal al-'Ilal,* is unfortunately lost. The first book, *Kitab al-Ghina wal-Muna,* which exists in at least 43 manuscript copies but has never been edited or published, is set out as a typical *kunnash* with the diseases from head to toe, a second section on external disease which we would now call skin diseases, and then a section on fevers, a typical ingredient of all the medical books of the time. All chapters are set out in the same way: first a description of the condition, followed by the signs and symptoms, then advice on diagnostic procedures, and ending with a variety of remedies. It is here that the material on foods and drinks is to be found. Thus, there may be references to single foods or to cooked dishes and the dividing line between their use as nourishment or as ingredients in medical prescriptions is often blurred. *Ghina wa Muna* is a particularly good example to use in this context because of its emphasis on therapeutics. A good proportion of the book is devoted to treatment and rather tedious lengthy prescriptions, and the longest part of each chapter is the one on therapy.

The place of diet in the treatment of disease according to classical Arabic medicine is well exemplified in the following passage from the famous fourth/tenth-century Islamic physician, al-Razi, cited in *Ghina wa Muna* by al-Qamari, who was a late contemporary of Razi and greatly admired him:

> Bodily strength is to the patient as provisions to the traveller, and the disease is as the journey. For this reason, it is incumbent on the physician to pay careful attention to preventing the strength from failing before the culmination of the illness by nourishing the patient, resting him, and making him happy…when the strength is good and the disease short, proceed to remove the cause…but when the matter is uncertain, let your inclination be more towards increasing the strength.[6]

In other words, attention is to be paid to keeping up the patient's strength so that he can fight his illness, and the physician's job is to see that the patient's nutrition is adequate.

In the treatment of vertigo, for example, al-Qamari says: 'Vertigo may be due to a weak heart and a lowering of strength. It is treated with the strengthening and building-up regimen.'[7] This contrasts strikingly with the tendency of modern medicine to ignore the patient's nutrition and concentrate on curative procedures instead. The idea of the body's innate strength, at some time called resistance, seems to have gone completely from today's medical thinking.

And thus it is that we find the names of foods and drinks in common usage at the time, in these sections on treatment. For example, in cases of meningitis:

> Let the patient's nutrition be lettuce, chard, artiplex, Jew's mallow, chenopodium, purlsane, cucumber and wild cucumber, skinned Indian peas and lentils, skinned barley, and Indian water melon. If he refuses, then give him mushed barley and mushed almonds and barley water to drink once or twice a day.[8]

We also learn about foods in an indirect way, when they are described as harmful. In cases of melancholy, for example, what we would call madness today, certain foods are to be avoided. Because it was believed that the condition was caused by an excess of black bile, certain foods were considered unsuitable. Al-Qamari says:

> Warn him against rich foods which engender the black bile, such as lentils, cabbage, aubergine, garden beans, dried meat, stale bread, chestnuts, beef, he-goat's meat, nag's meat, ass's meat, all game, and all salty, sharp, sour, or bitter things.[9]

Incidentally, melancholics were to be given the strengthening regimen referred to above, because, 'when they are fattened up, they will recover completely'.[10]

According to al-Qamari, cholera could be caused by certain foods. He says: 'It mostly occurs because of eating fresh fruit after food, and especially water melon.'[11]

Thus, diet in Arabic medicine played a vital role in the treatment and management of disease. It was important, as we have seen, for maintaining the patient's strength and restoring him after illness; certain foods were more beneficial than others for certain states, and some had positively to be avoided. In addition, foods played a significant role in the humoral theory of disease, for they were graded as cold or hot or dry or wet, and some were capable of producing certain humours within the body. Therefore, it followed that foods chosen correctly according to their qualities (in a humoral sense) could be therapeutic agents.

Early Arabic cuisine

What can we learn from the medical sources about the early Arabic cuisine? Al-Qamari's second book, the medical dictionary which I edited in 1991, turns out to be a most useful source. This dictionary is divided into ten chapters, each dealing with an aspect of medicine. Terms are defined briefly and succinctly. The author's aim, as his introduction states, is to provide both medical student and qualified practitioner with information on the meaning of medical terms which otherwise could only be obtained from a variety of disparate sources. Chapter 7 of the book is entitled 'On the names of foods and drinks', but there is additional information on the same subject in parts of Chapter 10, 'On those things which are in everyday use'. Some of the definitions of terms in these chapters are unfortunately too abbreviated to be illuminating, and many words, obviously well known at the time, are obscure to us now. Furthermore, some clearly show a Persian or non-Arab origin, and scholars of the subject have been led to speculate about the Persian antecedents of the Arabic cuisine.

The chapter on foods contains the names of 25 types of food, either as single ingredients or in combination to make a specific dish. Some of these are generic names which describe a style of cooking, as for example: 'roasts' which he defines as: 'all meats which are placed over the baking oven and roasted'. Or 'Fried foods', which do not turn out to be what we would mean today by fried. He says:

(This is) meat cut into pieces and put into a pot. Water is then poured over it and it is boiled until the water decreases and the meat is left moist and soft. To this are added what is necessary of herbs, spices, and *al-afâwiya* depending on the condition and the time.[12]

Fortunately, the term *al-afâwiya* is explained further on in the same chapter. These are 'aromatic medicines such as cloves, cinnamon, and galingale'.

The names of single foods are also included. For example, *al-hushkâr,* 'A type of bread, made of wheat which is ground as it is'. This is presumably what we might today call wholemeal bread. *Al-huwwârâ,* on the other hand, is 'wheat which has been wetted and skinned (by pounding) in the pestle and then ground. It is also known as table bread.' Generic foods include *al-tawâbîl* (condiments): 'that which seasons the cooking pot such as salt, vinegar and saffron'. And spices, *al-abâzîr,* which apparently included fresh and dried coriander and mint, as well as cumin and aniseed. Recipes are provided for the preparation of a variety of dishes, some quite simple, as for example soft-boiled eggs, whose name obviously derives from Persian: *al-bayd al-nimbirisht.* 'Eggs which are cooked until they are close to setting and are then drunk.' Or *al-kabâb* which is: 'meat that is cast onto burning coal to roast'. Similarly, *al-kirdanâk,* clearly a non-Arabic word, is 'meat which is skewered on a stick or iron and turned over burning coals until it is roasted'.[13]

More complex recipes follow, some of them for highly obscure dishes, for example *al-ihal* (or, *al-uhal*):

meat juices and herb juice mixed and cooked together, and this is known as the *khilbâj* essence (or, in other versions: *al-jilbâj,* or, *al-khlîbâj*). This name is taken from a term used among Bedouin Arabs who live in caves and in the tops of mountains.[14]

Al-hulâm is described as follows:

when meat is boiled in salt water until it is cooked. It is then removed and placed on a clean plate until all its juice is drained. Herbs as necessary are then boiled in vinegar. The meat is put into (this mixture) and removed from the heat. These dishes can be made in various ways, but all of them have the (same) basic ingredients of meats, herbs, condiments, spices, and vinegar.[15]

Another recipe describes a type of savoury bread. The dish is called simply 'vinegar oil' *(al-khall zayt):*

> bread is cut into pieces and cold greens such as lettuce, coriander, cucumber, purslane and the like are cut up over it. Sugar is melted in vinegar together with the juice of unripe grapes, pomegranate juice and the like as required. This is poured over the bread pieces, and then oil or almond oil or vinegar oil *[sic]* is poured on top.[16]

The chapter on substances in everyday use contains some interesting directions for various procedures. For example, how to heat food, how to make cheese, how to soften fat which has become hard and rancid, how to extract oil from vegetables, and several other procedures for making what we would call today marginal substances, which are not drugs as such but have a medicinal use as adjuncts to or solvents for drugs. Many of the substances described here are once again obscure to us, but one sees them referred to many times in medical books of the time.

The use of wine in Arabic medicine

No account of this subject would be complete without a reference to the widespread use of wine in medical treatment. There was a well-established tradition for the use of wine in disease. Al-Razi wrote a separate tract on the subject, called *al-Maqala fi'l-Sharab.* The use of wine was so widespread, as shown by the frequent mention of it in the treatment sections of most chapters in medical textbooks, that it is impossible to define a pattern of indications for its administration. It was often described as being white, light, and well-diluted with water, although the red variety of wine was also known.

Al-Qamari's small dictionary leaves us in no doubt about the importance of wine in medicine, and throws light on the meanings of wine terms seen frequently in medical texts. The section on wine appears at the end of Chapter 7 on foods and drinks. *Al-sharâb,* he says, is the name used for the sort of grape-juice which intoxicates. He then gives several alternative names for wine evidently in use at the time: *al-bâdhiq, al-khamr,* and fascinatingly enough, *al-qahwa,* which later of course changed its usage to mean coffee (and from which the word 'coffee' is itself derived), but which al-Qamari tells us is: 'light, white, diluted wine'. He then gives definitions for a number of wines in common use. *Al-sharâb al-rîhânî:* 'the grape wine with aloes, cloves and suchlike added'. *Al-sharâb al-murawwaq:* 'grape wine which is strained until it is pure and then set aside until it matures'. Or lastly, *al-sharâb al-'atîq:* 'wine which has been (fermented) a long time'.[17]

The interesting point here is that wine-drinking should have been an accepted practice in an Islamic society where alcohol was prohibited. It is likely that it was only acceptable in a medical context. For example, in an Arabic cookery book of the thirteenth century where a recipe uses wine, honey is suggested as a substitute. The origins of the medical wine tradition are almost certainly Greek; prescriptions for wine in Greek medical books are commonplace. Its adoption into Islamic medicine is an interesting demonstration of the secular nature of this medicine which was also free of magic and superstition. Of course, there was a well-defined corpus of astrological medical literature in the Islamic world at that time, but this did not represent mainstream medicine. The fact that there was in addition yet another medical tradition, namely the Prophet's Medicine, which came into prominence after the fifth/eleventh century and was clearly non-secular in its origin and practice, does not alter this fact.

Conclusion

I have argued in this chapter that Arabic medical works of the classical Islamic period provide us with a unique and untapped source of knowledge about the eating and perhaps other social customs of people living at the time. I have referred to only a small fraction of the potential medical literature for this material. A detailed study of the available Arabic medical works needs to be carried out and would, I believe, shed a fascinating new light on life during the early centuries of Islam.

Notes

1. Ibn Sayyar al-Warraq, *Kitab al-Tabikh,* (ed.) K.Ohrnberg and S.Mroueh (Helsinki: Finnish Oriental Society, 1987), cited by Manuela Marin, 'Beyond taste: the complements of colour and smell in the medieval Arab culinary tradition', in S.Zubaida and R.Tapper (eds), *Culinary Cultures of the Middle East* (London: I.B.Tauris, 1994), pp. 205–14.

2. Muhammad b. al-Hasan al-Baghdadi, *Kitab al-Tabikh,* (trans.) A.J.Arberry, 'A Baghdad cookery-book', *Islamic Culture* 13, 1939, pp. 21–47 and 189–214.

3. 'Ali b. al-'Abbas Al-Majusi, *al-Kamil fi'l-Sina'a al-Tibbiyya* (Cairo: Bulaq, 1877).

4. 'Regimen in acute disease,' in *Hippocrates,* (trans.) W.H.S.Jones (Loeb Classical Library, London: Heinemann, 1923).

5. Abu Mansur b. Nuh Al-Qamari, *Kitab al-Ghina wal-Muna,* unedited, unpublished MS (British Library MS Or. 6623; there is a study of this text in G. Karmi, 'The Arabic Medical Kunnash in the Tenth Century', unpubl. PhD thesis, University of London, 1979); *Kitab al-Tanwir fi'l-Istilahat al-Tibbiyya,* (ed.) G.Karmi (Riyadh: Arab Bureau of Education, 1991).

6. Qamari, *Ghina wa Muna,* f.257b, line 14—f.258a, line 5 (all quotations are taken from the British Library MS; translations are mine).

7. Qamari, *Ghina wa Muna,* f. 11b, lines 10–11.

8. Qamari, *Ghina wa Muna,* f.14a, line 17—f. 14b, line 3.

9. Qamari, *Ghina wa Muna,* f. 17a, lines 2–4.

10. Qamari, *Ghina wa Muna,* f. 17a, line 9b.

11. Qamari, *Ghina wa Muna,* f.90a, lines 12–13.

12. Qamari, *Kitab al-Tanwir,* p. 8 0.

13. Qamari, *Kitab al-Tanwir,* p. 80.

14. Qamari, *Kitab al-Tanwir,* p. 82.

15. Qamari, *Kitab al-Tanwir,* p. 82.

16. Qamari, *Kitab al-Tanwir,* p. 85.

17. Qamari, *Kitab al-Tanwir,* p. 86.

Chapter 5
Science and Technology in Islamic Building Construction*
Donald R.Hill

Medieval architecture: cities and buildings

In order to understand the place of science and technology in Islamic architecture we must first examine the meaning of the term 'architecture' in the medieval context and also consider the function of architects and other supervisory staff.

Before the eighteenth century the term architecture was not confined, as it largely is today, to the design of buildings. Islamic architects were not usually specialists. Their work included the design and supervision of buildings, both religious and secular: bridges, dams, irrigation works and other constructions. Indeed, in some of their roles Islamic architects would be more accurately described as engineers, although the idea of such a demarcation was quite foreign in the Middle Ages. This is not to imply, of course, that some architects did not acquire skills in specialized fields. For example, when Ibn Tulun, governor of Egypt in 868–845 wished to construct the harbour at Acre, he was unable to find anyone in thse immediate area who was skilled in marine works. He therefore sent to Jerusalem for Abu Bakr, grandfather of the famous geographer al-Muqaddasi, who constructed a splendid harbour for the port.[1]

Not only was the architect expected to turn his hand to a wide variety of structures, he was also responsible for the design, setting-out and construction of building projects. However, while one architect could manage to design and supervise a single building, larger projects needed a complete team of supervisory staff.

The foundation of new cities was regarded as a meritorious act in Islam, and a number of such foundations were made between the seventh and tenth centuries. Some of these cities grew out of military encampments. For example, Basra began in this way during the early conquests of the seventh century. It was at first an encampment of reed huts that were dismantled when the troops left for a campaign and then re-erected when they returned. Later the encampment grew into a city built largely of sun-baked bricks; many canals were dug from the Shatt al-'Arab to cater for the city's growing needs for water supply and irrigation.[2] On the other hand, several cities were planned in detail from the outset. Among these were Baghdad, founded in 762 by the Caliph al-Mansur, Fez in Morocco, founded in 808 by the prince Idris b. Idris, and Madinat al-Zahra near Cordoba, founded in 936 by the Umayyad Caliph Abd al-Rahman III.[3]

The story of the building of Baghdad is well known. It was ordered by the Caliph al-Mansur in 762 and completed in 766–7. It was a round city with four entrances through a double wall. From each entrance an

* This chapter is based on Donald Hill, *Islamic Science and Engineering* (Edinburgh: Edinburgh University Press, 1993), and is reproduced with the kind permission of the publisher.

arcaded road led to the central enclave containing the Caliph's palace and the mosque. The building materials were kiln-burnt bricks, gypsum plaster, mud-bricks and timber.

We know the names of many of the men who supervised the construction of the city. There does not seem to have been a chief architect over the whole project, although a certain al-Hajjaj b.Artat was responsible for setting out the city and for other important jobs, such as the building of the mosque. An engineer called Rabah was in charge of building the walls. The plan of the city, inside the walls, lent itself to a division into quarters, the building of each of which was supervised by a team of three: an agent, a representative of the Caliph and an architect. The agent seems to have undertaken the work as a contractor, whereas the architect took no part in contractual matters, labour relations or cost control. Al-Mansur took a close interest in the progress of the project, particularly in matters of cost. He fixed the rates of pay of supervisors and workforce and called the agents to account for their expenditure. He acquired the nickname of 'father of the farthings', though one assumes that one only used this expression behind his back.

The chronicles mention various professions and trades, including architects/engineers, surveyors, master builders, foremen, carpenters, masons, excavators and labourers. The workforce numbered many thousands and it is clear that as much thought was given to the organization of the supervision as on a modern construction project. One of the terms for the architect/engineer was *muhandis,* which is also the word for engineer in modern Arabic. It is derived from the noun *handasa,* which can mean either engineering or geometry. This indicates that the most important science used by Islamic architects was geometry.

Baghdad was built of bricks, but we are told nothing of how the builders were instructed as to how to interpret the architect's plans. On the other hand we are told how the city was set out. Al-Mansur ordered the lines of the buildings, streets and open spaces to be marked out with ashes. He then walked through the entire site, ordering changes as he saw fit. The lines were then sprinkled with cotton seeds upon which crude oil was poured and ignited. This showed him the layout; he ordered the foundations to be excavated along the burnt lines.

The components of masonry buildings in the Middle Ages consisted of three major elements: the arch (the dome is an arch in the round and the barrel vault is a continuous arch), columns and walls. Where beams were necessary, the architects met the problem that stone is very weak in tension. Beams were therefore either made of timber or, if of stone, they were over very short spans. None of these elements could be subjected to mathematical analysis—the means to do this were not developed until the nineteenth century. The analysis of arches, for example, involves complex mathematics. Nevertheless the medieval architects were able to erect many impressive structures. This is because they were imbued with an empirical knowledge of the materials and forms available to them for the expression of architectural ideas.

Geometry was not used to prepare working drawings. Such drawings as were produced were usually unidimensioned illustrations to assist clients to visualize the appearance of the completed buildings. These were not intended to be used for passing on the architect's designs to the builders. For this function, there was no alternative to constant supervision by the architect himself. Supervision of the masons in the task of cutting the stones was achieved by the use of wooden moulds. There was often a special room set aside for the architect and his assistants to draw the designs on boards, which were then cut to shape by the carpenters. Masons would then start work, using the moulds to cut the stones to the desired shapes and sizes.

In the Middle Ages the status of architects varied from place to place and from time to time. On the whole they seem to have been accepted as respected members of a skilled profession. Their names often appear on the inscriptions on buildings and bridges. Many of these inscriptions have survived.[4]

Surveying techniques

Having attempted to give a fairly general idea of the role of the architect/engineer in medieval Islam, we will now turn our attention to some techniques that originated in the Islamic world and mark important milestones in the history of building technology. The first of these is concerned with the development of surveying techniques. Since classical times, and probably earlier, levelling had been done using simple instruments, either primitive water-levels or levels using plumb-lines. Although these instruments could produce fairly accurate results, they were very slow and they usually required a surveyor and at least two assistants. In 1019 an engineer called al-Karaji, from the Iranian town of Karaj in the province of Jibal (the Media of the Greeks) completed a treatise that included a number of new surveying instruments. These were intended for use on hydraulic works but could also be used on large building sites.[5]

After mentioning the traditional instruments, al-Karaji describes one that is very similar to modern ones, except of course that there were no telescopic or electronic aids. It was a square or circular plate made of wood or brass and perfectly flat. In fact the illustrations show a circular plate and this was probably the usual shape. A fine hole was made in its centre. Then one made a perfectly straight copper tube, about 36 cm long, with a very narrow bore. It was slightly longer than the diameter of the plate. In its centre was a spigot that fitted into a fine hole that had been made in the centre of the plate, so that the tube turned freely. It was, says the author, similar to the alidade of an astrolabe. Two diameters at right angles were inscribed on the plate; at the end of one of them was a staple into which a ring was fitted.

A wooden 'gallows' was then made for suspending the level. The gallows was perfectly straight and about 100 cm long, just long enough for the surveyor to be able to look through the sighting tube, squatting on his heels, when the level was suspended from the gallows. The author makes it clear, in fact, that the apparatus was to be constructed to suit the measurements of the surveyor.

Now a level staff was made. This was a piece of wood about 2.2 metres long, absolutely straight and smooth and of uniform rectangular cross-section. At either end a distance of 12 centimetres was left blank, while the remainder of the staff was divided into 60 divisions. This staff had a round mark painted on it at exactly the same distance from the ground as the centre of the plate suspended to the gallows (see Figure 5.1).

To carry out the levelling, the sighting tube was brought to the horizontal along one of the diameters of the plate, and the staff was viewed through it from as great a distance as possible. If the circle on the staff coincided with the line of the sight, then the distance from the ground was the same in both cases. If the graduation visible in the sighting tube was a certain distance above the painted circle, then this was a measure of the vertical distance of the foot of the gallows above the foot of the staff. The reverse applied when the line of sight met the staff below the painted circle. The level was then moved to a new station, the staff remaining stationary, and another reading was taken. Both readings were of course recorded. The staff was then moved to a new station and the procedure was repeated. The algebraic sum of the figures on a longitudinal survey gave the total rise or fall from start to finish. On a large building site the level could be placed in a central position and a sight taken first of all upon a fixed bench mark. The staff could then be moved around the site and levels taken as required. The author ends this section of his work with a paragraph enjoining the utmost accuracy in constructing and graduating the instruments, in carrying out the levelling and in making the calculations. Nothing is said, however, about 'checking back', i.e. levelling back to the original start point or bench mark to verify that there is no discrepancy. This is the simplest and most reliable method of checking the accuracy of levelling.

Muslim surveyors commonly used triangulation for determining the heights and depths of objects and the widths of obstacles such as wide rivers that could not be measured directly. The usual instrument for carrying out these observations was the back of the astrolabe. There were two squares on the back known as

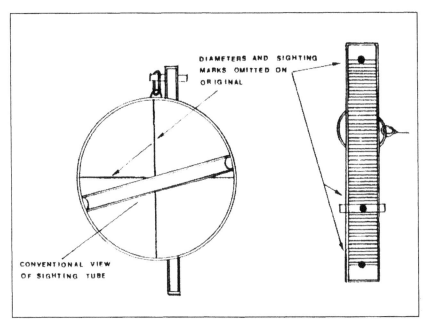

DIAMETERS AND SIGHTING
MARKS OMITTED ON
ORIGINAL

CONVENTIONAL VIEW
OF SIGHTING TUBE

Figure 5.1 Sighting tube and staff by al-Karaji. Note that the divisions of the staff are conventional and do not correspond to the divisions stipulated in the text (from Hill, *Islamic Science and Engineering,* Edinburgh University Press, 1993, p. 192; adapted from al-Karaji, *Inbat al-Miyah al-Khafiyya,* Hyderabad: Deccan, 1945).

'shadow squares', since they simulated the gnomon and its shadow, i.e. the tangent function of the angle. One square was divided into tenths, the other into twelfths, the subdivisions being known as 'fingers'. It was immaterial which square was used, since it was the angular relationships that mattered. When the alidade was sighted on a tall object—a tower for example—the sides of the triangle formed by the object and its horizontal distance from the observer were duplicated on the shadow square. If the horizontal distance 1 were known and the 'tenths' square, say, were being used, all that was necessary was to read off the number of fingers on the scale where it was cut by the alidade.

If this number was 'n' then the height 'h' of the object was given by

$$h = 1.n/10 \qquad\qquad (1)$$

plus the height of the observer's eye.

The great scientist al-Biruni (d. c. 1050), in one of his treatises, gave several examples of triangulation. To find the width of a river you stood on the bank, suspended the astrolabe in your right hand and then moved the alidade until you sighted the opposite bank. You then turned without changing your position and without altering the rule and looked through the sights for a recognizable object on the near bank. Measuring the distance between your position and the mark gave a direct measure of the width of the river. If you wished to find the height of a minaret the base of which could be reached, you took the altitude of the sun, and when it reached 45° you simply measured the length of the shadow cast by the minaret to give a direct reading of its height. If the sun did not reach 45° at the required time the alidade was set to 45° and you moved backwards or forwards until the top of the minaret was in your sights. The distance from your position to the base of the minaret again gave its height (see Figures 5.2 and 5.3).

It will be noticed that the surveyor in the field was required to do only very simple calculations. This was normal practice in Islamic surveying and constructional works. Very large numbers were employed in Islamic

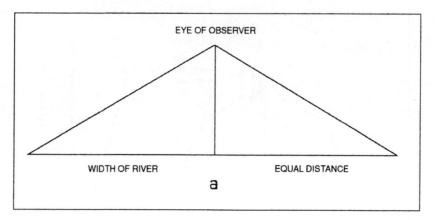

Figure 5.2 Triangulation method by al-Biruni (from Hill, *Islamic Science and Engineering,* p. 201, diagram by R.R.Wright 1934, *Book of Instructions,* original from Bodleian).

public works departments and it would have been very expensive and time consuming to have trained site engineers in the basic mathematical formulae that underlay much of their setting out and surveying. Calculations were therefore kept to a minimum, although scientists and senior engineers were of course fully capable of making geometric and trigonometric calculations when necessary.

The constructive approach is well exemplified in another of al-Biruni's triangulation problems, that of finding the height of a minaret the base of which is inaccessible. In al-Biruni's words:

> To find the height of a minaret, column or mountain the base of which it is impossible to reach, stand where you are and move the rule until you see the top of the object through both sights just as you take the altitude of a star. Then note the numbers of fingers in the quadrant of shadow to which it points and move forwards or backwards (according as the ground is most level); if forward place the rule-point at one finger less; if backward at one finger more and walk until the top is again visible through both sights. The distance between the two points of observation multiplied by twelve [or ten] is the height of the object, while the same distance multiplied by the numbers of fingers observed at the first point of observation gives the distance between that point and the base of the object. Similarly the height of any object in the air, such as a bird or a cloud which is stationary as to allow of the altitude being taken from two different points, can be determined by the same method, as well as the distance between you and a perpendicular dropped to the ground from the object.

The mathematics of this method can be expressed in modern terms by reference to the illustration (see Figure 5.4). If BS is the object to be measured and OB is known, then:

$$BS = OB tan\, \theta \tag{2}$$

which is identical to equation (1) given earlier. If OB is not known, angle is first measured, the theodolite is moved back from 0 to 0_1 and the angle $_1$ to the top of the object is measured. Then:

$$BS = \frac{00_1\ sin\,\theta\ sin\,\theta_1}{sin(\theta - \theta_1)}$$

(see Figure 5.5).

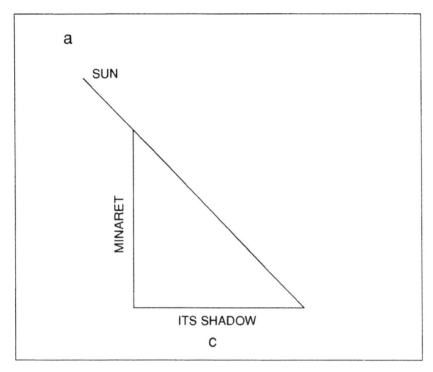

Figure 5.3 Triangulation method by al-Biruni (from Hill, *Islamic Science and Engineering,* p. 201, diagram by R.R.Wright 1934, *Book of Instructions,* original from Bodleian).

Dams

Dam building has a long history. The earliest known dams date from the third millennium BC in Sumeria and Egypt. Three dams with associated hydraulic works were built at Marib in the Yemen, the first in about 750 BC and the third in 115 BC. The Persians, in both Achaemenid and Sasanid times, were notable dam builders, as, of course, were the Romans, especially in their eastern provinces and in North Africa. The Muslims were therefore drawing on a long tradition, but they introduced several innovations in the construction, maintenance and usage of dams, as well as retaining the best elements of pre-Islamic dam technology. These points can best be illustrated by considering several Muslim dams, in Iran and in Spain.

An important dam was built by the Amir ʻAdud al-Dawla of the Buwayhid dynasty, which held power in Iran and Iraq from 945 until 1055. This dam, known as the Band-i Amir, was built in 960 over the River Kur between Shiraz and Istakhr (ancient Persepolis). To quote al-Muqaddasi:

ʻAdud al-Dawla closed the river between Shiraz and Istakhr by a great wall, strengthened with lead. And the water behind it rose and formed a lake. Upon it on the two sides were ten water-wheels…and below each wheel was a mill, and it is today one of the wonders of Fars. Then he built a city. The water flowed through channels and irrigated 300 villages.[6]

The dam still exists, though heavily silted up. It is some 10 metres high and 75 metres long. On top of it is a pointed-arch bridge, of later construction than the dam itself. The dam is built of masonry blocks throughout. In addition to the lead dowels, cement mortar was used in the joints, binding the whole structure

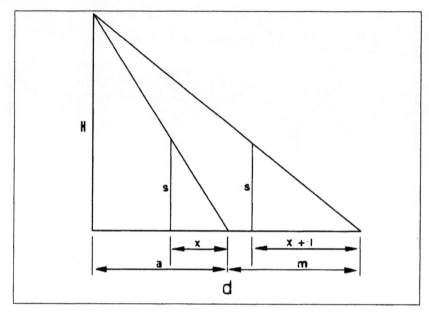

Figure 5.4 Triangulation method by al-Biruni (from Hill, *Islamic Science and Engineering,* p. 201, diagram by R.R.Wright 1934, *Book of Instructions,* original from Bodleian).

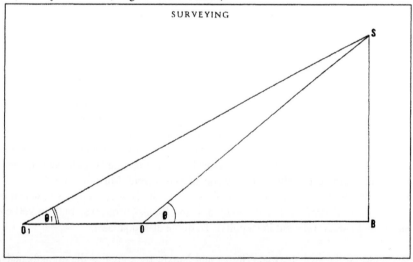

Figure 5.5 Geometry for measuring heights (from Hill, *Islamic Science and Engineering,* p. 199).

together and making it watertight. It is not surprising that the Band-i Amir has had such a long and useful life. It is also an example of the use of a dam to increase the power delivered to mills and water-raising wheels, a technique in which the Muslims were pioneers.

When the Muslims conquered the Iberian peninsula in AD 711, their armies included contingents from Syria, Iraq and the Yemen, among whom there were undoubtedly engineers skilled in hydraulic works. These engineers brought irrigation techniques to Spain and thereby laid the foundations of the agricultural prosperity which is one of the most impressive features of Islamic Spain. Nothing so elaborate and efficient had been seen before in Europe. The major irrigation schemes were in the great river valleys of the south, an environment similar to that of the Arabs' homelands in the Middle East.

Cordoba was the capital of Islamic Spain for nearly 500 years and it is here, on the river Guadalquivir, that we find what is probably the oldest surviving Islamic dam in Spain. According to the twelfth-century geographer al-Idrisi, it was built of Qibtiyya stone and incorporated marble pillars. It stands just downstream from the Roman bridge, the Puente Romano. It follows a zigzag course across the river so that its total length is about 425 metres, even though the river is only about 300 metres wide. This shape indicates that the builders were aiming at a long crest in order to increase the dam's overflow capacity. Today the remains of the dam are only a few metres above the river bed, but in its prime it was probably about 2 or 3 metres above high-water level and 2.5 metres thick.

There is rubble masonry everywhere, but we may assume that this was originally faced with masonry blocks, the Qibtiyya (or Egyptian) stone described by al-Idrisi. Al-Idrisi mentions three mill-houses below the dam, each of which contained four mills. The mill-houses still exist, but no trace of the original machinery remains. Also below the dam, and powered by the head of water it provided, was a large noria that raised water from the river and discharged it into an aqueduct which then carried it into the city. The aqueduct and noria have been restored, although the wheel is not operative. Here again, therefore, we have an example of the Muslim use of dams for powering mills and water-raising machines. As an additional bonus, the Cordoba dam has for 1,000 years protected the Puente Romano piers from scour.

The river Turia flows into the Mediterranean at Valencia. In the tenth century there were many small dams on the river, and eight of these, spread over 10 km in the province of Valencia, are of particular interest. All of them are similar in size, shape and design. The one at Mestella, the fifth in the series, can be considered as typical. It is 73 metres long and 2 metres high. The water face is vertical, the air face stepped, the crest is 1.2 metres wide and the base thickness 5.5 metres. The core of the dam consists of rubble masonry and mortar and the structure is faced with large masonry blocks with mortared joints. At one end the dam abuts on a masonry wall which extends downstream some 21 metres and is everywhere the same height as the dam and similarly built. Between this wall and the river bank a proportion of the Turia's flow is directed to the mouth of the irrigation canal. Two sluices are built into this wall, one half-way along, the other near the canal mouth. They served two purposes: during normal operation they were used as escapes to allow surplus water to drain back into the river; and occasionally they would both be opened to their full extent in order to desilt the approaches to the canal mouth. Such scouring sluices, closed with planks carried in grooves, are absolutely essential. Silt is bound to collect above dams of this type and must periodically be removed if the canal intakes and the canals themselves are not to become hopelessly choked and obstructed. All the Islamic dams on the Turia, and most others elsewhere, were equipped with desilting sluices. They were a Muslim development which later Christian Spanish dams were to utilize on a grand scale (see Figure 5.6)

These eight dams all have similar foundation works, which at first glance appear to be too massive for the superstructures. The masonry of each dam extends some 4.5 metres into the river bed. Below this, the whole structure is supported by rows of wooden piles, the tops of which are built into the lowest courses of the masonry. The combined depth of masonry and piles is 6 to 8 metres. The reason for building such solid foundations becomes clear when the behaviour of the Turia is considered. The river's flow, for most of the year, is only about 400 cusecs, but there are occasional dangerous floods when the flow is more than a

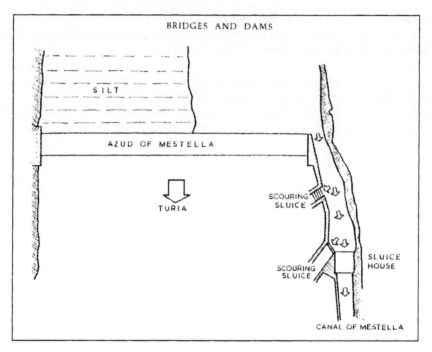

Figure 5.6 Mestella dam: desilting sluices (from Hill, *Islamic Science and Engineering,* p. 165; original diagram in Norman A.F.Smith, *A History of Dams,* London: Peter Davies, 1971).

hundred times greater. The dams are then submerged to a depth of nearly 6 metres and must resist the battering of water, stones, rocks and trees. Because they are so low and flat and are provided with deep and very firm foundations, the Turia dams have been able to survive these conditions for 1,000 years.

The dams on the Turia may appear to be small, unspectacular and a not particularly notable factor in the history of dam-building; but in fact, for the task they were required to perform and for the conditions under which they were required to operate, they turn out to be extremely practical. They continue to meet the irrigation needs of Valencia even today, and it is interesting to note that not only have no more dams been added to the system, but to add at all to it would be pointless anyway. Modern measurements have shown that the eight canals between them have a total capacity slightly less than that of the river. This raises, of course, the question whether or not the Muslims were able to gauge a river and then design their dams and canals to match.

At present it is not possible to answer such a question with confidence. It should be remembered, however, that the art of dam building had been practised for several millennia in the Middle East before the Turia dams were planned. It would be surprising if the knowledge accumulated over such a long period did not include empirical methods for estimating the flow of rivers.

Arches

For our final examination of a dam we return to Iran in the Ilkhanid period. First of all, we must define the three basic types of dam: gravity dams, arched dams and arch dams. The first, which includes the vast majority of dams built in antiquity and the Middle Ages, resists the pressure of the water by its weight alone. The second type is really a modification of the first; its arched plan is dictated by foundation conditions, but the main resistance to the pressure is still due to gravity. There are a few examples of early arched dams, for example, a Roman one at Glanum in southern France.

The arch dam is more slender than the other two types, and does not depend solely upon its weight. The arch itself carries the forces due to water pressure along horizontal lines to the sides of the structure. At the sides, the predominantly horizontal forces are resisted by normal forces and shear forces. Underneath the arch dam, the only vertical forces are those required to support its own weight. Clearly, therefore, the site of an arch dam must be chosen where the banks will provide secure anchorages.[7]

At the end of the thirteenth century a dam was built at Kebar, about 25 km south of Qum in central Iran. It was built in a roughly V-shaped gorge which suddenly narrows, about half-way down, to a deep gully, much deeper than it is wide. The rock is limestone, and there were no foundation problems. The dam, which has survived intact, is 26 metres high and 55 metres long at the crest. The crest thickness varies between 4.5 and 4.8 metres. The air face is vertical, except near the base where there is a slight slope in the downstream direction. Much of the water face of the dam is today obscured by the vast amounts of silt and debris which have collected in the reservoir. Where it can be observed at the top, the water face is vertical and it seems reasonable to suppose that this face of the dam is vertical throughout its height. The Kebar dam is a very thin structure, too thin to act as a gravity dam. It is in fact an arch dam, the oldest surviving example of this type of structure so far located. The radius of curvature of its air face is 38 metres at all points, the dam constituting what is known, in modern terminology, as an arch dam of constant radius.

The dam has other points of interest, in addition to its status as the earliest known arch dam. Up both sides of the dam and in the narrow bottom of the ravine, the limestone is cut away to form grooves into which the dam is built. There has been no cracking or slipping and the dam has remained watertight throughout. It has a core of rubble masonry set in mortar. The faces are finished with roughly-dressed rectangular blocks of varied size; they have mortared joints but are not closely fitted. The mortar which was used is called locally *saruj*. It was—and still is—made from lime crushed with the ash of a desert plant. The addition of ash makes the lime hydraulic and results in a strong, hard and impervious mortar ideal for dams, and undoubtedly an important factor in the Kebar dam's long life.

To summarize the developments in dam construction and usage in the medieval Islamic world, we have, first of all, the various constructional techniques which have ensured the survival of so many dams. The massive foundations of the Turia dams and the measures taken to keep the Kebar dam watertight, including the use of hydraulic mortar, point to a knowledge of the techniques of construction in hydraulic conditions of various kinds. The number of the Turia dams, which almost exactly corresponds with the flow of the river, suggest that the Muslims were able to gauge rivers and design their dams and canals to suit. The Kebar dam is the first known example of a true arch dam. Many Muslim dams in Spain incorporate desilting sluices, an essential feature if the dams and the mouths of their canals are not to become hopelessly silted up. Finally the Muslims made use of dams as a source of hydropower to drive mills and water-raising machines: cases we have cited are the Band-i Amir in Fars and the dam at Cordoba.

It is impossible to say which of these developments was originated by the Muslims. Given that dam-building has been an established practice since Antiquity, it seems certain that sound techniques of hydraulic engineering were passed on to the Muslims from their predecessors. These techniques probably included good constructional practices and perhaps also the gauging of rivers and the use of special materials of construction such as lead and cement mortar. The introduction of desilting sluices, the arch dam and hydropower seem to have made their first appearance in the Islamic world, and it is therefore difficult to see how these can be other than Muslim inventions. In stressing the innovative elements in Islamic dam building, we should not forget the basic constructional skills required in the erection of dams. These skills are more demanding than those needed for straightforward building work, or even for bridge building. It is not an easy task to build a barrage across a river, especially if the river is subject to sudden great increases in the rate of flow. With great out-of-balance forces to contend with, the structures have to be designed so that they resist overturning, fracture and slippage. The foundations must be protected from scour. Just because there are no Muslim manuals that put these techniques into writing, this does not mean that the Muslims were without a large body of available empirical knowledge.

The use of the semi-circular arch poses certain problems, one of which is common to all arches, namely that at its junction with a side wall or column it exerts both a vertical and a horizontal thrust. The first causes no difficulties, because masonry is well able to take compressive stresses, but the horizontal thrust can lead to overturning or produce tensile stresses in the supporting members, and masonry cannot withstand even moderate tensile stresses. These difficulties may be overcome in various ways. The structure above the arches may be lightened by introducing a second row of arches in the upper wall or by making domes out of wood instead of masonry. The load-bearing walls may be made massive, although this makes for a ponderous effect, or they may be supported by buttresses. Arched aisles on either side of the main part of the building were also used to reduce the horizontal thrust on the outer walls.

There is another disadvantage, this time peculiar to semi-circular arches, in that their height is rigidly determined by their span. This caused great difficulties to the builders of medieval cathedrals, as their height steadily increased and their ground plans became more elaborate. Something better than the semi-circular arch was needed to lighten the superstructure and to give more flexibility to the designs. The innovation that made Gothic architecture possible was the pointed, or ogival, arch. The question therefore arises as to whether the pointed arch was transmitted from outside, or whether it was an independent European invention.

There is no doubt that the pointed arch was used in eastern buildings long before its first appearance in Europe. It was first found in Buddhist India about the second century after Christ, but these early examples were of a decorative form. It reached Syria, possibly by way of Sasanid Iran, by 561, where it was used in a church some 80 km north-east of Homs, in four arches that supported a dome. A number of examples appear in Muslim buildings in Syria in the eighth century and in Egypt in the eighth and ninth centuries. Pointed arches are those in which the two halves are struck from a different centre. The less the separation of the two centres, the less the acuteness of the arch. The evolution of the pointed arch, i.e. the gradual separation of the two centres, can be observed in the Syrian examples, from one tenth of the span in arches in the Great Mosque in Damascus (AD 705–15) to one-fifth in two buildings dated to 744. The most acute arches in the early Islamic period occur in Egypt, with a separation of one-third of the span.[8]

All these ogival arches were unadventurous, being decorative rather than structural in their functions. The same cannot be said of the pointed arches in several Iranian bridges, of which the best preserved is the Pul-i Kashgan bridge over the Kashgan river, some 56 km west of Khoramabad (see Plate 1). The photograph, taken in 1936, shows five of the arches more or less intact. The arches were formed of three courses of burnt bricks. Here, as elsewhere, the builders of the bridge had chosen a spot where the river is closely approached by a high rocky terrace on one bank. This facilitated the approach to the top of the high arches which the mode of construction necessitated for spanning the actual river bed. Thus, on the left bank, the pier carrying the terminal arch was built straight against a wall-like cliff some 20 metres high. On the opposite bank no fewer than nine massive piers were needed to reach the full height of the bridge. The total length of the bridge was 190 metres.[9]

In this bridge we therefore have pointed arches that were used gradually to increase the height of the bridge without raising the vertical piers, which would have been necessary had the arches been semi-circular. And the arches were, of course, structurally important. This bridge and at least two others like it were built at the close of the tenth century on routes leading from the plains of Khuzistan to Luristan. The Pul-i Kashgan bridge carries an inscription which tells us that it was built on the orders of Badr b.Hasanwayh, a well-known Kurdish chieftain, between 999 and 1008.

The inscription on another bridge in Luristan attributes it to the same prince; it is dated to 984. Unfortunately, in neither case is the name of the engineer given.

Returning now to the question of the possible transmission of the ogival arch to Europe, the case for such a transmission was cogently put by the great historian of technology, Lynn White Jr:

> The pointed arch moved by about 1000 to Amalfi, a city intimately connected with Fatimite Egypt, and by 1071 a porch with pointed arches and pointed vaults graced Abbot Desiderius' new church at Montecassino. Structurally the Montecassino porch was no more adventurous than its Near Eastern prototypes... The great technological advance involving the pointed arch occurred not in Italy but in Burgundy. In 1080 Abbot Hugh of Cluny visited Montecassino, and there either he or his engineers, then working on the design of an enormous new church being planned for Cluny, realized that pointed arches and pointed vaults offered the key to solving the chief problems with which Romanesque architects had been contending. As a result of their insight, the church at Cluny, begun in 1088 and effectively finished in 1120, contained 196 pointed arches with more in the high vaults. The new Cluny was the most conspicuous church of northern Europe. In 1130 Abbot Suger of the French Royal Abbey of Saint-Denis visited it. Between 1135 and 1144 he and his engineers produced at Saint-Denis what is usually regarded as the first true gothic church. In doing so they realized the full possibilities inherent in the novel Cluniac development of oriental architectural ideas.[10]

White did not know of the existence of the Luristan bridges, and therefore assumed that the European architects, in adopting the pointed arch, converted what had been a decorative feature in the East to a key structural component of gothic architecture. His assumption may well be correct, since we have no evidence that the Iranian bridges were known about in Europe. At least, however, these bridges prove that the pointed arch was not used solely as a decorative feature in Islamic architecture.

Notes

1. al-Muqaddasi, *Ahsan al-Taqasim,* (ed.) M.J.de Goeje (Leiden: Brill, 1906), pp. 162–3.
2. al-Baladhuri, *Kitab Futuh al-Buldan,* (ed.) M.J.de Goeje (Leiden: Brill, 1866), pp. 345–71.
3. al-Khatib al-Baghdadi, *Tarikh Baghdad,* 14 vols (Cairo, 1349/1931), vol. I, pp. 66–79; 'Fas', *Encyclopaedia of Islam* (2nd edn) 2, pp. 818–23; Ahmad ibn Muhammad al-Maqqari, *Nafh al-Tib,* 8 vols (Cairo, 1355/1936), Vol. 4, pp. 272–82.
4. L.A.Mayer, *Islamic Architects and their Works* (Geneva: Kundig, 1956).
5. al-Karaji, *Inbat al-Miyah al-Khafiyya* (Hyderabad: Deccan, 1945).
6. al-Muqaddasi, *Ahsan al-Taqasim,* p. 444.
7. Norman A.F.Smith, *A History of Dams* (London: Peter Davies, 1971), pp. 75–101.
8. K.A.C.Creswell, *A Short History of Early Muslim Architecture* (London: Pelican, 1958), pp. 103–4.
9. Sir Aurel Stein, *Old Routes of Western Iran* (London: Macmillan, 1940), pp. 267–73.
10. Lynn White, Jr, *Medieval Religion and Technology* (Berkeley: University of California Press, 1978), pp. 231–4.

Chapter 6
Wind and Watermills in Iran and Afghanistan
Michael Harverson

Mills in the Middle East exhibit certain general characteristics in common with other working buildings in a vernacular mud-brick tradition.[1] Roofs are domes, except where wood is sufficiently available to support the construction of flat roofs, themselves thickly plastered with mud. There are few openings in the single-storeyed structure, apart from the door. The interior usually consists of a single space, concentrated on the stones. In mountainous areas, dry-stone walls replace mud-brick.

A horizontal mill contains an upright main-shaft with the stones at one end and the wheel revolving in a horizontal plane at the other, without the interposition of gears in most cases (see Figure 6.1). The power source is situated on the roof of these windmills and hidden below ground level in the watermills. As a result, windmills, rarely encountered, are instantly recognizable, whereas watermills, much more common, are easily mistaken for domestic or farm buildings. A similar situation obtains in Europe, except where prominent vertical waterwheels occur.

Fire, lack of maintenance and wet weather have been the downfall of British mills. In the Middle East, earthquakes and lack of attention after snow and rain cause the decay and destruction of mud-brick structures like mills, erected without the long-term permanence generally envisaged by a British builder. In both parts of the world the mills' economic usefulness is over, but the cultural value of preserving elements of the long milling tradition is so far only just about recognized in the one and neglected in the other.

Windmills

Traditional horizontal windmills are only found in the path of the 120-day wind, which blows with varying intensity from late June to mid-October down the border country between Iran and Afghanistan, from the Kara Kum desert in the north to Zahedan in the south of Sistan. They are not found east of Herat or west of Birjand (see Maps 6.1 and 6.2, pp. 113, 114). They are thought to be indigenous to this area and have a recorded history several centuries older than that of the dissimilar European vertical windmill., which is not found in the Middle East. (In the Near East, vertical windmills were common on the Aegean coast of Turkey, and a few were once found in Alexandria, Aden, Jerusalem and Syria.)

They are generally built on the edge of a village and resemble stretches of defensive wall as one approaches from the north. The ground in front of them needs to be flat and free of obstacles, either wasteland, fields or a graveyard. Their lofty frontage is broken only by a narrow vertical slit down half the height of each mill. From the south the wind-wheel, six metres high, looks like a huge revolving door. In Khorasan, mills are usually built in series, joined together like terraced houses; the longest, at Neh on the borders of Sistan, consists of over 60 mills in one unbroken line.[2] In Afghanistan, shorter runs existed, as at Ghôrîân, but single or paired mills were more usual (see Plates 2–4). The front wall of these Afghan mills has a pronounced angle in towards the slit. They also have a curving, stepped wall closely surrounding half

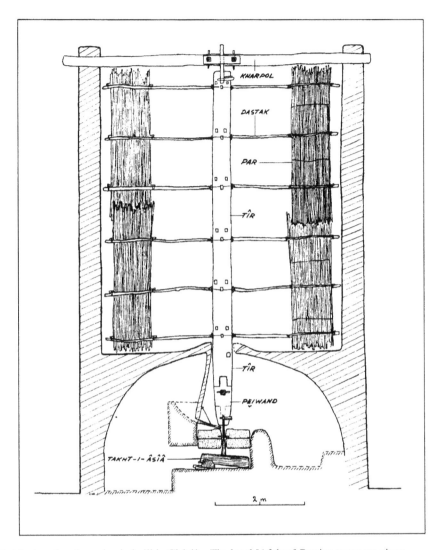

Figure 6.1 Sketched section through windmill in Ghôrîân. The local [Afghan] Persian terms are given.

the wind-wheel to enhance the momentum of this primitive turbine. Both these features are absent from the mills in Khorasan, possibly because the wind blows there with greater intensity and does not need to be exploited quite so cunningly.

Down below, in the mill-house, the wind-shaft protrudes towards the stones. Attached to it, an extension known in Afghanistan as the *peiwand* (or graft) contains in its lower end the iron thrust-pin which engages with the rynd and so turns the runner stone (see Figure 6.2). The whole weight of both wind-wheel and runner-stone is concentrated onto the centre of the rynd, whose underside is supported and balanced on a roughly-shaped, tall wooden cone which stands on the foot-beam. This is known as the *mosht;* it is greased with sheep's fat and wears down so rapidly that it has to be replaced every few weeks. Even in a watermill,

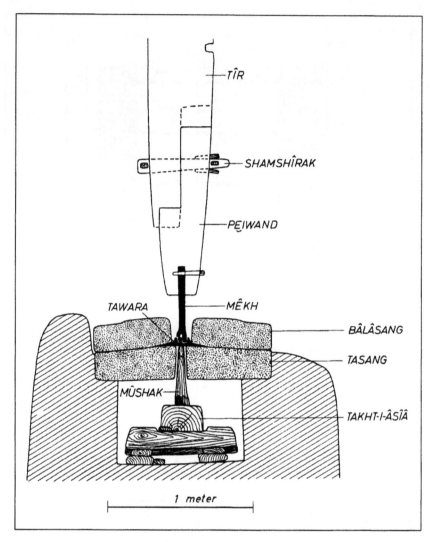

Figure 6.2 Detail of Figure 6.1, but in a section at right angles to it.

where the footbearing can be lubricated by water, one where iron and wood bear directly on one another is highly unusual, either stone or brass being much more common than wood. A thick Georgian penny used to play that role in some British mills, and a metal disc the size of a *dirham* coin serves the same purpose in Morocco.

Judging by Wulff's account of observations made in the 1930s, and by what could be ferreted out in the ruins of Neh 40 years later, the *mosht*, called by him the *tahtir* in the windmills of Sistan, was turned the other way up, with its point resting on the footbeam and the broader, flat end taking the weight of the thrust-pin and everything above it. A tallow-soaked cotton pad was inserted between wood and metal.[3] The *tahtir* stood in a tall recess beneath the stones, part of the mud-brick structure that supported them like the hurst frame in English mills. In Khorasan, the foot-beam on which the *mosht* stands lies in a short tunnel below the stones, with enough room to insert a lever when altering its position. The photos in Ferdinand's article on the windmills of Ghôrîân make this clear.[4]

Afghan mills are square-shaped, but those in Iran are rectangular: three shallow-domed bays or an equivalent length of mud-brick barrel vaulting. The hopper and stones are in the first, windward bay, while the miller spends much of his time in the third bay. Here is the door, which acts as the sole light source, and here is the winnowing eye, the termination of a low tunnel fashioned in one party-wall, which runs from a barred opening below the wind-slit at the front of the mill. It creates a fine draught and the miller squats beside it in the cool and shade of his mill to winnow each customer's grain.

Watermills

Horizontal watermills have a 2,000-year-old history, spreading from the Near East across Europe through the Balkans and the Alps as far as Scandinavia, the Iberian peninsula and the islands of the Celtic West; in Asia they are found from Turkey and Syria to Nuristan and Nepal, while in China they have been used throughout this time for varied purposes.[5]

They are mainly mills for mountainous areas, since they need a fall of water at the mill ranging between two and five metres, and they are designed to utilize much smaller flows of water than an under-shot watermill impelled by a river would require. Mills of the latter type once existed on the river Tigris, including the second earliest references anywhere to both tide-mills and boat-mills. Isfahan (see Plate 5) had vertical watermills in 1600 when Uruch Beg, in his book about Iran for Spanish readers, mentioned 'great numbers of waterwheels all along the banks of the rivers and lagoons, these being made after the fashion of the waterwheels and mills we see on the Tagus'.[6] Apart from millwheels, some of these would have been *noria* for irrigation. Similar vertical wheels once powered the complex of mills on the weirs at Dizful (see below).

In Iran there are horizontal mills powered by mountain streams, as at Abianeh and Estehban, but many more depended on the *qanat* systems, now almost universally decayed. They were placed either outside a village where the *qanat* emerged and before it irrigated the fields, or within the village, as at Taft or Ardestan, or even totally within the *qanat* system, as outside Zavareh. In every case the mill was hardly an afterthought; the precise and gentle gradient of a *qanat* does not lend itself to being tampered with after its initial construction. Papoli-Yazdi has described the now defunct arrangements for subterranean mills north-west of Yazd, and the series of such mills at Boshruyeh the other side of the Central Desert.[7]

Mills use, but also pass on, the water that drives them, so they fit well with the Quranic injunction that water be regarded as God's gift to all men. Water can be exploited by anyone over or under whose land it flows. So a landowner would incorporate a mill within his plans for a new *qanat,* while a philanthropic ruler, when he dammed a river to irrigate the fields of a new settlement, might insert a number of mills to take advantage of the fall of water he had created. Thus Azod ad-Douleh inaugurated the thousand-year history of the mills attached to his Band-e Amir in Fars, now sadly all destroyed by floodwater.[8]

Less venerable were the 30 horizontal mills below the dam built across the Ab-e Gerger at Shushtar in c. 1840 (see Plate 6). In such a situation, more powerful vertical wheels could have been installed, to make possible commercial milling on a large scale. Even so, a European visitor in the 1930s stated that each mill ground one ton per day.[9] Water flow drops markedly in the summer, but one suspects that the preference for horizontal millwheels derived from both a conservative attitude towards technology and the non-existence of a tradition of skilled carpentry capable of making and maintaining large, strongly-built, vertical waterwheels.

An apparent partial exception to this conclusion was once represented by the mills on the Sasanian weirs at Dizful in Khuzestan. These appear to have been powered by small, narrow *vertical* wheels, possibly of genuinely Vitruvian inspiration, as the Roman emperor Valerian's defeated army provided the labour force for major engineering works here and at Shushtar. Spring floodwater in this large river would have damaged these wheels unless they were dismantled at that time of year, as was the practice with some Portuguese mills which were similarly inundated when their rivers were swollen by melting snow and spring rain.[10]

The horizontal watermill of the Iranian plateau owes little to outside influences. Its wheel shape is primitive, with none of the careful crafting to be found in European examples stretching back to Irish finds as early as the seventh century AD, and with less tight an assembly than the wheels widespread in the Atlas mountains of Morocco.

The absence of gearwheels, something which is typical of almost all horizontal mills, wind and water, derives from the small power and low structural resistance of their waterwheels as much as from the limited skills of the local carpenter. After all, the *saqiyeh,* one of the earliest methods of raising water in the Middle East, which is often termed the 'Persian wheel', is based upon the principle of gearing a horizontal wheel to a vertically-mounted continuous chain of pots. (Its drive is of course in the opposite direction to that of a vertical millwheel linked through gear-wheels to its stones.) So the knowledge of gearing existed from an early date, to be utilized in mills if it was considered to be viable and profitable. Evidently it was not.

The drop-tower which creates and contains the head of water for Iranian mills, may be related to the Palestinian *arubah* (a Hebrew word for tube or chimney, popularized by an Israeli molinologist); it occurs also in Spain and on Crete. However, we do not know the ultimate origins of any of these examples of the drop-tower. Where it is found, it represents an intelligent response to the need to conserve and utilize efficiently a small water supply at a high head; the nozzle at its base concentrates the pressure from the column of water impounded in the drop-tower into a jet which turns the wheel. It is built of stone, with the central chimney sometimes brick-lined and always rendered. Unlike its more graceful and better-engineered cousin, the Spanish *cubo,* it is a massive, square-cornered structure, with a battered profile to withstand the pressure built up in the chimney. One side abuts the hillside along which the aqueduct or ditch acting as a leat conducts the head-race to the brink of the chimney. Occasionally two chimneys are built side by side within the main drop-tower, as at Salameh and above one paired mill at Estehban. At Shushtar, many of the drop-towers are carved from the living rock (see Plates 7 and 8).

Where there is no hillside, the drop-tower is largely or entirely below ground level and resembles a well, five metres or more in depth. In such cases, as at Fin, the grinding chamber of the millhouse is situated underground and the tail-race, arched over or tunnelled, may well run for a fair distance before emerging into the open. This is a predetermined feature of mills within a *qanat* system, ensuring that the precious water is not exposed more than necessary to evaporation in its course to the next mill and eventually to the point where irrigation is commenced.

In Azarbaijan and Afghanistan the drop-tower is replaced by hollowed tree trunks which lead the water to the wheels at an angle of 30–40°, or even by open chutes, as are found elsewhere in the world of the horizontal mill: Bosnia, Ireland and Morocco. These latter depend solely on the velocity of the water in the chute, while the former augment it with a weakened version of the pressure which a drop-tower would build up. Tree trunks are easily installed when a rural economy cannot contemplate the expense and labour of building a permanent tower. Penstocks of this kind have probably survived beside the Salang Pass and at Band-e Amir in Central Afghanistan, despite the guerrilla warfare and bombing since 1980 (see Plate 9).

The wheel-chamber under all these mills, inasmuch as it is possible to make out the details by torchlight as one crouches in the tail-race, is roughly lined with stone. It is largely filled by the blades of the wheel radiating from the hub whose foot-bearing rests on the beam half-buried in the pebbles and debris.

Directly overhead are the stones, fed from the hopper, which in mud-brick mills (and therefore also in all windmills) is an integral part of the structure. Wooden hoppers, similar to those found in European mills but suspended over the stones from above, are to be found in the stone-built mills in the mountains.

Few mills can boast the warren of interconnecting rooms which make up the Chogia mill at Qasr-e Dasht near Shiraz, where the miller has assembled a collection of lumber worthy of a rural Steptoe. However, mills often incorporate side-rooms, or at least alcoves, for sleep and for storage. The mill at Yazdkhast, near Shiraz, has a donkey stable built on at one side, while underground at Zavareh a similar facility lies beyond the first doorway on the right, complete with mud-brick mangers round the walls. This mill resembles a lofty, sloping tunnel, like a stairway to a cistern, with the grinding place 12 metres down at the bottom, and with stables, storage area and tearoom (with fireplace) leading off the main stairway in turn.[11]

Mill furniture and stones

Apart from the cutting out and initial dressing of the millstones and the fashioning of the three iron components of the mill-work, the whole of a Middle Eastern mill can be built by any determined and semi-skilled villager. His materials will be local and his designs based on the mills of his neighbours. The workmanship will be rough and ready, hardly craftsmanship. For example, the spokes of the wind-wheel will be branches cut to the right length, but they will not be straight nor planed smooth; the foot-bearing may be a lump of ironstone or even an old shoe (cotton *giveh* rather than leather); the cross-beam may be a cut-down section of superannuated windshaft (see Plate 10). No millwright's manual or scaled drawings are needed. But the smooth curves and straw-flecked mud plaster of walls and domes proclaim an assured handling of traditional materials for everyday purposes, in harmony with the other village buildings: mosque, bath-house, cistern, houses, even the walls round orchards and gardens.

Mills are seldom personalized in any obvious way. Perhaps this is due to a fear that a display of vanity will attract divine displeasure or the prying attention of officials who may seek to increase taxes and dues. Rather than individuality, anonymity and identification with the community are seen to be the safest stance when extending one's material possessions and thus offering one more hostage to fortune. Even God's blessing is seldom invoked visibly and permanently on a newly built mill. However, a poster of the Imam or a photo of a recent martyr may be displayed prominently.

The sole decorative feature of some Afghan windmills is the patterned brickwork on the western wall beside the wind-wheel: a simple rearrangement of the courses creates a latticed area which strengthens the structure, breaks the monotony of the surface and perhaps enhances the draught for one of the paired mills. Early this century, the ruins of one particularly fine example of such brickwork were photographed in Afghan Sistan.[12]

Pride of ownership may be expressed by the careful choice of thin planks for the sails, which otherwise are often composed of whatever orange-boxes have fallen off a passing lorry. The neatly-arranged reed mats in Ferdinand's photos of Ghôriân windmills in 1960 may be contrasted with the bulky sheaves of straw lashed to the spokes at Chahar Farsakh, near Neh, in 1977 (see Plate 11).

As usual with vernacular buildings in Iran, the mud-bricks are, at least in part, made from their collapsed predecessors: the structure is resurrected rather than replaced or repaired, for reasons which Malcolm noted in Yazd 90 years ago.[13] The wind-shaft may be an old telegraph pole or the trunk of a pine from the stands of trees planted beside the villages in the Bakharz. The hub of a waterwheel will be made of willow or plane, and the blades of poplar or mulberry, all common trees where irrigation is practised. The *mosht* or lightening cone will be of jujube or ash. The foot-beam and cross-beam may be made of turpentine. The journal for the top-bearing of a wind-wheel or within the bed-stone of a watermill will be of apricot wood.

The various woods are specific to each purpose and are readily obtainable; they are fashioned to shape with an adze rather than a carpenter's plane or spoke-shave.

The metal parts of the mill-work can be forged by any local blacksmith. The thrust-pin and the pintle wedged into the foot of the waterwheel present no difficulties, but the rynd, shaped like a bow-tie, needs to be made more carefully, so that it both fits in the groove of the runner stone and bears its weight in a balanced fashion. For one other detail, the steel wire used for lashing the spokes of the wind-wheel to one another, we are back in Steptoe's yard or the cartoons of Heath Robinson: it is salvaged from wornout lorry tyres.

Wind-wheels were at times and in places dismantled for the winter, but the more general view, either intelligent or lazy according to one's taste, held that any rain would swell the wood and help to hold the rickety contraption together. It is a source of some surprise that, even in ideal operating winds of 25 knots, they are not swiftly battered to pieces.

Millstone quarries are recorded near Natanz and at Khullar in Fars, but in practice any outcrop of a suitable stone might be exploited. The stones at Taft were said to come from Kuh-e Erdom; those at Neh from the mountains a dozen miles to the south; some of those stockpiled at Chogia mill were cut from the surface rock near Qasr-e Ghomsheh, a yellow brecciated stone. At Nishtafun one miller spoke of obtaining stones from nearby Kuh-e Sinu; he said it took a fortnight to cut them and it could be undertaken by anyone who had the time and inclination. In 1957 a pair of stones there cost 350 tomans (£17 then). By 1992 the price had risen to over 50 times that figure. Stones represented the major outlay in the construction and equipment of a mill. A farmer in a village of the Moroccan High Atlas itemized his expenditure on a small watermill built by himself and an unskilled labourer in 1984; the only item he bought was the runner stone, which at c. £60 represented more than a third of the total cost.

Most grinding in Middle Eastern mills takes place at a slow rate by British commercial standards, even amateur ones: well under half a ton a day. The stones in the windmills are large, about 1.50 m. in diameter, and revolve at 25–30 rpm, so the grain passes slowly between the stones and cool flour results. Watermill stones vary from a similar size down to a more usual diameter of 80 cm to 1 m, with a speed of 60–80 rpm. This is still below 120 rpm, the recommended optimum speed for production of stone-ground flour of the quality required by British bakers. The profile of Iranian stones varies from the regular, thick tablet-shape to an inverted soup-plate or cymbal, with the grinding surfaces being slightly dished downwards (see Plate 12). On both water and windmill stones, where examined, surfaces are roughened in random fashion all over, except at Fin, where some of the stones are dressed with the furrows common in European mills. Wulff reported stones with hewn-in spiral flutes in the 1930s, but at that time millstone dressing was still a full-time occupation for the occasional specialist craftsman.[14] It is no longer so.

One final point of detail at this stage: the damsel of British mills, revolving with the stone spindle, which ensures a regular feed to the stones and causes the clacking sound from which it receives its name, is replaced in Iranian windmills by a wooden trail-stick. This hooks over the feed-shoe (see Plate 13) and, as it rides up and down over the uneven upper surface of the runner stone, transmits the agitation to the shoe. They call it *laklak*, the stork. A similar but double device in the Atlas mountains is known as the 'dogs'. At Tashqorghan in northern Afghanistan, where a detailed study of the bazaar in the 1960s includes much on the 57 watermills of the town, this trail-stick is called *chapoldak*. There the carpenter who built a mill remained its millwright and stone-dresser and was paid one seventh of the weekly toll-flour.[15] Iranian watermills, however, are closer to British practice in this one respect: a stick attached to the feed-shoe is held in tension against the side of the eye of the runner-stone and sets up the necessary vibration.

The foregoing catalogue of mill furniture is brief. The interior of a small European mill can be compared to an outsize clock mechanism, where many of the cogwheels have wooden teeth; gears, shafts and belts distribute the power coming into the mill in various directions: to two or three sets of stones, to flour-dressing and bolting machines, to elevators which move the flour round the mill. None of this exists in an Iranian mill; there is just one pair of stones and direct transmission to it from one wind or waterwheel, so that the runner-stone turns at the speed of the wheel set directly beneath (water) or above (wind) it. The process of making flour from grain is visible, immediate and uncomplicated. No improving engineer has meddled with this most basic of all wheel-driven machines.

Simple technology

There are no machine-made parts in a Middle Eastern mill. The technology is of necessity very simple. The direct drive to the stones has already been described, together with the wooden *mosht* which takes the whole weight of the wind-wheel and runner stone. Its equivalent in a horizontal watermill is a metal spike, driven into the base of the hub of the water-wheel, which turns in a primitive bearing on the foot-beam, lubricated by the water pouring onto the wheel.

Water issues from the bottom of the drop-tower, through a nozzle wedged into an aperture. Nozzles of different sizes can be used, depending upon the availability of water to keep the tower filled and thus the waterhead as high as possible. Small nozzles therefore are inserted in the summer, while large ones serve the purpose in the winter. For maximum efficiency, the jet should strike the blades at an angle of 30–35°, so in many horizontal mills in other parts of the world the blades are driven into angled mortises in the hub, or alternatively the water is delivered to the blades down a sloping chute (see Plate 14). Iranian wheels seem to be constructed on less exacting principles, with broad, flat blades roughly perpendicular to the mainshaft of the water-wheel, rather like the so-called Norse wheels of the North Atlantic islands. These latter, however, can always rely on abundant water and so do not need to harness it in cunning fashion.

Few horizontal mills are designed or required to operate with anything remotely resembling scientific efficiency. Not only are they uncomplicated for reasons of expense and of ease of maintenance, but their purpose is principally to serve their owner's own domestic needs rather than to generate a profitable business. Where a large English village 200 years ago might have kept two or three mills occupied, a similarly sized Iranian one until very recently may have included ten times as many. Nishtafun/Nishtafeh in Khorasan had 23 windmills, and Fin, near Kashan, had 33 watermills. Such mills were relatively cheaply built, they could be owned in partnership, and there was no milling soke such as that which restricted the medieval English and French peasant to using his lord's mill, paying for the privilege and suspecting the professional miller of trying to cheat him in the process. Most Iranian windmillers were part-time farmers, grinding for customers by arrangement and not concerned to drum up business by running a donkey service, for example, to collect grain and deliver flour. Watermillers may have been occupied at their mills on a more full-time basis, depending upon the water supply and the number of competing mills it powered.[16] This is no longer easy to check, as so few traditional mills remain in even occasional operation.

In the Atlas mountains, on the other hand, milling remains a domestic chore and is regarded (by men) as women's work. They are expected to operate the mill themselves, though sometimes then without payment of any toll or fee. An exception is represented by the ten mills on the brink of the Cascades d'Ouzoud, the largest waterfall in North Africa, where men are in charge of a profitable enterprise and where a donkey park is provided for customers' beasts. Berber women have a good reason for welcoming the frequent trips to the mill: since there is (often) no hopper, they must remain to feed all their grain into the eye of the stones by hand, so cannot be required to undertake any other duties during all that time.

Herein lies another justification for extremely simple technology: there is little to go wrong, so the mill can also be left unattended for some while, even several hours, where a hopper has been installed, for grinding is a slow business: 100 kg may take all morning. Meanwhile, the miller, or the customer using the mill, can busy himself with other tasks or take a rest from his labours.

Gears would speed up the operation at the mill and facilitate the introduction of machinery for improving the product in ways the peasant farmers neither expect nor desire. This has happened in the towns, where commercial rather than custom milling is the rule, but by diesel engine or electricity! Wherever modern fuels are cheaply available, the traditional mills have gone out of business, 'asleep' *(khabideh)* as they said in Khorasan of many of their windmills in 1977. Having grain ground entails a cost on the household budget, and the fee paid can be used by the miller to contribute towards the repair of precision machinery and fuel. By contrast, the traditional horizontal mill was suited to a barter economy; the mill owner received grain or flour from his customers in return for his services and could exchange or sell any surplus in the local market.

Numerous mills lasted well into the second half of the twentieth century, because bread has remained the predominant item in the Middle Eastern diet and because, in large countries with scattered populations (despite several huge honey-pot cities like Tehran) and harsh geography, modern communications have only been put in place very recently to enable the majority of the population to gain speedy access to a large market economy. In the mountains south-west of Marrakesh, an unmetalled road leads to a valley where the villages hold nearly 6,000 inhabitants. Twice a week a lorry makes the journey, carrying, amongst other goods, sacks of flour and drums of diesel fuel for the mill at the central market. Not surprisingly, the horizontal watermills on the streams at the edges of the valley under the mountains are now little used, and remittances from the menfolk working in Casablanca help to pay for the household shopping which that lorry has made the new routine.[17]

Formerly a donkey trip of an hour or more to the nearest mill might have been a regular feature of the weekly round. Flourishing and well-used mills like those at Band-e Amir and the Cascades d'Ouzoud might have entailed a longer journey, involving a night spent at the mill. Migrating nomads also had to make longer journeys unless their tents were pitched near settlements which included a mill. They seem to have preferred to transport flour rather than quern-stones for grinding by hand at each night stop. Stones large enough to grind a sufficient quantity of flour of an acceptable quality, roughly comparable to the product of a watermill, would have represented a heavy burden for their pack animals.

Nevertheless, a century ago in the Middle East much grinding must always have been done by human muscle or by animal power. In dry countries, streams to drive mills have to be carefully husbanded, especially in the summer, and the windmills only ever operated in a limited area and for a few months in the year. Servants were used either to drive the donkeys to the mill or to grind the daily flour in the house. There are few records of such domestic arrangements, although Wulff describes the handmill installed in large households.[18]

It has been suggested here that the miller's role was never so prominent in the Middle East as in pre-industrial Europe. He was not seen as the ally of the landlord or as out to cheat his customers. He was often a part-time operator. Many mills were in group ownership, so that power was not concentrated in one man's hands. All peasant farmers, millers included, were conditioned to present a low profile to the forces that seemed bent on their adversity: government, landlord, soldiers, bandits, drought, locusts, etc. Unusually, at Neh there was the opportunity during the four windy months to grind for a passing trade, the pilgrim caravans proceeding to and from Mashhad. The grain itself had to be brought up from Sistan, so the miller's profits were perhaps small in any case. Sykes gives the pilgrim trade as the reason for the 50 windmills he counted in this town of 5,000 inhabitants in 1899.[19] That may or may not be true. Khaf had the same number of mills for half that population at the same date. Clearly those at Neh were more fully used and transacted profitable business whenever the caravans passed through the town.

Plate 17 The interior of the eastern tower of the Hazar Jarib: the central drum (1963).

Plate 18 Painted towers near Lenjan. Left, a cluster of four topped by a central turret. Right, a battery of 16. There was an ice-pool in its shade (see also Figure 7.4).

Plate 19 An ice-house near Sabzevar (at Za'farineh), in use in 1970. The ziggurat-like form results from the spiral step, which is designed to give easy access to the dome for maintenance.

Plate 20 An ice-house with its shade wall near Yazd, 1975. The photograph is taken from the south, so that the ice-pool is on the other side of the wall. A walkway runs along the wall below the decorative brick parapet. Access steps up to the dome can be seen above the porch which protects the entrance to the ice-pit.

Plate 21 Ögödey Qa'an with his sons (from *Djâmî' al-Tawarikh*, Bibliothèque Nationale, Paris. Supp. Pers. 1113, fo. 132 r).

Plate 22 Îlkhânîd tents, *c.* 1310, Rashîdîya (Preussischer Kulturbesitz, Staatsbibliothek Berlin, Diezscher Klebeband A., fol. 70, p. 18 top).

Plate 23 Îlkhânid tents, *c.* 1310, Rashîdîya (ibid. fol. 70, 8 top).

Plate 24 The great tent of Ghâzân Khân at Ûdjân, Adharbâidjân, 701/1302 (*Djâmi' al-Tawarikh,* loc. cit. fo. 239r.).

Plate 25 Transport of Ordos shrine tents (after Owen Lattimore, 'Douglas Carruthers and geographical contrasts in Central Asia', *Geographical Journal* 144 (2), 1978, pp. 208–17, pl. Va.).

Plate 26 The tents at Ix Ejen Xoroo *c.* 1909 (after Père Antoine Mostaert in F.W.Cleaves (ed.), *Sagang Secen's Erdeni-yin Tobci (Scripta Mongolica 2),* Cambridge, MA: Harvard Yenching Institute, 1956, Vol. 1, pl. 2.

Plate 27 The shrine tents of Çiñgiz Qan at Eĵfen Xoroo Museum in 1957 (after B. Rintschen, 'Zum Kult Tschinggis-Khans bei den Mongolen', in T. Bodrogi and L.Boglar (eds), *Opuscula Ethnologica Memoriae Ludovici Biró Sacra,* Budapest: Akademiai Kiado, 1959, ill. 3, 4).

Plate 28 Firuzkuhi trellis tent, Ghur, Afghanistan, 1959 (K.Ferdinand).

Plate 29 No ay cart-tents in 1793 (after Peter Simon Pallas, *Bemerkungen auf einer Reise in die Sudlichen Statthalterschaften des Russischen Reichs in den Jahren 1793 und 1794,* Leipzig, 1799–1801, Vol. 1, pl. vi).

Plate 30 No ay cart-tent, 1909 (after K.A.Inostrantsev, in G.BonchOsmolovskiy, 'Svadebnuie zhilishcha turetskikh narodnostey', *Materialui po Etnografii* 3 (1), 1926, fig. 2).

Plate 31 No ay wedding tent, 1904 (after Inostrantsev, in BonchOsmolovskiy, 'Svadebnuie zhilishcha', fig.3).

Plate 32 Al Na'im tent in northern Qatar at Murwab (Klaus Ferdinand, 1959).

Plate 33 Tent of the North Qatari type; photograph apparently taken in a settlement close to the coast between Hufuf in al-Hasa and Dohah, most probably in Qatar (Hermann Burchardt, see note 22).

The profitability of mill-ownership can be judged by the taxes extracted: 'Every watermill pays from one toman to twenty tomans a year or even more as taxes in proportion to the income of the mill owner.'[20] At that time the poll-tax per family was usually two tomans, with seyyeds, mullahs, bathmen and beggars being excepted. Twenty years later, in 1926, a new law established uniform land taxes, including one whereby mills had to pay 5 per cent of the owner's receipts.[21] By 1992 the last miller at Qasr-e Dasht outside Shiraz had ceased to pay this tax, which had once been 1,000 tomans and had then dropped to 600 as his business began to fall off dramatically. At this midway point in the mill's declining fortunes his total annual income would not have sufficed to buy a new pair of stones.

Six hundred tomans was the amount paid to the governor of Herat in 1833 by the monopolizer of water and windmills, equivalent to the monopoly of the Bokhara caravan and three times the figure paid for catching thieves.[22] It was a large figure, but it also indicates a considerable number of mills; the sum may be illuminated by the fact that at Nishtafun in 1903 each windmill paid an annual tax of less than one toman.[23] The governors of Herat and Khorasan were surely as rapacious or as realistic as each other.

Water power for industry

The waterwheel as prime mover of the Middle Ages in Europe initiated or improved a number of industrial processes. In the eighteenth century, one of these arrogated to itself the title *mill*, even though nothing was ground there by millstones; only the physique of the workers was ground down as they served the spinning and weaving machines whose bobbins and belts, cogs and shafts were driven by the waterwheel.

In the world of Islam the traditional waterwheel has seldom driven anything except stones for grinding grain. There are very scanty references to fulling mills and to trip hammers powered by water.[24] Brewing and malting had no place in Islam. Oil-mills were worked by animals.[25] There was insufficient waterpower for sawmills and cannon-boring mills, except perhaps in the Caspian provinces. Did the Sherley brothers advise Shah 'Abbas on the production of gunpowder by waterpower, as in Europe? James Morier certainly saw a water-powered powder-mill at Tabriz in the early nineteenth century, modelled on one at Constantinople.[26] Stone was ground for the production of colours, henna for cosmetic purposes, turmeric and saffron for cooking, sulphur for spraying fruit trees. Rice-hulling mills are still found in Afghanistan and Central Asia. The one large-scale industrial process, apart from flour-milling, powered by water in Islamic countries from an early date seems to have been paper-making. Samarkand, Baghdad and especially Cordoba, where the mills on the Guadalquivir still stand (empty), feature prominently in the early history of paper-making.

For reasons of geography and politics and due to a neglect of the application of science to technology, the Industrial Revolution came late to Iran and even later to Afghanistan, so late that it began there with the age of steam power in an already developed form. Water power has only been applied to industry in the modern form of hydroelectricity. (Or did the Kazeruni mills in Isfahan ever use waterwheels powered by the Zayandeh Rud in the years before the Second World War?)

Before the era of high dams, the volume of available water could not easily be increased. The small supplies were tapped inefficiently —totally so, for industrial purposes—by wooden wheels, which could not tolerate any greater strain than the pressure of a small jet of water and the torque of one shaft driving one pair of millstones. Metal parts., gears and precise, balanced and well-engineered bearings would have been necessary for the waterwheels of the Middle East to have become workhorses of early industrial progress.

In any case, it was not just a dearth of water that doomed any such plans in the nineteenth century. Traditional crafts were largely plied in the bazaar and protected by the conservative and jealous attitudes and trade practices of that powerful institution. Manual labour sustained those crafts, with a few animal-powered exceptions, like the camel-mills of Isfahan or Herat for oil and certain culinary products. There was little or no readiness to involve capital, even on a moderate scale, to turn to Iran's advantage the industrial developments pioneered in the West. Change did not begin to come until the modernizing regimes after the First World War.

Historical evidence

An informed interest in water-powered machines has a long history in the Middle East. The sketchbooks of the French architect and engineer Villard d'Honnecourt, dating from the mid-thirteenth century, are surpassed for detailed explanation by 'The Ingenious Mechanical Devices' of al-Jazari in Northern Iraq 50 years earlier. The Frenchman sought to power a saw, while the Arab designed water-raising devices and water-clocks. Three hundred and fifty years before that, the Banu Musa in Baghdad used a sophisticated version of the horizontal waterwheel, evidence of their advanced understanding of pressure, to operate a fountain.[27]

There are references to mills in the early Islamic period: the last Sassanian king was murdered in a mill at Merv in AD 651, and in a story recounted two centuries later by al-Tabari occurs the first mention of windmills when a Persian prisoner offered to build one for the caliph 'Omar. The mills at Dizful may date back even earlier, for the foundations of the weirs on which they stand were built around AD 260 by the Roman soldiers captured by Shapur. At Deh Loran in Khuzistan excavations have revealed drop-towers and subterranean mills on *qanat* systems from the Sasanian period.[28] On the southern shores of the Gulf of Oman, remains of similar mills from the tenth century have been discovered.[29] Otherwise the archaeological record remains slender so far, but that is hardly the fault of the archaeologist in a huge area so rich in the remains of ancient civilizations.

This same tenth century saw the historical geographies of al-Istakhri, al-Mas'udi, ibn Hauqal and al-Muqaddasi, which firmly establish the existence of wind and watermills at locations which include Band-e Amir in Fars, where the dam with its mills was newly built: ten waterwheels were installed close to the dam, with a mill under each of them.[30] In later medieval centuries the catalogue of mills was extended by, for instance, Hamdallah Mostoufi, who documented the grinding rate of the 40 mills at Nishapur and transmitted a local tradition linking the windmills of Ghôrîân to an Egyptian pharaoh.[31]

The earliest detailed description of the horizontal windmills of Sistan was written *c.* AD 1300 by al-Dimashqi. He states clearly that these windmills had under-driven stones, with the wind-wheel in the same relation to them as a horizontal waterwheel.[32] No other archaeological or literary evidence in the Middle East bears out this arrangement, fair though it is. It is not known whether al-Dimashqi wrote from first-hand observation or on the basis of second-hand information.

No other manuscript illustrations exist of these windmills, but horizontal waterwheels feature in several Moghul manuscripts of Persian legends and of the story of the murder of Yazdgerd. At much the same time, the early seventeenth century, there are several topographical references to windmills in *Ehya al-Moluk,* the continuation of the *Tarikh-e Sistan* to AH 1028.[33]

Chardin chose to state that there were no windmills in Persia, and, despite their long residence in the country, neither he nor Fryer make even passing reference to watermills. Unlike cisterns and pigeon-towers, mills were mundane buildings, of little interest to their potential readers back in England.

For one obvious reason, the appeal of the exotic and the unusual, windmills are better served than watermills in Victorian travel-books. Mohan Lal included the windmills of Khaf in the account of his journey in 1834, and Bellew, passing through Sistan in 1872, gives a valuable description of the windmills there and hints tantalizingly at their use for water-raising, the first such reference since al-Mas'udi 900 years earlier. Britain was interested in this corner of Persia as part of the Great Game against Russia. Useful first-hand descriptions around 1900 came from the two Yates, Savage-Landor and especially Tate in Sistan. Sven Hedin and later Alfons Gabriel in the 1930s travelled in this remote part of Iran, recording its geography; they mentioned windmills in specific villages where they were still to be found in 1977.[34]

The first detailed documentation of the horizontal windmills of Sistan since al-Dimashqi was published in Wulff's invaluable *Traditional Crafts of Persia,* largely researched in the 1930s. Klaus Ferdinand's article on the windmills of Ghôrîân, with numerous photographs and measured drawings, recorded them as fully working buildings in 1960, shortly before they fell silent and became objects of historical rather than ethnographic enquiry. A more recent study, drawing together previous work in this field and expanding the technical details from observations made at working windmills in Eastern Khorasan, appeared in 1991.[35]

Watermills were too plentiful and ordinary to merit detailed description until they had almost vanished. Binning, journeying through Persia in the mid-nineteenth century, and Stack 30 years later, include several brief references to mills, especially to those with vertical wheels on the Zayandeh Rud. Curzon, in typical encyclopaedic fashion, dwells on the Shushtar dam and its mills and on those on the weirs at Dizful.[36] Wulff again records a useful glossary of technical terms and itemizes the construction of both horizontal and vertical wheels.[37] The findings of the Danish expeditions to Afghanistan[38] and those of L.Edelberg in Nuristan add to our knowledge of horizontal watermills while they were still an essential part of the rural scene. Edelberg gives due prominence to those dimensions of the miller's role and of the place of his mill in the local economy that remain all too often untouched in the historical sources and the nineteenth-century travel books.[39] PapoliYazdi's article on the mills on *qanat* systems in the Yazd area and at Boshruyeh, most of which ceased operation around 1980, is well documented, with detailed measurements.

Mills in the modern world

The effect of deep wells upon the water table, and especially on the *qanat* system whose mother wells are linked to it, has doomed many watermills on the Iranian Plateau, as Papoli-Yazdi has made clear for the area north-west of Yazd. He also comments that formerly a mill often performed a valuable service in funding, through the tolls, the *muqanni* who maintained the *qanat*. However, once the daily labouring wage rose and parted company with the value of a few kg of flour, the mill could no longer fulfil its main *raison d'être,* so the *qanat* lacked maintenance and the mill stopped.[40]

Has the point of no return been reached for these traditional mills? Certainly they are no longer needed, except in the economy of the remotest villages. For the production of flour, such methods have been superseded, as in most other parts of the world. Only where cheap electricity is unobtainable and good road communications do not yet exist, do they hang on, as in parts of the Atlas mountains and probably the Hindu Kush. Iranians may dwell with nostalgia upon the cool flour and the tasty quality of stone-ground bread, but they patronize the new bakeries or use bought flour to prepare bread which they bake in gas-fired ovens themselves. The effort of producing flour by traditional means, when mass-produced bread is cheap and readily available, is not viewed as worthwhile by those who might even now be prolonging the useful life of the small mills.

Migration from the villages into the towns and the rapid growth of Iran's population have raised the demand for urban facilities and encouraged a life-style where the old, slow pace of life and traditional customs are increasingly viewed as outmoded. The Iranian government has subsidized and fixed the price of bread, making it as advantageous as it is necessary to eat the shop *nan,* processed by gleaming machines powered by gas or electricity.

In Hamadan, the mills which supplied much of the city with flour even as recently as 1960 could not cope with the changed state of affairs and within 20 years vanished without trace. Below Isfahan the mills were inundated by the waters of a small hydroelectric scheme. Even at a country town like Estehban in Fars, only two out of 11 mills remain on the abundant stream in the valley above the town. Neither of them any longer produce flour. They are reduced to the occasional grinding of *sefid-ab* and henna. The primitive, old-fashioned technology of the mills, which was not inappropriate to Middle Eastern rural society before 1960, is condemned as backward and not even regarded as quaint. Only their water supply is appreciated as the backdrop to Friday outings.

When the movement begun in the 1970s to safeguard Iran's vernacular heritage regains momentum, as it surely will, it may be too late for many of these buildings. Mud-brick needs maintenance. So it may be a question of constructing copies, examples that illustrate aspects of a once-lively vernacular architectural tradition; a theme-park rather than an outdoor museum.

Some mills should be saved now, kept weather-proof, retaining their equipment and their working atmosphere as much as possible, and put into operation periodically to maintain an awareness of the purpose and tradition in the locality which they once served. But who will organize and pay for that in a country which, understandably, has other priorities, and which does not attract more than a handful of discriminating tourists?

A modern highway carries heavy traffic along the north side of the great line of windmills at Neh. Those at Khaf have been turned into garages or storage sheds. The famous watermills at Band-e Amir have been left in an almost totally destroyed state after a disastrous flood in 1977. Those at Shushtar suffer from similar neglect, despite an optimistic official notice. The windmills between Herat and the Iranian border have been razed by Russian bombs and rockets.[41] In Sistan, their original homeland, windmills have long since disappeared

The relevant government department should pay several of the millers at Fin to continue operating their watermills, at least on the part-time basis obtaining in 1992. Their proximity to the great potential tourist attraction of the Bagh-e Fin should ensure them a stream of visitors in the future. Band-e Amir and Shushtar deserve to be restored to limited operation, as also one of the lines of windmills at Nishtafun. A nation is the poorer for losing its heritage, especially those aspects of it which were once so vital to the everyday life of the whole population. There is no denying that preserved vernacular architecture is a luxury, and one which we ourselves in the developed world are only just able to afford. The interest and enthusiasm our traditional working buildings arouse, in more than a trickle of paying visitors, suggest that one day the Middle East might belatedly admit it was the poorer for letting its own similar heritage disappear into history.

Notes

1. E.Beazley and M.Harverson, *Living with the Desert* (Warminster: Aris and Philips, 1982) concentrates on such buildings on the Iranian plateau, including both wind and watermills.
2. Hans E.Wulff, *The Traditional Crafts of Persia* (Cambridge, MA: MIT Press, 1966), p. 286.
3. Wulff, *The Traditional Crafts of Persia*, p. 286.
4. Klaus Ferdinand, 'The horizontal windmills of western Afghanistan', *Folk* 5, 1963, pp. 71–89, and 8–9, 1966/7, pp. 83–8.
5. Joseph Needham, *Science and Civilisation in China* (Cambridge: Cambridge University Press, 1965), Vol. 4, Part 2, pp. 356–405.
6. Guy Lestrange (trans.), *Don Juan of Persia* (London, 1926,) pp. 50–51.

7. Mohammad Hosain Papoli-Yazdi, 'Asyab-ha'i ke be ab-e qanat kar mikonand', *Majalleh-ye Daneshkadeh-ye Adabiyat* (Mashhad) 18(1), 1364/1985, pp. 3–30.

8. E.Wiedemann, *Aufsätze zur arabischen Wissenschaftsgeschichte* (Hildesheim: Georg Olms, 1970), Vol. 1, pp. 288–9; see also plan reproduced in E.Reza *et al., Ab-o Fan-e Abyari dar Iran Bastan* (Tehran, 1971), pp. 267–8. See also Hill's chapter in this volume.

9. Lawrence Lockhart, *Famous Cities of Iran* (Brentford, 1939), p. 89.

10. F.Galhano, *Moinhos e Azenhas de Portugal* (Lisbon: Associação Portuguesa dos Amigos dos Moinhos, 1978), pp. 55–9.

11. See further, M.Harverson, 'Watermills in Iran', *Iran* 31, 1993, pp. 149–77.

12. G.P.Tate, *Memoir on the Ruins of Seistan* (Calcutta: Government Printing, 1910), pp. 160, 251–4.

13. N.Malcolm, *Five Years in a Persian Town* (London, 1905), p. 28.

14. Wulff, *Traditional Crafts,* p. 279.

15. Pierre Centlivres, *Un Bazar d'Asie Centrale* (Wiesbaden: Reichert, 1972), pp. 106–7.

16. Papoli-Yazdi, p. 20.

17. See M.Harverson, 'Watermills in the Atlas Mountains', *Transactions of the 8th International Symposium on Molinology* (Aberystwyth, 1995), pp. 117–26.

18. Wulff, *Traditional Crafts,* p. 278.

19. P.M.Sykes, *Ten Thousand Miles in Persia* (London, 1902), pp. 413–14.

20. P.M.Sykes, *Report on the Agriculture of Khorasan* (Simla, 1910), p. 5.

21. A.K.S.Lambton, *Landlord and Peasant in Persia* (London: Oxford University Press, 1953), p. 183.

22. Munshi Mohun Lal, 'A brief description of Herat', *Journal of the Asiatic Society of Bengal* 3, 1834, p. 11.

23. Ludwig Adamec (ed.), *Gazetteer for Meshed and N.E. Iran* (Graz: Akademische Druck und Verlagsanstalt, 1981), p. 533.

24. D.R.Hill, *Islamic Science and Engineering* (Edinburgh: Edinburgh University Press, 1993), p. 112; al-Biruni, in F.Krenkow (ed.), *Kitab al-Jamahir* (Hyderabad, Deccan, 1936), pp. 233–4.

25. E.O'Donovan, *The Merv Oasis* (London, 1882), Vol. 2, p. 308.

26. James Morier, *A Second Journey through Persia between 1810 and 1816* (London, 1818), p. 231.

27. Donald Hill, *A History of Engineering in Classical and Medieval Times* (London: Croom Helm, 1984), pp. 146–52, 160.

28. J.A.Neely, 'Sassanian and early Islamic water control and irrigation systems on the Deh Luran Plain, Iran', in T.F.Downing and McG.Gibson (eds), *Irrigation's Impact on Society* (Tucson: University of Arizona Press, 1974), pp. 31–4.

29. P.M.Costa and T.J.Wilkinson, 'The hinterland of Sohar', *The Journal of Oman Studies* 9, 1987, pp. 56–7, 66–75.

30. Wiedemann, *Aufsätze,* pp. 288–9.

31. Guy Lestrange (trans.), *The Geographical Part of the Nuzhat al-Qulub* (London: Luzac, 1919), pp. 147, 151.

32. Wiedemann, *Aufsätze,* p. 218. Different diagrams in two versions of this work illustrate the point.

33. Ghiyath al-din Sistani, *Ehya al-Moluk* (Tehran, 1966), pp. 127, 299.

34. M.Harverson, *Persian Windmills* (The International Molinological Society, 1991) pp. 17–25.

35. Harverson, *Persian Windmills.*

36. G.N.Curzon, *Persia and the Persian Question* (London, 1892), Vol. 2, pp. 304, 373.

37. Wulff, *Traditional Crafts,* pp. 278–91.

38. Johannes Humlum, *La Géographie de l'Afghanistan* (Copenhagen: Gyldendal, 1959), pp. 314–9.

39. Lennart Edelberg, *Nuristani Buildings* (Jutland Archaeological Society Publications XVIII, 1984), pp. 197–212.

40. Papoli-Yazdi, 'Asyab-ha', p. 27.

41. Nick Danziger, *Danziger's Adventures* (London: HarperCollins, 1992), p. 199.

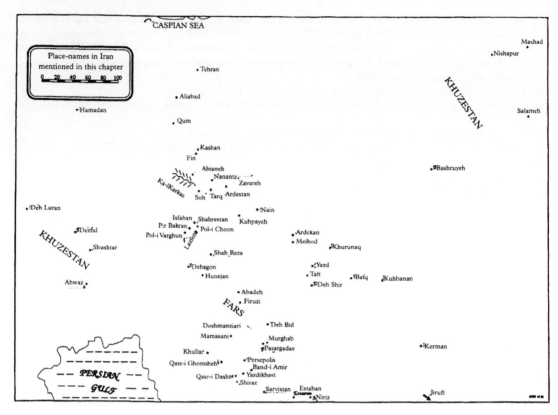

Map 6.1 Place-names in Iran mentioned in this chapter.

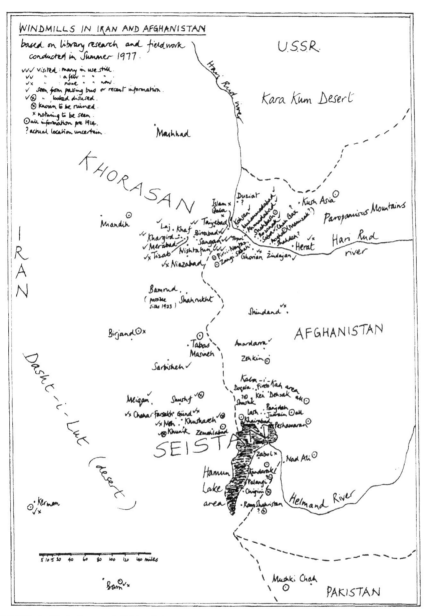

Map 6.2 Windmills in Iran and Afghanistan.

Chapter 7
Pigeon Towers and Ice-Houses on the Iranian Plateau
Elisabeth Beazley

Of the many buildings designed by the ingenious Iranians to make life more civilized in the harsh climate of the plateau, ice-houses perhaps take pride of place. Their pigeon towers are equally astonishing.[1]

Pigeon towers *(borj-e kaftar)*

Their function and distribution

The distribution of pigeon towers is, naturally enough, a direct consequence of their use. By far the greatest number survive within the oasis of Esfahan (there are only isolated groups elsewhere). Afghan examples, near Herat, are in country which was part of Iran until two centuries ago, on the opposite edge of the plateau to Esfahan, in another fertile river valley near what was then another royal capital.

The general absence of pigeon towers is at first sight very surprising, but it can probably be accounted for by the fact that the squabs (young birds) were not used for food as they were in Britain and many other parts of Europe. The towers were built for the collection of pigeon manure, which was found to be particularly beneficial to the cultivation of melons, a fruit much prized in the hot, dry climate. A capital city produces a concentration of wealth which makes it profitable to intensify the agricultural output of a region which serves it; a steady demand for the luxury of melons over a long season would necessitate heavy use of fertilizer. Its production was the *raison d'être* of the pigeon tower, which might today be termed a fertilizer collection centre. It was not until after Esfahan ceased to be the capital that many of the towers began to fall to ruin. Elsewhere, in most places away from the capital, the individual landowners and peasants could grow enough melons in season without going to the expense and trouble of building a pigeon tower in which to collect the relatively small amounts of fertilizer that might be needed.

The other use for the dung, for the manufacture of gunpowder, must not be forgotten. This too would lead to the siting of towers within easy reach of the capital city, where an important part of the Shah's army would be based.

The success of a pigeon tower must also depend on the food available to the pigeons foraging for themselves on both crops and uncultivated land. A rich oasis like Esfahan or a river valley like that of the Hari Rud would supply both, something which could not be claimed by many places on the plateau. Nor could many regions supply sufficient water; melon crops depend on an exceptionally large supply for their irrigation.

It was the rare juxtaposition of these diverse factors which made the building of pigeon towers worthwhile; demand for melons over a long season at up-market prices had to be centred in a region where the birds could successfully forage and the fruit be generously irrigated.

Figure 7.1 Plans of the towers of the Hazar Jarib.

The towers have long been landmarks in the Esfahan oasis. 'I don't think there are finer Dove-cots in any part of the World', wrote Sir John Chardin in the sevententh century.[2] Even in ruin they are spectacular, and hundreds, I hope, still dot the hazy green sea of orchards and gardens which surround the city. Massive in scale, these structures seem to be incongruously out of context; they might be Martello towers stranded hundreds of miles inland, or chess-men awaiting the master mind of a remote giant.

The bigger towers are free-standing but many of the smaller ones, built into the walls of the gardens, are deceptively akin to bastions or corner towers in a defence system. Others brood protectively, but unstrategically, over the flat mud roofs of village houses. Their useful but unromantic purpose, the collection of manure, makes the sculptural form and the fascination of pattern in the interiors of these utilitarian structures the more astonishing.

As in all traditional building, dating is difficult. The only two (see Figure 7.1 and Plates 15 and 16) to which even a period is ascribed are thought to have been built during the reign of Shah 'Abbas (1587–1629) in the great royal gardens of the Hazar Jarib ('thousand acres'), but since these have more highly developed plans than any others now extant it must be assumed that a considerable tradition lies behind them.

Unfortunately, there is a dearth of travellers' reports in the period preceding that of Shah 'Abbas, when they appear, architecturally, in full flower. They were first noted by the seventeenth-century traveller, Thomas Herbert (1628) between Shahreza and Esfahan (in Mahyar): 'albeit their houses were neat, yet they were in no wise comparable to their dove-houses for curious outsides'.[3] For the next 300 years traditional designs

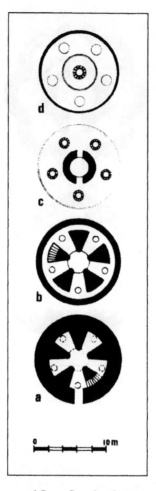

Figure 7.2 Plans of a 'typical' tower. (a) The ground floor: five giant buttresses, like the spokes of a wheel, support the drum of the central turret. Steps lead to the upper galleries. (b) The first and second floors: the galleries are pierced by holes which allow the birds to fly down from the pepper-pots on the roof, from which they enter the tower. (c) The main roof is topped by five pepper-pots. (d) The upper roof: one pepper-pot crowns the central turret.

seem to have been handed down within each family or village, but although the aim of the builders and the unit on which they worked, the pigeon hole, were identical, no towers were the same.

Single round towers are typical, but amazing inventiveness has gone into the solution of the basic problem: the provision of the maximum number of pigeon holes with the minimum amount of building material, mud-brick or mud. This requires ingenuity. Timber is rarely used, so the whole structure must be designed to be in compression, minimizing tensile stress. Circular ground plans, which are by far the most common, are important in this respect. The variety of plans within the basic concept of a circle, with their curving vaults and pierced saucer domes, produce fascinating sequences of solid and void (see Figures 7.2 and 7.3).

Basically, the towers consist of an outer drum, battered for stability and buttressed internally to prevent collapse and to gain lateral support from an inner drum which rises perhaps half as high again as the main

Figure 7.3 A section of a 'typical' tower.

structure. The main drum is divided vertically by the galleries which cut the buttresses and are connected by a circular stair. The galleries are supported on barrel vaults and saucer domes. Between the buttresses (which look like the spokes of a wheel on plan) the domes are pierced to allow the birds to fly up and down; similarly the inner and outer drums are connected by open arches at every level. The pigeons enter only through the sides of the domed cupolas or 'pepper-pots' of honeycomb brickwork. One of these crowns the inner drum while others usually ring the flat roof of the main drum below. They vary in number according to the ground plan; half a dozen would be usual, but one tower (still in use in 1961 at Chahar Borj) had 20, plus four on its central drum.

Size varies considerably. A big tower might have a base diameter of 12 metres (*c.* 39 feet) and an overall height of about 20 metres (*c.* 66 feet). The Chahar Borj—the biggest seen—was 22 metres (*c.* 72 feet) across.

Most builders seem to have been content to build the outer wall as a simple drum; it is the way in which it may be alternatively hollowed out and buttressed internally which provides its architectural fascination. However, the two towers attributed to the late sixteenth or early seventeenth century in the Hazar Jarib (see Plates 15 and 16) have the further refinement of a corrugated outer wall which increases the stability of these large towers without increase of wall thickness. This also increases the surface area of the wall and hence the number of pigeon-holes. The eastern tower could be thought of as a cluster of eight small drums round a larger central drum.

The mesmeric character of the inside of the towers comes from the repetition on every vertical surface, whether or not it is curved on plan, of the standard pigeon-hole, 20×20 cm by 27 deep (*c.* 8× 8×11 inches) with its mud perch below (see Plate 17). Much of the sculptural quality of the structure is due to these perches; contrast the comparative flatness of those interiors where they have fallen away. Each is made of an asymmetrical mud pyramid of four unequal sides. When in position, the smaller top side of the pyramid forms a horizontal perch and the other sides slope away, making access to the neighbouring holes easier for the pigeons next door. This perch allows the bird to alight clear of the nest and droppings to fall clear to the floor below—an important point since the function of the tower was to collect manure.

Clustered towers

Although the vast majority of towers are single drums, two unusual designs in which drums adjoined were seen in the village of Kelisan near Lenjan (in 1970). One consisted of a cluster of four small turrets of about 3 metres (*c.* 10 feet) in diameter crowned by a central drum (see Plate 18).

The other, built on the edge of an orchard, consisted of a battery of linked turrets which was about 38 metres (*c.* 125 feet) long, each turret having a diameter of about 2–3 metres. The last two turrets at each end had two more attached, making a cluster like the one already described (see Figure 7.4). These projections gave shade to the ends of an ice trench that had been excavated in the lee of the wall (see below).

Rectangular towers

Big rectangular pigeon towers of quite different design were found in use (in 1971) in the Khunsar-Golpayegan region, 125–200 kilometres to the north-west of Esfahan. They were reminiscent of small forts. Some were sited singly; others were grouped; none seen was built into garden walls. A typical tower measured 12.3×4.5 m (*c.* 40×15 feet) at the base and was 7–8 m (*c.* 23–26 feet) high. The walls, which were battered at the base, were decorated by a broad plastered band 2–3 m (*c.* 7–10 feet) above the ground. This smooth surface was probably introduced to prevent the entry of reptiles (see below). The top of the walls was crenellated. It was not possible to enter any tower to make a plan, for the cheering reason that they were in use.

Snakes and decoration

The towers are entered once a year for the collection of manure, after which the small doorway (occasionally there are two) is bricked up for the next 12 months. High-level entrances are not uncommon; they are almost certainly positioned to reduce the danger of snakes and rats getting into the tower. The cause of structural cracks was said to be the tremendous vibration set up by the wings of hundreds of terrified birds if a snake got in. Some cracks may have been caused by earthquakes, but most of those in the many disused towers still standing were probably caused by rain. Deterioration would be swift, once the long

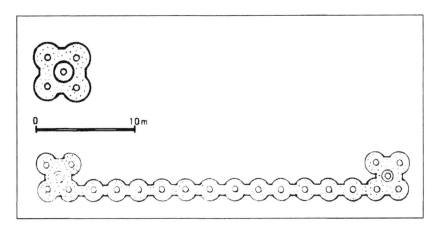

Figure 7.4 Plan of Lenjan towers; see Plate 18.

wooden water spouts which take the water clear of the battered walls had gone; they are seldom left in an abandoned tower.

External decoration varies according to the grandness of the tower and the whim of the owner, but even at its most exotic it probably derives from the function of keeping out snakes and rats.

A band of smooth plaster, about a metre wide, often coloured in lime-wash or red ochre, decorates the main wall. It would prevent a snake getting a grip; it might otherwise creep up the battered drum of the tower on the rough mud and straw plaster with which it is rendered. Projecting courses of brick and plastered cornices and friezes, besides giving an effective decorative capping to the wall, also provide projections which snakes would find difficult to negotiate. Painting is now relatively rare, but Morier (in 1810–16) noted that towers 'were painted and ornamented' and that 'more care appears to have been bestowed on their outside than upon that of the generality of dwelling-houses'.[4] The cornice of even the simpler towers usually has a 'spoon' pattern moulded in the plaster; this seems to be the remains of the idea of finishing the tops with stalactite decoration which was so popular among Muslim builders.

The only modern example seen where the tradition of painting survived is on the groups of towers already described (Lenjan) to the south-west of Esfahan. Here the tradition was very much alive. Astonishingly vigorous decoration in cobalt blue, black and red ochre on white depicts stylized birds, pomegranates on twining branches and, surprisingly, a man (the owner?) in a big black hat. The battery of towers nearby was decorated in a similar way but here the head of a woman appears and she is unveiled, which further suggests that the towers were owned by an Armenian. However, immediately below the cornice is a painted frieze of decorative script giving the Islamic date, 1335 (AD 1916); a brick inscription on the battery could be read as 1324 (AD 1906).

These designs also typify the traditional Iranian enjoyment and masterly management of pattern and colour; the painted bands which are densely filled with elaborate decoration are boldly contrasted with areas of blank wall space.

Strikingly painted pigeon towers have also been recorded in Afghanistan in the Hari Rud valley between Herat and the Iranian frontier. Square, rectangular, round towers and even an octagonally-topped one were described and illustrated.[5] The square tower was decorated by two huge cats which confront each other below a broad frieze painted with zig-zag lines; it was claimed that leopards are known to protect pigeons.

Ice-houses (*yakh-chal*)

The storage and use of ice

The popular use of ice and snow for cooling drinks and food in Iran was reported by several European travellers in the seventeenth century. 'They mightily covet cool things to the Palat wherefore they mix snow or dissolve ice in their Water, Wine or Sherbets', Fryer recorded of his stay in Shiraz; and later of Esfahan, 'the Poor, have they but a Penny in the World, the one half will go for Bread and dried Grapes, or Buttermilk, and the other for Snow and Tobacco.' He described hunting expeditions on which they took '*Yoqdans* (ice-chests) for provisions'.[6] Sir John Chardin was surprised to find that, although 'the Cold is dry and penetrating more than it is in any part of *France* or *England,* yet the greatest part of the People drink with ice as well in Winter as in Summer'.[7]

Thomas Herbert's (1628) description of Esfahan has a tantalizing throw-away line which remains unexplained. Having described the town as being 'of no great strength', he goes on: 'towards the outside of the city, a large castle; unflanked but moated about; and several houses within; which guard the treasure, arms and ice there stored'.[8] This certainly suggests that ice was precious, even if it throws no light on the method of storage.

Fryer reported that the ice was stored in 'Repositories' (outside Shiraz) which unfortunately he merely describes as 'fine buildings'. These were probably similar to the huge domed pits still to be seen in parts of Iran, which were in common use until the introduction of modern refrigeration and road transport after World War II. Only one such pit seen on this survey appeared to be in use (at Za'farineh, near Sabzevar) in 1970 (see Plate 19), but it was sealed, so we could not go inside it. The doorway of an ice-house is bricked up until the ice is needed.

The practice of storing ice was probably long established in Iran by the seventeenth century. It may have been introduced as a result of the thirteenth-century Mongol conquest which brought China and Iran into closer relationship. Ice-houses were known as early as the eighth century BC in China; these were probably small thatched buildings like their successors there.

In Britain the idea of keeping ice in an ice-house does not seem to have been introduced until the seventeenth century. Its popularity among the landed classes spread and it became widely accepted as a necessary adjunct to a country estate. Henry Hoare, who had an ice-house at Stourhead, regarded 'Ice in Summer' to be 'one of the fruits of Industry and application to Business', listing it with 'Temples, Grottos, Bridges, Rocks and Exotick Pines' as 'the envy of the indolent'[9]—a rather different point of view to that then prevalent in the Iranian bazaars. Ice in Britain was not considered to be a common necessity for a long time, and it was certainly not for the poor, but in Iran its popularity persisted. An Englishman, Dr C.J.Wills, who worked with the Indo-European Telegraph Department in 1866–81, was struck by its ready availability:

A great thing in such a warm place as Shiraz is the cheapness of ice; for about fifteen shillings in dear years and five in cheap ones, ice can be obtained all through the warm weather... A huge block is thrown down in one's doorway each morning by the ice-seller...so common is the use of ice that the poorest are enabled to have it, a big bit being sold for a farthing, and even the bowls of water for gratuitous drinking at the shop doors are cooled by it.

He continues:

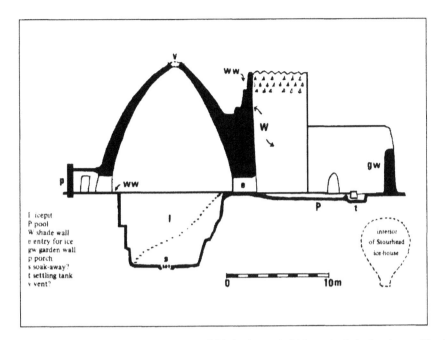

Figure 7.5 Section of the ice-house near Yazd. The size of this ice-house is fairly typical; the interior profile of a good English example (Stourhead, Wiltshire) is drawn for comparison. The Yazd ice-house was disused so was becoming dilapidated. The corbelled brick dome seems to have had ventilation at the crown and there may have been a soakaway in the floor. The wall and pool were in a fair condition. The pool was fed by water from a surface channel which ran through a small settling tank before entering it.

> The Persians well understand the art of making water-ices and icecreams, and various ices unknown
> to us are made by them, as tamarind juice, pomegranate and cherry-water ices; iced 'mast' or curdled
> milk, and various ices of pounded fruits, as apricots and cherries, which are very good.

The quantity consumed, or anyway offered, amazed Wills, when he went to call upon the *muschir;* 'four conical ices, the size and shape of an ordinary sugar-loaf, were placed in handsome Chinese porcelain basins before each of us'.[10]

Ice used in such quantity needed considerable storage space. The great demand led to structures of monumental scale and size. Figure 7.5 shows the Stourhead ice-house (diameter 5 metres, *c.* 16 feet), one of the larger English examples, drawn to the same scale as a typical Iranian ice-house at Yazd (diameter 12 metres, *c.* 40 feet). However, the principles governing the design of each are the same: the ice had to be insulated and kept dry. The differing climates made insulation a far greater problem on the fiercely hot but very dry plateau, and drainage of prime importance in damp, temperate Britain.

The drainage of ice-pits was vital to the storage of the ice. Probably most Iranian pits had some sort of soakaway in the bottom. It is mentioned by one or two travellers[11] but it is a difficult point to check because disused ice-houses soon begin to fill with sand or rubbish. On the other hand, seepage through the sandy ground into which the pit was dug may itself have given efficient drainage of melt water.

The mud-brick vaults and domes covering the ice-pits gave good insulation. The great height of the domes meant that there was plenty of space above the packed ice into which the relatively warmer air could rise, leaving the cold air lying immediately above the ice. The low humidity as well as the temperature of this air is vital to the preservation of the ice: it should be kept as dry as possible. The superiority of ventilated ice-houses is described in a letter to the *Gardeners' Chronicle,* 1849: 'it is the vapour arising from the slow wasting of the ice that is the real cause of it melting fast'.[12] The writer, a gardener in the UK, had designed very successful ice-houses with ventilators. The moisture content of the air in a sealed ice-house, as was common in Britain, could rise considerably over the months. In Iran some ice-houses have a ventilation hole *(hava-kesh)* of about half a metre in diameter in the crown of the dome; the wind blowing across the dome would suck air out. Unfortunately, the ruined state of the crown of the domes makes it impossible to say just how they were protected from the weather; presumably, before a rainstorm, sacking would be wrapped round the sides of the *hava-kesh* to keep the water out. Whether or not a *hava-kesh* is provided, constant evaporation occurs through the permeable mud-brick shell of the dome, thus reducing both humidity and temperature.

In thatched ice-houses (see below) constant ventilation could be simply achieved.

Ice making

Obtaining the ice was a much more difficult matter in Iran than Britain, where it was skimmed from a handy lake or pool and packed away early on a cold morning—a job traditionally organized by the head gardener. On the plateau, water itself is not only in short supply, it is often saline; even a low degree of salinity would reduce its freezing temperature, so the siting of ice-houses was limited by the availability of a pure water supply, a *qanat* being a likely source.

Extremes of temperature add to the difficulties. In winter, in the desert, even when the temperature drops to freezing at sunset, the sun can be hot by mid-morning, which further reduces the chance of collecting enough ice to fill the vast pits. To make ice, a spot was chosen to which water could be diverted whenever it was needed; here a long shallow pool was dug out, about 50×10 metres and 40 to 50 cm (2 feet) deep. The excavated earth was used to build a high wall along the south side of the pool, which shaded it from the sun and protected it from wind; the width of the pool was governed by the protection given to it by the wall. The pool was lined with baked brick tiles to make it watertight and to stop the water becoming muddy, and perhaps to insulate it from the ground (see Figure 7.6 and Plate 20). C.J.Wills probably gives the best first-hand description of ice-making:

> The delicious Ab-i-Rookhni ('stream of Rookhnabad') is diverted from its course during the first cold night. A few inches of still water is collected in the pool, by morning it is frozen; at night the water is again admitted, and another inch or two of ice made. When three to six inches thick, the ice is broken and collected for storage in a deep well (ice pit) on the spot: and so day by day the process goes on during the short winter until the storehouses are full.[13]

Iranians who remembered the work in the ice-houses told how, on clear frosty nights, the water would be diverted to the ice-pool and the ice formed was skimmed off in layers of 2 or 3 cm (*c.* 1 inch) thick. The thickness must have varied depending on the cold, and methods of collection seem to have differed from place to place.

Chardin (in Iran 1762–77) described how in Esfahan a deep hole (an open ice-pit) was dug, and:

> before it they dig deep squares of sixteen or twenty inches, like so many little Basons; they fill 'em with Water over Night, when it begins to freeze, and in the Morning, when all is frozen, they break it

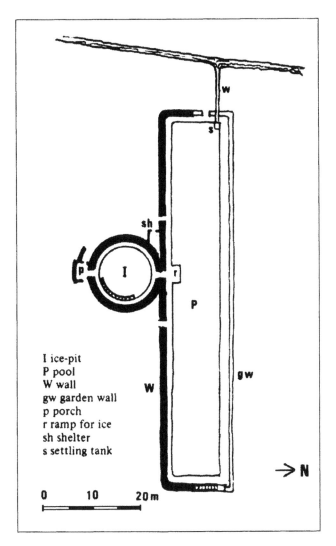

Figure 7.6 Plan of the ice-house near Yazd.

to Bits, and put all these Pieces together in the Hole (the ice-pit), where they break 'em again into little Bits, as well as they can; for the more Ice is broken, the better it is.

At night more ice was made in the 'basons' and the broken-up pieces of ice in the big ice-pit were themselves watered,

to the End, that they may hold the better together. In less than eight Days Working after this Manner, they have Pieces of ice five or six Foot thick: and then they gather the people of the Quarter together, who with loud Shouts of Joy, and Fire lighted upon the Edges of the Hole, and with the Sound of

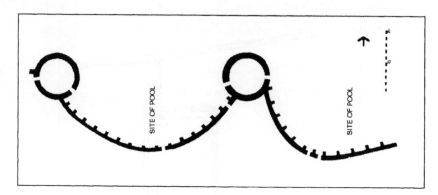

Figure 7.7 A pair of ruined ice-houses with curved shade walls near Sirjan (1975).

Instruments to Animate them, go down into it, and lay these Lumps of Ice one upon the other, which they call *Codrouc,* as much as to say, Basis or Foundation, and throw Water between, to make them hold together the better.

Great care was taken to sweep away any snow that might happen to fall but, all being well, in 'six Weeks time, an Ice-house of a Fathom or more deep, and as broad and long as one will, is fill'd to the very top with Ice'.[14] The ice, once rammed down in the pit, was insulated by layers of reed or straw, or 'a sort of Sea-Rush, which they call Bazour' and then the door was sealed and the ice kept safe until needed in the summer. This system does not seem to have altered much over the years.

Chardin's observations of the cheerful Esfahan customs continue: 'In the Summer when they go to open the Ice-House, it is another Festival for that Quarter... What is very Remarkable, as well as Agreeable in their Ice, is its beauty and clearness'. This is more than could be claimed of ice skimmed from some lakes in Britain in the early years of the twentieth century.

At first sight the only function of the wall would seem to be to protect the pool from the sun. Walls are built along the long south side, with short lengths continuing east and west (Figure 7.7), so in winter, when the sun is lower in the sky, they completely shade the pool, thus minimizing the warming of the tiled bottom and the ground under an empty pool, or the thawing of ice in one that is in use. This allows for the collection of ice after sunrise, which saves the difficulties of working in the dark.

The second function of the wall is to protect the pool from the wind. Moving water, even if only ruffled by a breeze, freezes more slowly than still water, and temperatures will only fall markedly when the air is still. Then each layer of cooled air near the surface stays where it is, because it is more dense, and so takes another turn of cooling, giving very low temperatures near the ground, perhaps several degrees lower than that of the air only a metre or so above it.

The importance of protecting the pool from the wind was stressed by the diplomat James Morier, on an excursion made from Shiraz: 'A wall is built the whole length of the reservoir to screen the ice from the south wind which is hottest.'[15] No mention is made of shade from the sun. The French architect Maxime Siroux gives a variation between the shade and the sun temperatures of the order of 15–20 degrees Centigrade (27–36 degrees Fahrenheit).

The line taken by the walls varies considerably. The straight ones already described seem to have been typical, but others are curved; perhaps the most fascinating ones seen consisted of two curved walls and two ice-pits, like some strange winged creature (Figure 7.7).

Thevenot, who was in Esfahan at about the same time as Chardin, gives a similar description of ice making, adding 'This is an easie invention at Isfahan where the Air is very dry, and where there is little moist Weather'.[16] The ice in Thevenot's description was stored in a long trench along the north side of the wall, 'three fathom deep' and 'three to four feet' wide. This does not seem to have been roofed with mud-brick but, when the ice in it was 'a fathom and a half high', it was covered by a two to three foot thickness of straw and reeds (and perhaps it was also thatched to throw off the chance rain). Thatched pits or low buildings such as these could quickly be submerged in sand when they were no longer used. This might account for some of the huge free-standing walls with no obvious function which were still to be seen outside Tehran (near the Esfahan road) in 1961. They may have been ice walls.

Notes

The fieldwork involved in this and other research concerning vernacular building was made possible through the encouragement and practical support of Professor David Stronach OBE, then Director of the British Institute of Persian Studies. I am particularly grateful to him, and to many others too numerous to mention. This work resulted in E.Beazley and M.Harverson, *Living with the Desert* (Warminster: Aris and Phillips, 1982), a small part of which includes the pigeon towers and ice-houses described here.

1. Beazley and Harverson, pp. 49–54, 103–16. Elisabeth Beazley, 'The Pigeon Towers of Isfahan', *Iran* 4, 1966, pp. 105–9, and 'Some vernacular buildings of the Iranian plateau', *Iran* 15, pp. 90–3.
2. Jean Chardin, *Sir John Chardin's Travels in Persia* (London, 1724; reprint Hakluyt Society, 1927), p. 177.
3. Thomas Herbert, *Travels in Persia 1627–9,* ed. Sir William Foster (London: Hakluyt Society, 1928), pp. 120.
4. James Morier, *A Second Journey through Persia…in 1808 and 1809* (London, 1818), pp. 140, 141.
5. P.I.Zestovsky, 'Esquisses d'architecture afghane', *Afghanistan* 4 (3), 1949, p. 17.
6. John Fryer, *A New Account of East India and Persia being Nine years Travels 1672–81,* ed. W.Crooke (London: Hakluyt Society) vol. 3 (1915), p. 135 and vol. 2 (1912), p. 48.
7   Chardin, *Travels,* p. 239.
8   Herbert, *Travels,* p. 127.
9   Geoffrey Locke, 'Ice-houses', *National Trust News Letter* no. 24 (autumn 1975), p. 20.
10. C.J.Wills, *The Land of the Lion and the Sun* (London, 1891), p. 240.
11. Including M.Siroux, *Caravanserails d'Iran et petites constructions routieres* (Cairo, 1949), p. 132.
12. D.Beaton, Letter to the *Gardeners' Chronicle,* 13 January 1849.
13. Wills, Land, p. 241.
14. Chardin, *Travels,* p. 239.
15. Morier, *Second Journey,* p. 123.
16. A.Lovell (trans.), *Travels into the Levant by Monsieur de Thévenot* (London, 1687), p. 96.

Chapter 8
Sustainable Buildings: Middle Eastern Traditional Systems for the Future
Susan Roaf

Central Asia and the Middle East have the richest stock of building types in the world. They are shaped by a wide range of constraints including geographical, social, material, technological, climatic, religious and temporal influences, and are characterized by design features that give them unique regional identities. They can be viewed from three historical perspectives; those of the past, the present and the future. While many see them in the context only of museum pieces, they have an important role to play in the development of future buildings. For global, economic and political reasons, we will need, in the new century, buildings that are more culturally and climatically appropriate than those modern buildings that are fashionable throughout the region today and that are so destructive of the environment.

The past

This region of the world is home to the oldest civilizations on earth. The earliest excavated settlements such as Jericho date from around 9000 BC, and it was in Mesopotamia, the Cradle of Civilization, that the first cities, civilizations and religions grew.[1] This antiquity enables us to see the history of building types in the region with a depth of view that clarifies the processes underlying the creation of regional building traditions. I shall outline briefly some of those forces, particularly those of climate, that have shaped the varied building types of the region.

The relationship between the productivity of land and the density of settlement on it is well understood. The richer the land and its climate, the more people it will support, and this may lead in politically stable regions to more villages in a well-defended region or larger cities with protected hinterlands (see Figure 8.1). As regions swing from periods of political stability to instability, settlement patterns will change to reflect the dependability of agricultural space. The impact of land productivity on settlement patterns was well illustrated by Yagi in his study of Syria.[2]

The steepness of slopes also influences settlement and house form. In mountainous areas, buildings tend to be two- or multistoreyed, with store rooms and stables on the ground floor. In his study of Lebanese buildings Ragette shows that houses can vary stylistically between forms using the *aiwan* and the *riwaq,* but the underlying two-storey mountain house form prevails in this region, to which it is eminently suited.[3] Perhaps the most spectacular of high-rise cities is that of Sana'a in Yemen where the mountain homes rise typically to seven and eight storeys high.

Climate influences house form at many levels. Bonine demonstrates that factors such as wind direction and solar access have influenced town forms on the Persian plateau, along with other factors such as water sources and land slopes.[4] Solar access is one of the prime determinants of house form in the region, and where houses face in one direction only, the preferred orientation is to the south. An important house type,

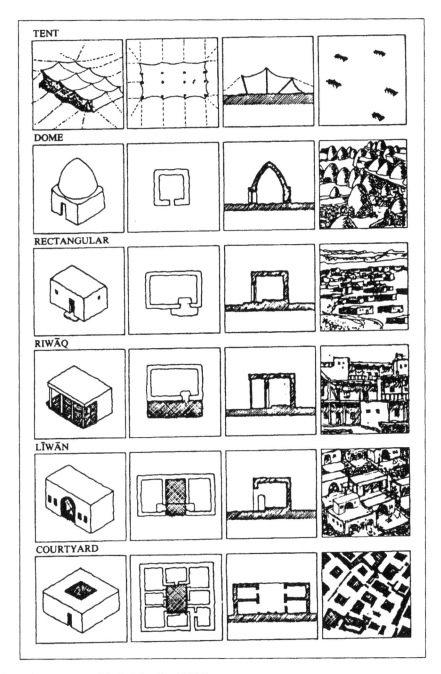

Figure 8.1 The settlement types of Syria (after Yagi 1983).

the courtyard house, has the main summer rooms facing north away from the sun and the winter rooms facing south towards the sun.

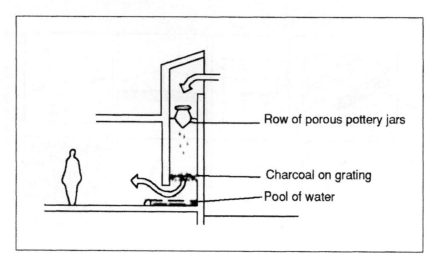

Figure 8.2 The stereotypical windcatcher of the Middle East (after Roaf, 'The windcatchers of the Middle East', PhD thesis, Oxford Brookes University).

Wind direction not only influences street patterns, where it is desirable to have cooling breezes channelled through streets and alleys in densely built settlements, but also house orientation. It is preferable to have courtyards and windcatchers facing directly into the path of the prevailing wind, so as to enhance the windspeeds within them and to optimize their cooling potential in the house.[5]

Rainfall influences buildings in a number of respects. In areas with high rainfall, roofs are often pitched and eaves typically extend over walls to protect them from running water. Wall foundations are often raised on stone footings around 1 m high to prevent damage to the base of the wall from rain splash ricocheting up from the ground, which is particularly bad for mud-brick walls.

Summer and winter temperatures are perhaps the most important of all influences on building form in this region. Much of the region is very hot, summer temperatures approach the upper limits of thermal comfort and it is very dangerous to build climatically unsuited buildings in hot temperatures. In temperate regions it really does not matter whether a building is hotter or cooler than the one next door, because a few degrees here and there will not threaten the comfort, or even the life, of the occupants at all. In very hot regions, however, particularly in humid climates, slight increases in temperatures can threaten the very lives of building occupants as they approach heat stroke. The subtlety of the physiological thermal thresholds that underlie the evolution of climatically appropriate regional building types was well understood by traditional local builders, but is seldom appreciated by modern builders. This is well illustrated by the case of the windcatchers of the Middle East.

The traditional preconception of the windcatcher is that it looks like the example in Figure 8.2. This stereotype is dangerous, however, in that it can lead to the construction of large windcatchers on modern buildings where they would, at worst, introduce extremely hot air into summer living rooms. In fact, every windcatcher built varies for reasons of macro, meso and micro climatic considerations (see Figure 8.3). In very hot regions, such as southern Iraq, windcatchers are used only for ventilating basements, as they would bring scorching air into summer living rooms during the afternoons. On the Persian Plateau and in Middle Egypt, large windcatchers are used to introduce air movement through living areas to cool people through convection and evaporation of heat from the skin. At night they also draw heat from the structure of the building. In the hot, humid regions of the Gulf and Sind, windcatchers are large, because, even though

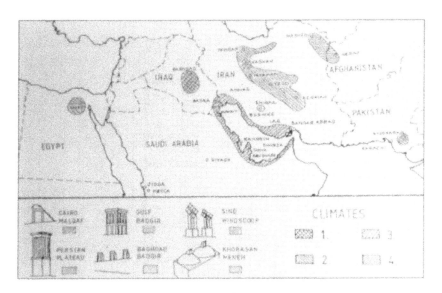

Figure 8.3 The windcatcher types of the Middle East (from Roaf, 'The windcatchers').

during the day the air temperature may be higher than skin temperature, the only method of cooling people was to move air as fast as possible over the skin and lose heat, not by convection—which is not possible when skin temperature is higher than air temperature—but by evaporation of moisture from the skin. In the Plateau lands of north-east Iran and western Afghanistan, where the cooler climate negates the need for a great deal of cooling, the cowl windcatchers are small and used to provide ventilation and light in addition to summer cooling. Thus, very real thermal thresholds exist in the design of local windcatcher types, as they do in the design of house types in the region.

Although climate is a very important determinant in building form, there is considerable flexibility of possible building types in most areas. The most characteristic of these are the village compound houses, where rural homes are typically constructed in a high walled compound with rooms banked one deep, typically with the main room facing south and a variety of combinations of flanking rooms, depending on the size of the house or family, the slope of the ground, or a family's wealth. Figure 8.4 shows compound houses in Syria similar to those found throughout the region. Another strong model form is that of the courtyard house, usually an urban model. In hot regions these houses are often single-storeyed, with basements where possible, and largish courtyards with gardens such as the house in Yazd, Central Iran, shown in Figure 8.5. In very hot regions such as Baghdad the houses have two or three storeys, to prevent the heat penetrating down to the summer living rooms on the ground floor (see Figure 8.6).[6] In the hottest regions the courtyard is omitted and houses are often multistoryed, to remove the living quarters as far as possible from the heat of the sun. Light and ventilation wells take the place of courtyards, as in Madina in Saudi Arabia (see Figure 8.7).[7]

Local building styles will also be influenced by availability of materials. For instance, the town houses of northern Iraq are largely built of stone from the foothills of the Taurus mountains, while the buildings of southern Iraq, where local building stone is lacking, are predominantly of mud-brick. However, traditions of craftsmanship also influence building types, and one can see this in Peshawar in northern Pakistan, where local eighteenth and nineteenth-century builders were very highly skilled carpenters, as demonstrated by the beautiful woodwork of the Sethi houses of the city (see Figure 8.8). The coming of the British in 1817 led to

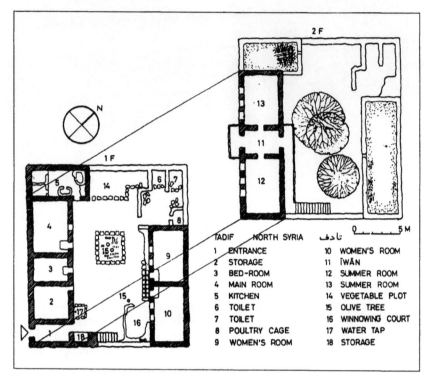

Figure 8.4 Compound houses in Syria (after Yagi 1983).

the demise of this tradition and replaced it with solid brick, British colonial buildings, which also used available local building materials in a different way (see Figure 8.9).

Local building types change over time. In Mesopotamia, in a fairly constant climate with the same local materials, house types changed radically over history. The Ubaid monolithic house of the fifth millennium BC is very different to the garden houses of the ninth century AD in Samarra and the courtyard houses of Baghdad in the eighteenth century. Yet each house type was comfortable for its occupants at the different periods.

From the fourteenth century in Yazd there was a gradual change in house form until the twentieth century. The deep spaces of the houses surrounding the courtyard gradually became shallower, and windcatchers grew in height. The greatest changes in the evolution of house form were due to the introduction of new technologies and materials. Around 1800, coloured glass became available in the city, and the open walls of aivans often were walled in as talars, with french doors or sash windows glazed with brilliant coloured glass that could be opened where fresh air was needed and closed when it was not. The second revolution occurred in the 1930s when the ceiling fan was introduced, which meant that smaller rooms could be kept cooler without the enormous thermal mass that had to be built into the nineteenth-century summer rooms. This has subsequently been superseded by the swamp cooler or air-conditioner, which has further reduced the extent of the passive cooling contribution required from the fabric of the building.

In parallel with these changes over time in Yazdi house form, there also exist in the city different cultural stereotypes of house forms, such as the Zoroastrian houses which were noticeably different from Muslim

Figure 8.5 Courtyard house in Yazd, Iran (Roaf).

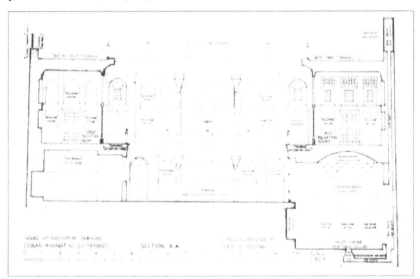

Figure 8.6 Nineteenth-century courtyard house in Baghdad (from Reuther 1910).

homes in many ways, with physical forms in the houses often having symbolic meanings that have possibly endured through the many centuries of the faith.

It is very rare for individual building types to prevail unchanged for centuries; the only authenticated example I can think of in the Middle East is that of the reed houses of southern Iraq, which we know from cylinder seals have been built since the Late Uruk period in the fourth Millennium BC.[8] However, if the

Figure 8.7 The traditional Makka house (Fadan 1983).

reports coming out of the region are correct, it appears that the continuation of this ancient unique building type is threatened by current political forces.

The reason why Marsh Arab dwellings have remained unchanged for at least 6,000 years is that, using the rich resource of local reeds, they provide the only inhabitable form of shelter for this intensely hot and humid region. In this climate the only way to prevent heat stroke is to provide shade from the sun and air movement over the skin, to encourage evaporative cooling of the body. For a whole range of reasons, such as ease of transport of building materials in the marshes, and the ability to erect light houses rapidly on small islands, the *mudhif,* or reed house, is uniquely suited to the marshes, the climate and the culture.

There are three types of settlements in the Middle East: settled, nomadic and transhumant. The lines between these types are often very fine. Nomadism is a way of life that takes advantage of marginal land that will not support agricultural settlements all year around but is adequate for pastoralism with some light cropping. Many nomads move from cooler upland camps in summer to warmer lowland sites in winter, fattening flocks on grasses along the spring migration road. They choose a site and location for a comfortable climate, whereas settled populations in this region practise intra-mural migration around a house, selecting a room for comfort within the house. The material of which a tent is made is influenced by climate, with the warmer felt yurts predominating in Central Asia and the cooler black goat-hair tents in the Middle East. Tent types in adjacent areas may differ significantly in design, for instance in the arrangements of tent poles and forms of tent cloths and walling materials. In addition, the tent form is adjusted in different seasons with walls and roof opening up in summer to provide shade and breeze and closed down in winter to exclude the weather. So, site and dwelling form, use and materials are all significant variables in the success of the tents as shelter in different regions.

Transhumant populations live in one permanent house but will move to tents or temporary shelters at some distance from their village to graze flocks on spring and summer pastures. Transhumance is often associated

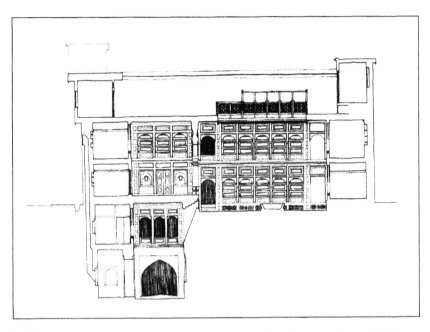

Figure 8.8 The Sethi House in Peshawar. An example of the timber Arabic building tradition of Pakistan (drawn by students of Oxford Brookes University).

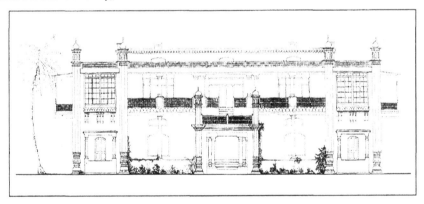

Figure 8.9 A nineteenth-century brick Raj house in Peshawar, Pakistan (drawn by students of Oxford Brookes University).

with a fixed regional house type and an interesting assortment of temporary dwellings, such as the brushwood houses of the transhumant villagers of Ras al-Khaima on the Gulf.

Change is inherent in the evolution of regionally appropriate buildings. We have seen how, for one climate, a range of different architectural solutions can provide adequate shelter over time, as in Mesopotamia, with the Ubaid, the Samarran and the Baghdadi house. We have seen how, in Yazd in the second half of the second millennium AD, rather than architectural change resulting from major cultural changes, this isolated regional architecture has evolved gradually into new forms. There are many reasons for this, such as the importation of new materials and technologies. It is also possible for a number of cultural models to exist side by side with each other, such as the very different Muslim and the Zoroastrian houses of Yazd, which occupy the same location and climate. Lack of change in regional architecture is a rare exception. The traditional architecture of every region is unique in its form and in the ways in which it is used. But all this itself is changing.

The present

The buildings of Central Asia and the Middle East are a product of the land, the climate and the enormously complex cultural currents that have ebbed and flowed through the region for millennia. Nothing in Europe approaches this contextual complexity. In recent decades these buildings have been threatened by processes of 'Westernization' and the perception that all that is modern is better. Two factors are accelerating this decline: better communications, and air-conditioning—which allows modern designers to get away with increasingly poor standards of climatic design.

Here I illustrate my concerns about what is happening to the traditional buildings of the region with a case study of Peshawar, a city in the North West Frontier Province (NWFP) of Pakistan that stands with one foot in the Middle East and one in Central Asia. Over the last decades, the traditional buildings of central Peshawar have been rapidly demolished or allowed to decay for a number for reasons, many set out in The Pakistan National Conservation Strategy 1993, including:

1. urbanization trends;
2. poor conservation;
3. environmental pollution;
4. neglect due to:

    lack of awareness;

    socio-cultural constraints;

    lack of education;

    economic constraints;

    lack of co-ordination between authorities;

5. absence of firm criteria for selecting and grading heritage resources; and
6. natural hazards.

The result is that in the historic heart of this and many other cities in the region, the historic buildings, are rapidly being lost. A key factor here is that many old buildings would be costly to conserve, as was the case with the project to restore a number of old houses in Baghdad, where houses cost around £80,000 each to restore.[9] Old buildings are difficult to air-condition, and businesses often prefer modern, more air-tight buildings, despite the fact that they are typically over-glazed and less comfortable than the old, non-air-conditioned buildings.

Recently there has been an increase in awareness of these traditional buildings and their potential economic importance to communities. The following issues are central to the new view of a possible future role for old buildings in the region:

1. Without these buildings, little visible evidence will be left of the material culture and history of a region.
2. Traditional buildings provide important models for the way in which architecture has evolved to meet local requirements of culture, materials, labour and climate. They can provide a valuable alternative to the inappropriate imported Western architectural styles now common in many cities of the world.
3. When these old buildings are pulled down, the modern buildings that replace them are often no match for the original in design quality or detail. A grading system is needed to ensure that at least the finest examples of regional architecture are preserved, as a matter of some urgency.
4. Building conservation is labour-intensive, creating employment, and keeps both the large and the small builder busy. It is preferable, in benefits to the local community, to the pursuit of comprehensive redevelopment, relying more on factory-made parts and mechanical assembly, which only a few large builders can accommodate.
5. Conservation protects and encourages local traditional skills, such as carpentry, that would otherwise be lost, denying them to future generations who may be better able to use them.
6. New uses abound for many old buildings whose original function is redundant, new uses which could generate local economic opportunities, for instance in opening up the heritage and tourism industry, as well as for commerce.

The future

Modern Western buildings are generally inappropriate for use in the Middle East because they are often not suited to the local building industries of this region and they are very demanding in terms of energy consumption because of poor climatic design. This can also contribute to high levels of thermal discomfort in them. The Western heating and ventilating industry has tried to foist its own inappropriate indoor air-temperature comfort standards on other countries,[10] but the folly of this is being recognized internationally. After all, why should people in the hot regions of the Middle East cool their buildings to 22 degrees centigrade, by generating energy they cannot afford and creating peak demands for power that are difficult to meet in any country, when they are perfectly happy in temperatures of 28 degrees, which would cost 60 per cent less energy and be much easier to generate on hot afternoons?

A team from Oxford Brookes University, under the direction of Fergus Nicol and Michael Humphreys, has been working in Pakistan on new indoor air-temperature standards, based on field studies of the temperatures local populations are comfortable at in the five different climatic regions of Pakistan. The resulting standards should be the first in the world based on comfort temperatures of locally adapted populations.[11]

There is an urgent need to understand more of climatically appropriate buildings, in view of global warming processes which will lead to temperature rises in the region of 2–8 degrees centigrade by 2050.[12] These increases will force buildings that are climatically inappropriate into more and more profligate consumption of energy. In turn, this will further exacerbate the greenhouse effect and deplete the ozone layer. Such considerations reinforce the need to preserve examples of good local regional architecture as models for future designers.

The Oxford/Peshawar Project—one way forward

One way forward is the use of historic buildings for new functions such as eco-tourism. This will preserve them for future generations and demonstrate their climatic performance to a wide range of visitors from the locality and abroad.

An example of such a project is the Peshawar Heritage Trails Project. To stem the destruction of the old historic centre of Peshawar and other settlements in the area, to save for posterity samples of the rich heritage of building types in the NWFP, Oxford Brookes University, in conjunction with ENERCON, the Energy Conservation Unit of the Pakistani Government, has proposed the development of a Sustainable Infrastructure of Heritage Trails for the NWFP These could be developed through the incremental implementation of a selective programme of conservation and preservation of the historically and culturally important buildings of the province.

The Heritage Network Trail is based on a system of Heritage Centres or nodes of different sizes linked with a transport infrastructure which includes road, rail and air links. Nodes can be at the level of an individual building or tourist facility such as a hotel or restaurant. Any village or city with two or more nodes will be considered as a Heritage Centre. Financial support will be considered for the conservation of buildings, or nodes, and the responsibility for upgrading the routes between the nodes will be taken on by the local community who can choose to be, or not to be, part of the Heritage Trail. The process will thus be community based, and all major trail developments will undergo environmental impact analysis. Where possible, renewable energy systems will be used to power development so as to minimize environmental impact. Waste and sewerage systems will be carefully designed, and transport systems will be chosen with their environmental impact in mind.

The initial report on the Heritage Trails was included in the Sarhad Provincial Conservation Strategy for the region. Under the stewardship of IUCN, the Canadian Environmental Agency, a sum of around £1.2 million has been allocated for cultural tourism, to include the development of the Cultural Heritage Trails. Thus we can look to the North West Frontier Province as a pioneering application of the concept of giving vernacular buildings a new economic meaning in rapidly developing cities.

Once the trails are open they will provide a source of education on the historic buildings for national and international tourists, schools and universities, and businesses who may choose to use these facilities for conferences, etc. Giving the buildings an increased economic status in the region will not only continue to preserve them but will also raise the profile of local appropriate architecture. For the next generation of building designers and users, this may provide a strong enough model to combat the globally destructive movement towards the universal model of 'modern buildings' at the expense of traditional appropriate buildings.

It is essential that we see this rich resource of historic buildings, of this and any region, as an economic as well as a cultural asset, because to see them only as museum pieces is to underestimate the importance of the lessons of appropriate regional design that these buildings have to teach us for the buildings of the future. These are the fundamental lessons of sustainable settlements.

Notes

1. M.Roaf, *Cultural Atlas of Mesopotamia* (Oxford: Facts on File, 1990).
2. KojiYagi, 'Traditional houses and living patterns in Syria', in Aydin Germen (ed.) *Islamic Architecture and Urbanism* (Saudi Arabia: University of Dammam, 1983), pp. 343–62.
3. F.Ragette, *Architecture in Lebanon* (New York: Caravan Books, 1974).

4. M.Bonine, 'The morphogenesis of Iranian cities,' *Annals of the Association of American Geographers* 69, 2 (June 1979), pp. 208–23.

5. Roaf, *The Windcatchers of Yazd* (PhD thesis, Oxford Polytechnic, 1989).

6. Figure 8.6 is taken from Oscar Reuther, *Das Wohnhaus in Baghdad und anderen Stadtendes Irak* (Doctoral thesis in Engineering, Technische Hochschule, Dresden; Berlin: Ernest Wasmuth, 1910).

7. Figure 8.7 is taken from Yousef Fadan, 'Traditional houses of Makka', in Germen, *Islamic Architecture and Urbanism,* pp. 295–323.

8. M.Roaf, *Cuhural Atlas.*

9. J.Warren and I.Fethy, *Traditional Houses of Baghdad* (Horsham: Coach Publishing House, 1983).

10. S.Roaf, 'The ozone loopholes', *Proceedings of the World Renewable Energy Congress, Reading* (Oxford: Pergamon, 1994), pp. 1870–75.

11. F.Nicol and S.Roaf, 'Pioneering new indoor temperature standards: the Pakistan Project', *Energy and Buildings* 23, 1996, pp. 169–74; M. Humphreys, 'An adaptive approach to the thermal comfort of office workers in North West Pakistan', *Proceedings of the World Renewable Energy Congress, Reading* (Oxford: Pergamon, 1994), pp. 1725–34.

12. S.Roaf and P.Howes, 'Climate change and passive cooling in Europe', *Proceedings of PLEA Conference, Auckland* (1992).

Chapter 9
From the Rashîdîya to the Ordos: In Search of Early Mongol Tents

Peter Alford Andrews

Introduction: at the Rashîdîya

Very few early representations of tentage survive. In the copy of Rashîd al-Dîn's *Djâmi' al-Tawârîkh* at the Bibliothèque Nationale, which was probably illustrated at Herat in about 1430, there is a particularly fine series of paintings showing tents. They depict the lives of Çiñgiz Qan and his successors.[1] Although the paintings are Timurid, and reflect the style and ornamental preferences of the time, comparison with other manuscripts of the same work[2] suggests that, in composition and to a limited extent in detail, they may be based on book paintings originally prepared at the studios of the Rashîdîya in about 1310, which seem in this case not to have survived.

Most of the tents in the Timurid version are recognizable as trellis tents (so-called yurts), and in some cases the trellis is actually visible through the door to confirm this (see Plate 21), but they differ from the usual Timurid type in their roof profile. Instead of being domed, it appears quite consistently as a rather tall cone, with a rounded apex over the roof wheel, and a sinuous curvature at the sides, convex above the wall, but concave at mid-slope. This would necessitate a set of roof struts with double curvature between the top of the cylindrical trellis wall and the rim of the roof wheel. Since Mongolian trellis tents today invariably have straight roof struts,[3] and their conical roofs are relatively low, the shape in these paintings is unexpected. There is some evidence from early Mongolian paintings that the roof slope was once steeper, though these seem to date at the earliest from the seventeenth century. It would be reasonable to assume, then, that the tents in the manuscript must show, not Mongolian tents, but Turkic ones, which generally have curved struts: they might well represent a particular type of Timurid tentage.[4]

There are, however, a set of displaced and unattributed miniatures in the Diez albums at Berlin, which can be recognized at once as being in the Rashîdîya style, and may have been taken from an Îlkhânid *Djâmi' al-Tawârîkh*. Among these are three which show tents, and in the background of two, only partially visible, is the roof of a trellis tent. In one of these (see Plate 22) the roof wheel is uncovered, and is clearly recognizable as the Turkic type, of bent wood with thin arching spokes, and not the present Mongolian type of heavier, cut-timber sections. We can also see one of two wooden door leaves, and part of the trellis wall within; the roof profile is convex above the wall, and the webbing felt-ties on the outside are like those in the Timurid version. In the other (see Plate 23), only the upper part of the roof slope can be seen, showing a slightly concave slope, and the same crowsfoot of webbing ties above the door. Putting the two together, it seems we again have the sinuous roof profile. Raised above the opening is a rectangular flap, with a rosette in a typically Mongolian quilting pattern,[5] and an edge trim. Above this in turn is a curious fan-shaped extension, apparently of white felt like the rest, which flares out into a convex top edge wider than the roof wheel, which it obscures. This has no parallel in trellis tents today. Its sides are continuous with the flap below, and it seems to be an extension of it. Just behind the bottom of this flap is the end of the door flap rolled up at the lintel. If we compare this with the Timurid scene from Ghâzân Khân's festival at Ûdjân in 701/1302 (see Plate 24), we can see that the top of the trellis tent there is treated in a comparable way, though its distortion shows that the later artist did not understand what he was copying: we can assume that it was no longer familiar at the Timurid court. Nor, to my knowledge, does it appear in a book painting again. As an indication of cultural change this is intriguing in itself. It also seems that the roof profile of the Îlkhânid tents was Turkic too, rather than Mongolian: not quite what we would expect. It is possible, incidentally, that the Îlkhânid picture represents the same event, where Ghâzân Khân had particularly impressive tents pitched for Qur'ân readings.

As it happens these two features can be related to particular tent types at the two extremes of Central Asia, which can both be regarded as cultural relics: the shrine tents of Çiñgiz Qan at EǰEn Xoroo in the Ordos (the great bend of the Hwang-Ho) in the east, and the tents of the No̤ay in the north of the Caucasus. I have traced the known history of the Eǰen Xoroo tents elsewhere:[6] here it is enough to say that the shrine does seem to have existed in the region since the death of Çiñgiz Qan in 1227, together with a set of eight tents, though they have been moved around, and have at times been pillaged. I then concluded that they were unlikely to be trellis tents, since their plan was a square with rounded corners, incompatible with the folding of a normal trellis section. It was then impossible to deduce more without information from the spot. Now that has become available.

The Shrine of Çiñgiz Qan at EǰEn Qoro̤a

The importance of the tents at EǰEn Xoroo is that they appear to be the last representatives of an archaic type of Mongol dwelling. This is not to claim, of course, that the tents, as they survived until the 'Cultural Revolution', were the original ones. They did, however, incorporate a tradition which may well have been continuous since the burial simulated there in 1227. A felt-tent frame can be expected to last for up to 50 years, but the felts for at best ten. We can therefore assume that the tents were regularly renewed. As a parallel for such periodical renewal one can cite the Ise Shrine in Japan, which has survived, preserving an archaic form, nearly twice as long.[7]

The shrine tents are now called çomçṳ, a word which does not however appear in the *Secret History*, nor, to my knowledge, is it recorded until relatively recent times. Significantly, these Ordos tents could be mounted intact on carts, and indeed this was the way in which they were regularly brought to the site for annual festivals, as described by Lattimore.[8] His photograph shows the camel-carts with shafts running straight through into the sides of a flat-bed frame set on high spoked wheels which rotate inside the walls of the tents (see Plate 25). We know, of course, that in the *Secret History* the cart-tent, *ger-tergen,* is represented as the normal dwelling of the Mongols in the time of Çiñgiz Qan, and that even the large tents of his own court were *ordo-ger tergen.*[9] The trellis tent, it seems, had not yet been adopted by the Mongols in general, and the word *terme* occurs only in the context of the Tangut and, as *altan terme,* as the golden tent of the Kereyit Oñ Qan.[10]

I believe that the distribution of the trellis tent was closely connected with the distribution of the camel as a beast of burden, for the folded trellis sections fit the flanks of a camel so well that it seems plain that they were designed for it. We know from the *Secret History* that Çiñgiz Qan made particular efforts to obtain camels, and extorted them from the Tangut as tribute. Once they were available, the development of the trellis tent could follow. The transport of intact çomçṳ on carts corresponds, of course, to the descriptions given by emissaries to the Mongol armies a generation or two later, as in Hsü T'ing, Carpini and Rubruck, but it seems now to be without any parallel elsewhere in the Mongol world.[11] It does have a parallel, though, in the cart-tents of the No ay on the Kuban and Terek, which are now the only examples of an ancient type to have survived in the Turkic world. A comparison is therefore relevant to any enquiry into the origin of Mongol (and Îlkhânid) tent design.

Remarkably enough, no adequate description of the structure of the çomçu appears to have been published in the West. It emerges that the reason for this is that, for a casual visitor, it was invisible: the walls were covered with felt outside, and a lining inside. We have only Potanin's rather cursory description of 1883, in which he remarks upon the squareness of the space inside, wooden walls, and a flat ceiling.[12] The only ethnographic treatment it has received in Western sources was from Gafferberg, who drew attention to the parallel between the pointedness of the Ordos tents and those of the Hazâra in north-western Afghanistan, suggesting that the latter might represent an archaic type too.[13] She failed to notice, however, the outstanding feature of the çomçu , that in plan it is a square with rounded corners, and she also misread the scale on Potanin's photograph. Nor do the photographs help us with more than an idea of the profile, whose pointedness seems to be the origin of the term çomçu itself.[14] Potanin's picture is so heavily touched up that one is left in some doubt as to whether it is really a photograph at all, but fortunately it is confirmed by Father Mostaert's picture of a rather battered set of tents at Ix Ej en Xoroo in the first quarter of this century (1909?) (see Plate 26), and Duilikov's of 1956.[15] All three show the peculiar square plan, and the dome rising from the wall in a convex curve which reverses into a concave one before reaching the rather pointed apex; this in turn seems to require a rather conical profile in the roof wheel. The details are shown more clearly in Rinçen's photographs (1957) of the tents within the museum built for them (see Plate 27). All, too, show the long extensions of the top felt reaching down the dome to the wall on the four sides. This reverse curve is now represented in the nomadic world only among the Çahâr Aymâk of Afghanistan (who are Persian-speaking), including the Hazâra mentioned above, who appear to have a Mongolian connection in their history, the Fîrûzkûhî (see Plate 28), and the northern Taimanî.[16] There is a general resemblance to the tents in the Timurid pictures, though there the roof wheel is hemispherical rather than pointed in profile, and there is no indication that the tents are not round as usual. The çomçu , then, remain idiosyncratic in both their plan and their pointedness.

On 15 April 1990, Professor Sagaster was kind enough to interview one of the Darxad, Sayinj ir al, at Ej en Xoroo, with the guidance of a list of questions about the çomçu which I had given him. The answers largely confirmed the conclusions I had reached before, but add some important new detail. As had been feared, the tents were indeed destroyed in the 'Cultural Revolution', and those now ranged in the museum are only simplified substitutes, made to look like the originals but in a non-traditional way, by ordinary carpenters using modern materials including screws, wire, and nylon fabric. The tape-recorded testimony of the Darxad is therefore particularly important, as it draws on his experience of the tents as they used to be, before their destruction, and is, so far as I know, the only analytical description available. The answers he provided can be compared with the relatively short description in his recent book:[17] the two are to some extent complementary.

Firstly it was confirmed that the çomçu are unique to the Ordos, and quite distinct from the usual trellis tent—so much so that Sayinj ir al always referred to the latter as Mon ol ger. Furthermore, the tents had indeed been renewed regularly every three or nine years by a family of craftsmen who had carried out this duty from generation to generation in a traditional way: they have now unfortunately died out, though Sayin j ir al had interviewed the last two for his book. The work was supervised by the Darxad. There were special reserves of birch trees for this purpose at Jun ar: no one else was allowed to fell timber there. The felts were also made by specialists, toloxçin, under the supervision of the Darxad. Since the Darxad have lived at the shrine since its inception, it seems likely that the tradition of tent building was unbroken there, and this Sayinj ir al claims himself. This likelihood is reinforced by a detail given in his book:[18] punishments were prescribed for anyone altering the dimensions of the tent frames, their felts, or their cordage, and also for anyone providing inferior materials. Those guilty of altering the size were to be given 25 lashes and fined a three-year-old sheep. Those guilty of using inferior timber or felt would receive 50 lashes and be fined a three-year-old gelding.

There was no normal trellis, and there were therefore no lath crossings. Instead, the wall was of a type known in different districts as *sam xana,* 'comb or grille wall', *saralǰin xana,* 'bristling wall', or *šolooñ xana,* 'simple or straight wall'.[19] Conversely the normal Mongolian trellis is called *oqšiñ xana.* The structure is essentially framed between an upper ring, *mörübč* and a lower ring, *ulabč,* literally objects connected with a shoulder (Ordos *mörö*) and a sole (Ordos *ula*) respectively, at the top and bottom of the wall. It may be noted that in Turkic tent terminology *egin* 'shoulder' is still used for the haunch of the dome just above the top of the wall (as in Türkmen *egin*). Both these rings were pierced with slots to receive the wall structure, the door posts, and, in the case of the upper one, the struts of the roof structure too. The plan was a square with rounded corners. The laths joining the upper and lower rings were originally round; the corners were formerly built of felt. Normally the frame was not taken apart, as this involved a great deal of work: it was, however, divisible in four sections, or six if the two short sections either side of the door were separate.[20] The exact nature of the laths in the wall is unfortunately unclear: one needs a drawing. The names suggests parallel upright bars projecting at the top.[21] In the book (p. 12) this structure is described as a wall of upright timbers, *silu un modun xana,* 5 cubits high (i.e. *c.* 2.5 metres): a figure which seems too large unless it is taken to the shoulder of the roof struts. The number of these standards, *boso a modu,* for the normal *çomçu* was nine each on the east, west, and north, including the corners, and six on the door side (south): the numbers are obviously auspicious.

The roof struts were actually flat planks touching one another at the edges. They were curved strongly at the bottom, and had a slight reverse curve at the top. Their butts engaged in the slots of the upper wall ring, and their tips supported the roof wheel as usual. There was no definite number, as this depended on their width; they were not interconnected, except by the rings. The book adds (p. 13) that the struts were 6 cubits long (*c.* 3 metres), or longer, at 6½ cubits (*c.* 3.5 metres) at the corners as might be expected.

The door frame was in one piece, and the lintel, *ennix,* was pierced to receive the bottom ends of the roof struts: this was of willow, *xal as.* The wooden threshold was not particularly high. Two door leaves opened outwards. We know from Duiluikov's description that many of his party had to stoop to enter, so the door-frame, and the wall itself, cannot have been higher than 1.7 metres.[22]

The roof wheel, *tôno,* was formerly like an *aru* (Xa. *ara*) (the basket used for collecting *ar al* fuel), that is to say strongly domed. It had a single thick rim drilled with round holes for the tips of the roof struts, and spokes, *xegees,* spanning from side to side. It may be noted that an *ara* is formed from two sets of strongly-bent 'spokes' crossing one another to form the rounded bottom: it is thus structurally similar to the bentwood type of roof wheel general among Turkic groups, but also among Mongols in western Mongolia (*çamxraa toono*). Its honorific name here was *xala asu.*[23]

Çomçu at Ix Eǰen Xoroo and ǰüngar Xoroo were properly of two different sizes. A large *dabxar çomçu,* 'double *çomçu*', had four centre poles, *tul uur:*[24] this type no longer exists. The other, dañ *çomçu,* 'single *çomçu*', with no poles, is the present type: this was of different sizes at Ix Eǰen Xoroo and ǰüngar Xoroo. Such use of four centre poles is still normal for very large tent frames in Outer Mongolia, as in the reception tent at Gandan Monastery. The *dabxar çomçu* was an interconnected type, in other words two tents set up in tandem so that one formed the antechamber to the other, as described by Potanin.

Typically for the Mongols, little emphasis is given to the horsehair cordage. There were three external girth ropes around the walls. Two large felts, *deever,* covered the roof, in two layers, together with a felt lining, *dotor deever* or *xöšig,* inside the struts. The walls were covered with a single long piece of felt, *tooro* (cf.

Mo. *tu ur a,* Xa. *tuur a,* 'wall felt'); again there was a lining felt, *ba a xöšig,* 'small curtain', within the wall frame. There was a small, round felt cover for the top. A door flap, *isgii üüd,* was hung outside the wooden doors on the usual hair ropes. The felts could be decorated with a 'cloud application', *üülen xultïru* or *üülen xee,* in blue on the white, symbolizing the blue sky. This of course is consistent with the image of the tent as a microcosm. The honorific name for felts is *tolo isgei.*[25]

We have evidence, then, of a structure which, despite the uniqueness of the plan shape and silhouette, is clearly related in its roof struts, roof wheel and door frame, to some extent in its terminology, and in the hot-bending technique by which it was made, to the current tradition of trellis tents in Central Asia. The most marked difference from this tradition is in the hooped wall structure. Sayinǰir al, following Vladimirtsov and Gafferberg, draws attention to its pointed top, comparing this to a neck, *küǰügüü,* as described by Rubruck. These may indeed be the vestiges of the cart-tent once typical of the Mongols. By 1235–36 Hsü T'ing recorded that there were two types of tent in use among them: the simpler was made in the steppe, but the more complicated, probably a trellis tent, as made at Yantsin (Peking): possibly the technique had been developed there under the Xidañ.[26]

The Noǧay cart-tent

The way in which the *çomçu* was mounted intact on a cart had only one parallel at the beginning of this century, and that was among the Noǧay, a Turkic-speaking offshoot of the Golden Horde who now survive in a few small groups in the northern part of the Caucasian isthmus, notably in the Kuban and Terek river basins. The Noǧay had at one time been a numerous and powerful people in the South Russian Steppe, until they were reduced by internal dissensions and the plague, and displaced by the incursions first of the Qalma and later of the Russians. Their use of the cart-tent in this steppe is well documented at intervals from Ibn Baṭṭûṭa's observations on the Horde under Özbek Xan in about 1331 onward.[27] By the early fifteenth century Schiltberger claimed that there were 100,000 tents in the xan's camp under the Mangït emir Edigü:[28] it was the Mangït who were to become known as the Noǧay. Cart-tents were still used by the Qazaq, too, as late as 1509. It is an interesting reflection on the rapidity of change in material culture that the Özbek of Bukhârâ, who defeated the Qazaq at that time, were fascinated by the cart-tents they captured, evidently having forgotten them entirely.[29] After the break-up of the Horde in the 1420s, there are several rather unsatisfactory descriptions, from which it is clear that tents were round, domed, and lifted onto carts for the migration. The draft animals were camels, oxen or horses, according to size and weight. Some continuity can be established through old accounts.

The first really comprehensible description was given by Cornelis de Bruin, who visited the Tatars three or four kilometres from Astrakhan in 1703.[30] His information is the more valuable as he tells us in his book that he sat down and drew the tents on the spot; his sketches are reproduced as engravings (see Figure 9.1). His competence as a draftsman can be assessed by the boats he shows. which are convincing. What emerges is the following. The tents are circular in plan, with a cylindrical wall and a low dome forming about a quarter of a sphere. The junction of dome and wall is marked by a distinct convex welt in the felt covering. The covering reaches only part of the way down the wall, and what can be seen of the remainder reveals a double hoop of timber at the bottom of the wall, probably made from a sapling split in half: the end of this timber can be seen where it is tucked inside the hoop from above. The welt can thus be interpreted as a second hoop at the top of the wall. De Bruin states that the structure, made like a parrot cage, is built with flat timbers three or four fingers broad. Between the two hoops he has in fact shown vertical bands which appear to represent these boards placed edge to edge, or nearly so: it therefore seems that the wall is built rather like a barrel, with these staves confined by hoops outside, and probably inside too, at the two levels.

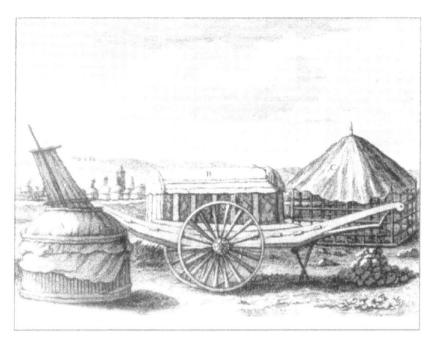

Figure 9.1 No ay tent and cart in 1707 (after Cornelis de Bruin, *Reizen over Moskovie door Persie en Indie,* 't Amsteldam, 1714, pl. 36–7).

The only other interpretation appropriate is that the vertical bands represent the reed matting which he says is used round the wall when felts do not reach the ground. Although rush screens in this Qalma region are indeed banded in such a way, they seem to be precluded here by the appearance of the hoop, which they would normally cover at the bottom. De Bruin, in any case, shows another welt at the apex of the dome forming the rim of the smoke hole, where one can assume there is a third hoop as usual.

Out of the smoke hole projects a pole, to which an elongated cloth flap is fastened by means of a short cross-yard at the top and a longer one acting as a spreader at the bottom just above the smoke hole. This could be turned according to the direction of the sun or wind, so as to screen the smoke hole as required. We are told in other accounts, such as that of Olearius on the Tatars at Astrakhan in 1636, that this flap could be let down over the smoke hole to seal the tent in cold weather, once the fire was out. As will be seen, later representations of this flap suggest that it may be connected with the puzzling raised flap which appears in the paintings from the *Djâmi' al-Tawârîkh* already mentioned[31]—a detail hard to interpret on its own, but which begins to make sense once compared with the No ay flap (Plate 31 and Figure 9.5).

Some caution is required where the structure is concerned, as Guillaume Le Vasseur, Sieur de Beauplan, a military engineer and cartographer who served the King of Poland from 1632–48, published a plan and section of the Tatar tent which remain to this day the only ones available (see Figure 9.2). Unfortunately there is no description relating to this illustration, though he apparently intended to give one: it is, however, clear from his text that the cart-tent he illustrates was used by Tatars in the region of Bucaq and in the Crimea as well as by the No ay between the Don and the Kuban.[32] What he shows conforms in outline to Olearius's and de Bruin's information, as a stilted hemisphere set on a cart with its wheels within the walls, but the structure is shown as a series of seven circumferential hoops, which with those at the base (not shown) and

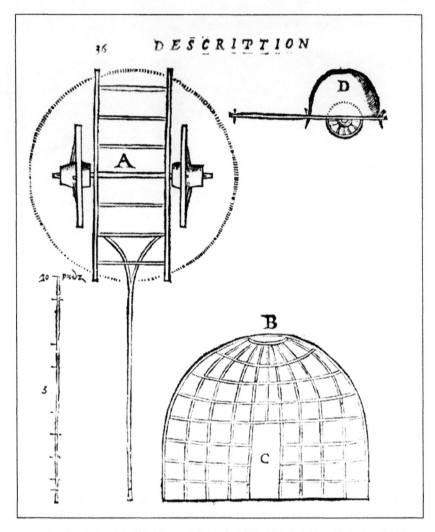

Figure 9.2 No ay cart-tent, c. 1645 (after Guillaume Le Vasseur, Sieur de Beauplan, *Description d'Ukrainie, qui sont plusieurs Provinces du Royaume de Pologne,* Rouen, 1660, p. 36).

at the smoke hole would make a total of nine. Outside these, and at right angles to them, run a second set of 18 radial struts converging on the smoke hole: the doorway is made between two of the struts, and three of the hoops are interrupted at this point. The scale of feet provided shows the tent to be 9 6 (2.90 m) in diameter overall and 7 4 (2.23 m) high, with a smoke hole of only 1 9 (0.53 m) diameter, and a doorway 3 6 (1.07 m) high. All the frame members seem to be slender, at about 1.5 (38 mm), much less than the 3–4 mentioned by de Bruin. This frame would indeed fit de Bruin's comparison to a parrot cage, but one is then left to wonder where the flat timbers were used, unless in the wall cladding. The cart itself has a bed only 3 6 (1.07 m) wide and 9 6 (2.90 m) long, with a draft pole projecting a further 9 6 , and wheels 48 (1.42 m) in diameter.

Although the details of this cart correspond to the familiar Central Asian build, the tent frame seems oversimplified, and the omission of the essential bottom hoop confirms that impression. If Beauplan was unable to see much of the structure, he may have guessed at the rest, or relied on his memory when later preparing his material for publication between 1648 and 1660. Nor is there any indication of a special hoop reinforcing the top of the wall. Yet he was an engineer, and we must place some credence in his competence, even if some details may be defective. Sir John Chardin in fact confirms a little later (1672) that the Tatars at Duzlah (Tuzla), 80 km from Kaffa in the Crimea, have tents made of round rods crossing one another.[33] We know, too, from Giovanni da Lucca that tent frames 'made of wicker' were sold on the market at Kaffa in 1633.[34] The comparison to basket- or wicker-work occurs often enough in a succession of authors to show that it must be taken seriously, and is not due simply to poor description. One is reminded of Rubruck's description of the wall as of *virgis cancellatis* in 1253.[35] Possibly the frame varied in detail from one area to another. The hoops remain in any case as a constant factor.

It seems, then, that in 1700 the basic structure of the No ay tent was the same as that of the *çomçu* , that is that both require hoops at top and bottom of the wall, with a third for the smoke hole above. The structure in between the wall hoops is unfortunately somewhat uncertain in both cases, though vertical slats may have been used in either. De Bruin and Beauplan show clearly that when the tent was placed on the cart bed, the upper quarter of the wheels would pass neatly inside the cylindrical wall. The unusual boat-like curve of the side timbers in de Bruin's drawing is quite different from the more usual flat cart-bed shown by Beauplan.

In 1773 Peter Simon Pallas visited a group of Tatars from the Kuban region who returned to migrate on the Aqtöbe (Achtuba) river. He refers to them as Mangït (Mankatten), but notes that they call themselves Qondïruv (Kundurau). His description is the most circumstantial yet:

Their yurts are very different in form and structure from those used by the Qalma and other Asiatic nomads. They cannot be taken to pieces, but are built much more lightly, and only so large that they can be placed on a large cart, that is to say somewhat over four or five ells in diameter. Their round wall is a trellis of very thin sticks, and the roof quite a flat vault of bent staves, one end of which is fastened in the trellis and the other around the rim of the smoke hole. The walls are covered with a reed mat, and the whole hut with light felt in such a way that this cover, too, cannot be taken off. In order to transport these tents, they put them on a tall, two-wheeled cart, so that they rest on the side timbers at the front and back, and cover the cart and its wheels like a sunshade. They load their modest possessions, chests of clothing, utensils etc. on the cart with their wife and children, and set off with everything. Rich people have two or more of these yurts, depending on the size of the family, besides a cart with a sleeping-hut of carpentry-work, where they sleep with their wives. If they are not to pasture for long in a place during the summer, they do not take the yurts and household down from the carts, but sit under them like Gypsies, and do their work in the shade of the yurt.[36]

Although he emphasizes that the structure is different from the usual trellis tent, he does not explain adequately where the difference lies, except in the lightness. The roof structure, with bent struts placed around the roof-wheel rim, is no different in principle, so the peculiarity seems to be in the wall, with its very thin rods *(sehr dünnen Stöcker)*. It is noteworthy that he describes the roof struts *(Stäben)* as fastened with one end *in* the trellis *(im Gatter),* not to or on it. In lieu of the disturbingly variable German ell it seems that the Russian *arshin* is meant (see below), at about 71 cm, giving a diameter of rather over 2.84 m—say 3.0 m: the same as Beauplan's figure.

In 1793–34 he returned to the same group, and found that 'their peculiar felt tents shaped like baskets *(korbförmige Filzgezelte),* which cannot be taken apart', as used by the other tribes of No ay, were no longer their only form of dwelling as before, as they had begun to adopt the trellis tent like that of the Qazaq. If a family possessed two tents, one of the old type was reserved for its women. It took the lead on migration, drawn by a span of two of their small cattle. Pallas also provides us with what is clearly an authentic as well as beautiful engraving of No ay tents, both encamped and on the move (see Plate 29).[37] Here the profile of the tent is the same, with the same distinctive welt, though the wall is shown sloping in slightly towards the top. The scale of the tents is more apparent, with the welt about shoulder-high. The smoke flap has changed in shape somewhat, and is now broader at the top than at the bottom, with an ogival point, and rounded shoulders: furthermore, it can be seen in some cases to rise from the level of the welt at the eaves. In these two respects it is reminiscent of the Rashîdîya picture. The carts are straight-sided, like Central Asian carts today. Subsequently he remarks on the No ay near the Volga estuary, who then migrated between the Berda and Molochnaya, and lived in the same type of cart-tent, *yüs* (a corruption of *üy*, 'dwelling'), noting that they were four to five-and-a-half *arshin* in diameter at the most, and could be lifted onto the carts by two men. He adds:

> The side walls of these huts are generally covered with reed mats, and the woodwork there is usually, like that of their carts, very old and smoke-impregnated, since they entirely lack workable timber, and, although they are not rich, have to buy it from the Crimea (Taurien) for both. (Note) The staves of their huts are generally of hazel, from which the Crimean mountain Tatars make lucrative sales to the No ay at Koslof, where they bring wheat to market.

Although they had no camels, their small draft cattle trotted just as lightly and quickly.[38]

As hazel rods are unlikely to be more than 15–20 mm (¾) in diameter, especially if coppiced, these would be about half the size of the normal trellis lath. It would appear that these No ay trellis rods must have been anchored in the hoops at top and bottom. As nothing is said of any fastenings at the crossings, there may have been none. Given the shortage of timber, the broader wooden slats seen by de Bruin were probably no longer available.

This indication of the structure can be linked directly to the specimen collected by Inostrantsev in 1904 (see Plate 30).[39] The cart-tent itself seems unfortunately to have been destroyed during the war, but two photographs of it survive, together with the more decorative elements of the covering, in the State Museum of Ethnography at St Petersburg. Besides these, there are several photographs he took among the Qara No ay in the field.[40] Here again the welt at the top of the wall is quite apparent in both photographs, with the inward slope of the wall shown in Pallas's plate; in one (3349:1.1) the bottom hoop can be seen too, below the ragged edge of the felt: it was probably about 6 cm (2½) in diameter. The line of both roof struts and trellis is clearly visible through the felt, which clings tightly to them. The most striking peculiarity is that the roof struts do not correspond to the trellis heads in number, as usual in a trellis tent, but seem to be about twice as frequent, to a total of perhaps 44. They are evidently anchored in the top hoop, as deduced. The trellis, with its wide mesh, is four rhombic interstices high. The roof wheel is traversed by two rods in a low arc from side to side, with a third at right angles under them running from front to rear, in the usual Qipçaq Turkish form, as in the Rashîdîya painting.

Closer inspection shows that the trellis laths seem not to be in two distinct layers pinned together at their crossings, but of rods woven in and out of one another, so that now one is on the outer surface, now another: comparison with a photograph taken in the field (334–2) appears to confirm this. In this, too, it can be seen that the trellis feet project only a little before engaging in the lower ring. If the trellis is woven, then the structure is indeed unique, and explains the recurring comparison to basket work. It also explains how,

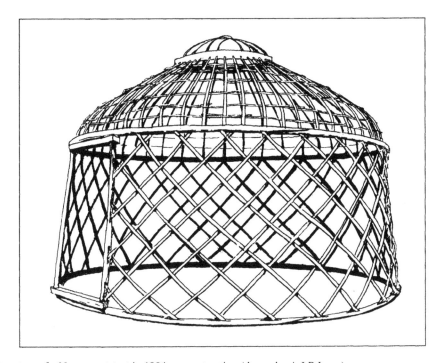

Figure 9.3 Structure of a No ay cart-tent in 1904: reconstruction (drawn by A.J.P.Jansz).

when it was light, it was made rigid enough to be lifted intact (see Figure 9.3). It does not correspond, though, to the framework drawn by Beauplan.

Another photograph from the field (334–3) (see Figure 9.4) helps to reconcile the two. In this a young woman is sitting with her baby in front of a trellis wall, only part of which can be seen. The large mesh of the trellis (*c.* 20 cm) is framed by a system of vertical standards (*c.* 6 cm) at alternate joints, crossed on the inside by similar horizontal laths, also at alternate trellis joints, to form a series of square openings: three horizontal laths are visible, pinned where they cross each vertical, and probably pinned though the trellis joint behind. If this really represents the inside of a cart-tent wall—and the presence of the woman supports the possibility—then it is the only picture available. We have a combination of the network of horizontals and verticals shown by Beauplan, with the diagonal trellis mesh visible in the external photographs. Though the absence of any roof structure here restricts comparison, the only aspect which does not fit Beauplan's scheme is the discontinuity of roof struts and wall evident from the exterior.

The findings can be set against the only systematic description available, recorded by Arkhipov in 1850. Unfortunately the Russian syntax is not as clear as it might be, but the sense appears to be as follows:

The *otaüy,* or true No ay kibitka, consists of a hoop, *ergé,* at the middle and one at the bottom, of an upper one, *ya araq,* of smaller ones, *ektal,* placed between the upper and the middle ones, of longitudinal rods, *tevetal,* of lower, longitudinal bars, *calqan,* of cross rods, *asyamay,* of two door-leaves, *e ik,* of a threshold and lintel, *bosa a* and of a pole, *sroq,* on which the upper quilted roof cover, *tünülük,* is fixed. The patterns stitched on the upper roof cover of the *otaüy* are called *kögälä-tünülük,* and those on the door flap *kögälä-esik.* To the doorway, *esek,* is fastened the door flap, and to the roof cover are fastened woollen, and sometimes even silken webbing, *tünülük— baw,* to which

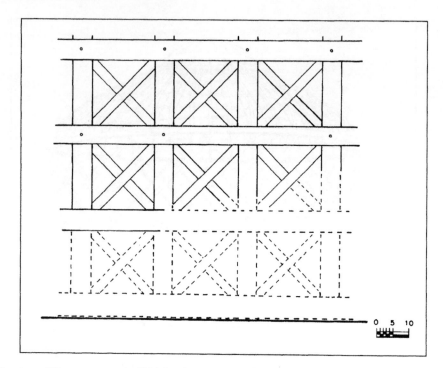

Figure 9.4 Structure of No ay cart-tent in 1904, interior: reconstruction (after K.A.Inostrantev, GME Narodov Rossii, Coll. No. 334–3; drawn by Mügül Andrews).

tassels, *ök*, of different colours are sewn. The *otaüy* is the wedding kibitka, and is never taken to pieces during transport.[41]

The terms given are apparently in the Central No ay dialect.[42] It seems that Arkhipov first visualizes three horizontal hoops placed at different levels in the structure, and then gives further elements from top to bottom, before mentioning two elements in the covering. Of the terms used, *ergé* can be identified with literary No ay (N) *irge*, 'wall' or 'foundation', as already used in the Secret *History of the Mongols,* where Mostaert identified *irge* as the skirting at the foot of the tent wall,[43] and as in Qalmag irge, 'the lower edge of the tent' or 'the felt covering the lower edge'. This is not now to be confused with *erüke~örüge* for 'roof wheel' or 'smoke hole', though the use here suggests that the two Mongolian terms may have the same origin in the sense of 'hoop'. The hoops seem to be those at the top and bottom of the wall. *Ya araq* is recognizable as a metathesis of N *a araq*, 'roof wheel'. *Esik~esek* is the usual term for door, *bosa a* is of course the common Mongolian for 'door frame', as generally adopted in the Turkic world for lintel and threshold, and *sroq* must be intended for N *sïrïq* 'pole'. *Tünülük* is the equivalent of N *tünlik,* 'smoke flap' or 'top felt', and *tünülük baw* the ties for this. The Russian gloss 'door leaf' is probably a slip for 'door post': there is no other information to suggest this light tent had doors as such.

Interestingly., the other terms are totally unfamiliar in the general tent vocabulary. *Tal* on its own means 'willow', and appears in that sense here or as 'withy'; it seems likely, given its position, that *tevetal* is intended for *töbe-tal*, 'top withy', and that *ektal* means something like 'edge withy', as *ek* means 'boundary limit'. *Calqan* is a dialect equivalent of N *yalqïn,* defined as 'the bars on either side of a cart, serving as support for the body', and thus tending to confirm that by 'longitudinal' Arkhipov means 'vertical' in this context, as would be expected from 'small posts': these are standards of some kind, low down in the structure. The *tevetal* must also be vertical, then, and are likely to be the roof struts. Arkhipov's phrasing leaves it uncertain whether 'placed between the upper and the middle one' refers to *ektal* or to *tevetal,* but, as verticals are required, he is likely to have meant the *tevetal*. The function of the *ektal* is unspecified, but given the fact that he mentions them immediately after the roof wheel, and then works downward, they might be the spokes within the roof wheel, which are certainly small, or lesser hoops in the roof structure. A *yamay (~asaraay?)* is puzzling: possibly the first part is to be connected with Qazaq and Tatar *esiyä,* 'edge, bank, surrounding',[44] as the limiting wall or its horizontal framing.

The appearance of *irge* here is of course most significant in providing the sought-for connection with an early element in the Mongolian tent vocabulary, though it is disappointing that it bears no relation to the recorded vocabulary from Eǰen Xoroo: it remains possible that it has simply been omitted, for it does survive in the Ordos, as shown by Mostaert. *Bosa a,* too, could date from this period, though it could also have been adopted from the Qalma . The appearance of *ya araq~a araq* and *e ik* supports the early use of these terms: an equivalent *ça araq* for '(roof) wheel rim' is attested in the Ordos too.[45] The lack of correspondence of the remaining structural terms with the usual Turkic trellis tent vocabulary is also significant, as it indicates the largely separate development of this tradition. Though this is now a mainly Turkic vocabulary, the presence of *irge* and *bosa a* for two major frame elements suggests that the type may have been of Mongol origin.

By Arkhipov's time the *otaüy* was preserved mainly as a wedding tent (see Plate 31), and even in 1900 its decoration was particularly striking. The appliqué-work, as collected and photographed then, was confined mostly to the door flap, and the smoke flap, now exaggerated in size, though still spread on two battens as before, served as a signal of its special purpose. The concentration of decorative webbing around the door is also found in the trellis tents of the Qaraqalpaq, another early offshoot of the Golden Horde now in the Aral Sea region, showing that it must once have been a common feature. It seems likely that it draws attention to and protects the transition into married life represented by the threshold. The style of ornament itself (see Figures 9.5 and 9.6), with due allowance for abstraction, is not hard to associate with the multi-coloured appliqué-work depicting vines and trees, as seen by Rubruck on door flaps in the mid-thirteenth century.[46]

Conclusion

Whatever the unresolved contradictions in detail, the evidence shows a correspondence between the cart-tents of Eǰen Xoroo with those of the No ay in the use of hoops at the top and bottom of the wall, curved roof struts, a small roof wheel of bent wood, and the basic principle that the structure could be lifted intact and placed on a flat-bedded cart to overlap the two wheels. These features, then, were probably common to the cart-tents of the Mongols and their subject peoples in the time of Çiñgiz Qan, both in Mongolia itself and in the far west of Asia. From the Rashîdîya painting we can see that the erect smoke flap may have been used then, at least in special circumstances. The decorated felts recorded then have also survived in the west, but not in the Ordos. Different aspects of the same original dwelling, as well as common ones, have survived in the two regions.

Furthermore, the evidence suggests, whether in the Mongolian or the Turkic context, that the original structure was at least as complicated as that of the trellis tent, if not more so: the development of the collapsible trellis wall may have represented a simplification, in the elimination of the hoops and their supports, and the direct relation of struts to trellis heads. This depended on the concept of the flexible girth of rope or webbing. It is possible that the girth of long wooden arcs, *iti,* connected in series, as collected by

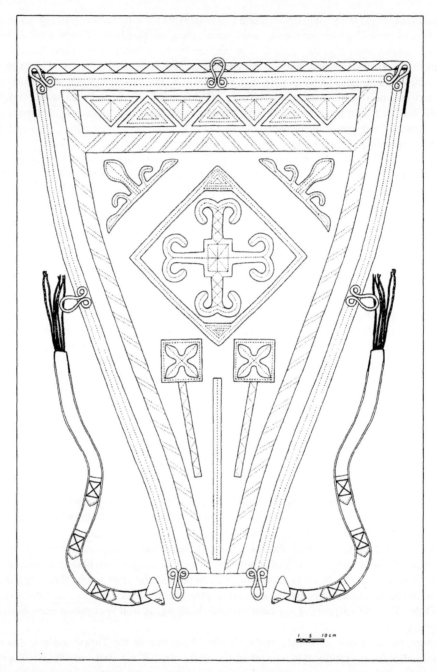

Figure 9.5 Smoke flap of Noʔay wedding tent, 1904, from a tracing made in 1993 (GME Coll. 333) (drawn by Mügül Andrews).

Haslund Christensen among the Xorçin Mongols,[47] is a vestige of this transition. The presence of the curved

Figure 9.6 Door flap of No ay wedding tent, 1904 (GME Coll. 333) from a tracing made in 1993 (drawn by Mügül Andrews).

roof strut shows that the seemingly simpler straight Mongolian roof strut, as used today, was developed later on. In this case, it may well have been the serpentine roof strut, as shown in the paintings, which generated it. Appearances can be deceptive.

Notes

I am most grateful to Prof. K.Sagaster for presenting my questionnaire at EJen Xoroo, to Čimeddorǰi for his mediation in interpreting it, to Sayinǰir al for answering it, and to Tömörtogoo for translating his answers: all of them showed admirable patience in the course of an hour and a half of questioning on my behalf. I am also most thankful to Hurcabaatar Solongod for lending me Sayinǰir al's book, and translating the relevant text. For the latter, see note 17.

The standard transcription system is used for Mongolian, the Ortak Türk Alfabesi for No ay (N), and the *Encyclopedia of Islam* system for Persian and Arabic.

1. Bibliothèque Nationale, Supp. persane 1113, fos 16v., 44v., 65r., 85v., 239r., etc.
2. For example, those in the Asiatic Society of Bengal and the Rampur State Library, and the fragments in the Topkapı Sarayı. Cf. B.Gray, 'An unknown fragment of the Jâmi' al-Tavârîkh in the Asiatic Society of Bengal', *Ars Orientalis* 1, 1954, pp. 67–75.
3. N.Kharuzin, *Istoriya Razvitiya Zhilishcha v Kochevuikh i Polukochevuikh Tyurkskikh i Mongolskikh Narodnostey Rossii* (Moscow, 1896).
4. Peter A.Andrews, 'The tents of Timur', in P.Denwood (ed.), *Arts of the Eurasian Steppelands (Percival David Colloquies on Art and Archaeology in Asia* 7, London: Percival David Foundation, 1978), pp. 143–87.
5. Cf. Krystyna Chabros, 'Quilted ornamentation on Mongol felts', *Central Asiatic Journal* 32 (1–2), 1988, pp. 34–61: fig. 10.
6. Peter A.Andrews, 'The tents of Chinggiz Qan at EJen Qoriy-a, and their authenticity', *Anglo-Mongolian Society Journal* 7 (2), December 1981, pp. 1–49.
7. The Ise Shrine, built in AD 685, is renewed every 20 years.
8. Owen Lattimore, *Mongol Journeys* (London: Cape, 1941), pp. 39–60.
9. Peter A.Andrews, *Felt Tents and Pavilions: The Nomadic Tradition and its Interaction with Princely Tentage* (2 vols) (London: Melisende, 1999): Mongols I i 5 and IV iii 3.
10. Andrews, *Felt Tents:* I i 1 and III.
11. The Xorčin and other groups in Inner Mongolia still transport their tents on high-wheeled carts, but dismantled: the carts here are needed to carry the large roof wheel with hinged struts typical of the region, which is divisible into two halves. This appears to be a later, though still perhaps early development. The tents are trellis tents.
12. G.N.Potanin, 'Pominki po Chingis'-Khane', *Izvestiya Russkogo Geograficheskogo Obshchestva* 21, 1885, p. 304.
13. E.G.Gafferberg, 'Khazareyskaya yurta khanai-khuirga', *Sbornik Muzeya Antropologii i Etnografii* 14 (Moscow), 1953, pp. 90–92.
14. An etymology for *çomçu* was proposed by the Dilova Xutu tu, in reply to a query from Owen Lattimore, and sent to Klaus Ferdinand in a letter dated 29.5.57: this is cited in full in Andrews, 'The tents of Chinggiz Qan', p. 12. He derives it from a stem meaning: 'to squat on both heels, to kneel, either on one or both knees', with a parallel between the bent back in this position, and the bent struts of the tent dome. There is a parallel form in the Ordos, *çomços,* with this meaning: it can be compared with Lessing's *çomçui-*: 'to greet by bending the knee' etc. (Ferdinand D.Lessing (ed.) with Mattai Haltod *et al.* (comp.), *Mongolian-English Dictionary,* Berkeley and Los Angeles: University of California Press, 1960). The more usual explanation, however, is that the word refers to the pointedness of the tent profile (due to the reverse curve), as in Lessing's *çomça* : 'tent with a pointed top… hair gathered into a tuft'.
15. Antoine Mostaert and F.W.Cleaves (eds), *Sagang Secen's Erdeni-yin Tobči (Scripta Mongolica* 2, Cambridge MA: Harvard Yenching Inst., 1956), Vol. 1, pl. 2; S.D.Duiluikov, 'Edzhen-Khoro,' in G.D.Sanzheev (ed.)

Filologiya i Istoriya Mongolskikh Narodov. Pamyati Akademika Borisa Yakovlevicha Vladimirtsova (Moscow: Izd. Vostochnoi Literatury, 1958), p. 231. Mostaert (p. 21, notes for pl. 2) appears to indicate that he may have taken the photograph on 22.8.1909. The original print of the photograph, as presented to the Verbiest Foundation by Prof. F.Isono in 1993, is labelled Ix Ejen Xoroo on the back. The particular value of the photograph provided by Duilikov is that he was apparently the last scholar to visit the four tents before they were placed in the Museum in 1956.

16. Peter A.Andrews (ed.), *Nomad Tent Types in the Middle East* (Tübinger Atlas des Vorderen Orients, Beiheft B 74, Wiesbaden: Reichert, 1997), Part 1, *Framed Tents,* types b and c. Cf. Klaus Ferdinand, 'Ethnographical notes on Chahâr Aimaq, Hazâra and Moghôl', *Acta Orientalia* (Copenhagen) 28 (1–2), 1964, pp. 175–203; Alfred Janata, 'On the origin of the Firuzkuhis in Western Afghanistan', *Archiv für Völkerkunde* 25, 1971, pp. 57–65; Janata, 'Aimaq', in R.V. Weekes (ed.), *Muslim Peoples* (Westport and London: Greenwood, 1978), pp. 8–12; Janata, 'Appendix on Châr Aimâq', unpublished conference paper, SOAS, London, July 1979.

17. Sayinjirgal and Šaraldai, *Altan ordun-u tayilga* (Beijing, 1983).

18. Sayinjirgal and Šaraldai, *Altan,* p. 10, fn. 1.

19. Lessing, *Mongolian-English Dictionary;* Gustav John Ramstedt, *Kalmückisches Wörterbuch* (Helsinki: Suomalais-Ugrilainen Seura, 1935), p. 313b, cf. p. 214b; Sir Gerard Clauson, *An Etymological Dictionary of Prethirteenth Century Turkish* (Oxford University Press, 1972), p. 930b, *yalñûs.*

20. This seems to be a mistake for five (three whole sides plus two half sides at the front), rather than four units incorporating the corners, plus two at the door jambs.

21. The present tents appear to be built with a wall 'like a picket fence', according to M.Yahuda of the LSE, who kindly ran his hand over the outer covering for me in 1988.

22. Duiluikov 'Edzhen Khoro', p. 233 fn. 20.

23. For the distribution of the bentwood type, see B.Rinčen (as Rintchen) (ed.), *Atlas Ethnologique et Linguistique de la République Populaire de Mongolie* (Ulaanbaatar: Academy of Sciences, 1979), maps 151, 152, 153b.

24. Cf. Antoine Mostaert, *Dictionnaire Ordos* (Monograph 5) (Peking: Monumenta Serica, 1941–44); also Lessing, *Mongolian-English Dictionary,* s.v. *tul a uri.*

25. Saynijirgal, p. 12, fn. 1.

26. Hsü T'ing, *Meng-ta Pei-lu und Hei-ta Shih-lüeh,* (eds) Peter Olbricht and Elisabeth Pinks (Wiesbaden: Harrassowitz, 1980), p. 105.

27. Muhammad b.'Abdallâh, ibn Baṭṭûta, *Riḥla,* (ed.) C.Defrémrery and B.R. Sanguinetti (Paris, 1855–58), Vol. 3, pp. 361–2, cf. pp. 380ff.

28. Johannes Schiltberger, *The Bondage and Travels* (trans. and ed.) J.Buchan Telfer (London: Hakluyt Society, 1879), p. 35; (German edn, Franckfurt am Mayn, 1554, p. 30 r).

29. Fd-Allâh ibn Rûzbehân, *Mehmân-nâmeh-ye Bokhârâ,* (ed.) Manuchehr Sotûdeh (Tehran, 1341/1962), pp. 222–3.

30. Cornelis de Bruin, *Reizen over Moskovie door Persie en Indie* ('t Amsteldam, 1714), p. 90 and pl. 36–37.

31. These may both represent Ghâzân Khân's great festival at Ûdjân.

32. Guillaume le Vasseur, Sieur de Beauplan, *Description d'Ukrainie, qui sont plusieurs Provinces du Royaume de Pologne* (Rouen, 1660), p. 36; though the numbering implies that a description should have been provided, and the text (p. 29) states this intention, it is absent in the facsimile reprint (Rouen n.d., 1985). The text refers to cart-tents as used by the unsubjugated Tatars in Bucaq (between the Dniestr and the Danube) (p. 29), those subject to the Xan in Crimea (pp. 33, 35), and by implication the No ay subject to the Russians (p. 37).

33. Sir John Chardin, *Travels…into Persia and the East Indies through the Black Sea and the Country of Colchis* (London, 1686) p. 74; cf. his *Voyages* (Paris, 1811), Vol. l, p. 40.

34. Giovanni da Lucca, 'Relation des Tartares, Perecopites et Nogaies etc.', in J. de Thévenot (ed.) *Relations des Divers Voyages Curieux* (Paris, 1663), Vol. 1, pp. 18–19, 25.

35. Willem van Rubruck (Guillelmus de Rubruc), 'Itinerarium', *Sinica Franciscana i, Itinera et Relationes Fratrum Minorum saec. xiii et xiv,* (ed.) Anastasius van den Wyngaert (Florence/Aquae Clarae: Quaracchi, 1929), p. 172, ¶2.

36. Peter Simon Pallas, *Reise durch verschiedene Provinzen des Russischen Reichs* (Frankfurt and Leipzig, 1776–78), Vol. 3, pp. 381–2.

37. Peter Simon Pallas, *Bemerkungen auf einer Reise in die südlichen Statthalterschaften des Russischen Reichs in den Jahren 1793 und 1794* (Leipzig, 1799–1801), Vol 1, pp. 144–5 and pl. vi, cf. caption p. xxvi.

38. Ibid., pp. 507–8.

39. State Museum of Ethnography, St Petersburg (GME) collection no. 333, from Terek Oblast, Kizlyar division; see G.Bonch-Osmolovskiy, 'Svadebnuie zhilishcha turetskikh narodnostey', *Materialui po Etnografii* 3 (1), 1926, pp. 101–10. It is not entirely clear whether the frame was collected or merely photographed.

40. GME Narodov Rossii, Coll. no. 334, K.A.Inostrantsev 1904: (a) Envelope 3349:1.1, *otaw,* front view (coll. 333); 1.2, same, three-quarter view from r.h.s. (b) Album 83:334–2, *terme* and *otaw* in Qarano ay Steppe; 334–3, interior showing part of the trellis frame.

41. A.P.Arkhipov, 'Domashnyaya utvar' Nogaytsev Stavropol'skoy Gubernii', *Geograficheskiya Izvestiya* 1, 1850, p. 75.

42. The vocabulary here, from the Stavropor' region, differs from the literary No ay (N) parlance in the only dictionary available (N.A.Baskakov (ed.), *Nogaysa-Orïssa sözlik/Nogaysko-Russkiy slovar'*, Moscow: Karachay-Cherkessk Institute for Scientific Research in Language, Literature and History, 1963), making identification of the terms rather more difficult.

43. Antoine Mostaert, 'Sur quelques passages de l'Histoire Secrète des Mongols', *Harvard Journal of Asiatic Studies* 14 (3–4), 1951, pp. xlvii, ¶230, p. 386; cf. Mostaert, *Dictionnaire Ordos,* p. 387a.

44. W.Radloff, *Versuch eines Wörterbuchs der Türk-Dialekte* (The Hague: Mouton, reprint 1960), Vol. 1, p. 876.

45. Mostaert, *Dictionnaire Ordos,* p. 692a. *Ca arï* and its cognates are used for 'roof-wheel rim' in most East-Mongolian dialects, as well as in Dörböt and Sartul.

46. Rubruck, 'Itinerarium', p. 172, ¶2.

47. Nationalmuseet, Copenhagen, R vii 90a, 1–6: there are six curved rods corresponding to the six trellis sections, each about 210 cm long.

Chapter 10
Material Culture of Pastoral Nomads: Reflections based on Arab and Afghan Materials
Klaus Ferdinand

This chapter examines the material culture of two bedouin groups typical of Qatar, particularly the two types of 'black tent', and other specifically nomadic features, and their modernization.[1] In addition, I present contrasting material on Afghan nomads collected over nearly three decades, with the aim of generalizing about the material culture of pastoral nomads.

Nomads of Qatar

The two Qatari groups are, first, the short-range bedouin of the Al Na'im tribe, who make few and limited movements within their territory of north-west and central Qatar, and second, the long-range bedouin of south Qatar, who make frequent and long migrations, and enter Qatar from the south in early spring. The latter are particularly of the Al Murrah tribe, whose main territory lies immediately south of Qatar in Saudi Arabia and the United Arab Emirates.

Before oil, Qatar's main source of significant income was pearls from the surrounding waters. Compared to other Gulf countries, Qatar had the greatest proportion of its inhabitants engaged in pearling. The population of Qatar falls by tradition into groups dependent on either the uncultivated interior or the sea, or a mixture of both. It was peculiar to Qatar that there was no permanent settlement in the interior, and no cultivation. The settled population of the villages and towns of the north-west, north, and east was occupationally oriented towards the sea and its pearl fisheries, while the interior was the grazing ground of the bedouin and of some of the settled populace, which for a period of the year were tented in the interior.

Culturally, Qatar belongs to a larger area comprising the southern portion of the Arabian/Persian Gulf and adjoining parts of the Arabian mainland. This is also evident from their language, where the bedouin of the Al Na'im and the Al Murrah fall within two dialectical groups. The Al Na'im, with the Al Manasir, the Bani Hajir and the Bani Khalid, belong to a group of tribes that have lived along the Gulf littoral for a long time, whereas the Al Murrah are relative newcomers, together with their neighbours the Ajman, and are ascribed to the southern Najdi, i.e. the dialect of the region of Najd in central Arabia, west of their present area, a region from which they are said to have emigrated about 150 years ago.[2]

The bedouin of north and south Qatar are markedly different in their migration patterns, ranging from a nearly stationary life to frequent movement. Many other cultural differences may be related to this fact.

Pastoralism among the Al Na'im of north Qatar

The nomads of the north have used lorries for their movements since about 1950, while donkeys were otherwise the most common means of transport. The group of Al Na'im we knew best spent six to eight months (February-March to October) at their summer quarters, where they had stone houses to move into during the hottest period. At the beginning of autumn they moved 30 km inland, spending about three months before finally staying a further three months at Murwab, where we visited them first. Thus, they kept themselves all the year within the Al Na'im tribal territory.

In 1959, the Al Na'im were still basically dependent upon and influenced by their livestock keeping, even though they had a settled existence most of the year. The range of livestock kept was comprehensive: it included camels, although they were not nearly as common as in former times. Sheep and goats were the basic items of their nomad economy, often with the addition of a few cows, and always with donkeys for day-to-day transport work; now and then, a little poultry, and occasionally (surprisingly) pigeons. Unusually, they kept no dogs to guard the camps, though some of them had Arabian greyhounds *(saluqis)* for hunting.

In general, it was a range of livestock which could have been found among settled farmers. The vicissitudes of life which Al Na'im had undergone since the war of 1937, when a great number went to Bahrain and Saudi Arabia, whence some of them had only recently returned,[3] may have contributed to increasing their settled character, as employment by the oil companies probably has too.

Pastoralism among the Al Murrah of south Qatar

The nomads of south Qatar showed a completely different pattern. Their way of life was first and foremost characterized by mobility and frequent movement. The camel was the beast of transport, and it was in fact the universal animal of the bedouin, who were adapted to life in the great sand deserts of South Arabia. The yearly pattern could therefore involve long migrations into these deserts. The bedouin came up to Qatar in the late winter and early spring. This was the good time of the year, with abundant grazing for the flocks, and with opportunities for hunting and truffle-gathering, as the bedouin explained. In the hot summer they had stationary camps near wells to the south of Qatar, where they assembled in larger groups. Spring, in contrast, was characterized by small camps.

At the beginning of February 1959, bedouin started coming into Qatar from the south. We contacted a little group of five to seven tents of closely interrelated Al Murrah people, exclusively camel herders, who also herded the Ruler Shaykh 'Ali's camels. The bedouin in south Qatar gave the impression of being much more traditional in their way of life than those of the north. The camel dominated their lives: besides being their beast of burden, it was their riding animal and their milch animal, and in addition practically everything from it was used; its urine for washing hair and for tanning, its dried manure as excellent fuel and (if crumbled) a fine absorbent inlay for babies' 'nappies', its meat, especially from a young foal, as a prestige food (we tasted it as guests of the shaykhs), its wool spun and twined for weaving and for knot looping into stockings, etc. Lastly, the skin was used, in particular for a large variety of transport bags and containers and in earlier years also for big water-containers.

The Al Murrah camp-group studied had previously kept sheep and goats as milch animals, as did other bedouin of south Qatar, but their importance was minimal compared to that of the camels. The milk was soured in skins and churned to butter in a skin hung from a tripod. The buttermilk was boiled out, drained in a cloth, dried for a couple of days on the roof of the tent, and then stored away for later use. This was, in brief, a process also met in north Qatar, which is widespread among cattle- and sheep-keepers all over the Middle East.

Camel-saddles

In Qatar four types of camel-saddles were in use:

1. Women's riding saddle, the litter, with curved wooden bows to carry a rug as cover and to protect the rider. It was seen in two forms, both basically of the North Arabian *shadâd-type*.[4] This was only met among the Al Murrah.
2. The well-known South Arabian riding saddle, *al-hawlânî*, where the rider sits on a separate U-shaped pad behind the hump. The curved wooden saddle-bows were said to come from Oman.[5] This type was in use among Al Na'im and Al Murrah, and was the common riding and racing saddle in Qatar.
3. The pack-saddle *al-misâma* of Al Na'im, in form and structure closely related to the combined pack and riding saddle of Al Murrah of the *shadâd-type*.[6]
4. The true North Arabian riding saddle *al-shadâd* was also met with among Al Na'im, whereas Al Murrah seemed to manage with the combined saddle referred to above.[7]

This pack and riding gear corresponds well with Qatar's geographical and cultural position more than half way down the Gulf where influences from north and south meet.

Hunting and collecting

Hunting was clearly a tradition, but was little practised in northern Qatar in 1959. Wild animals and other game were no longer common. Hunting hounds, *saluqis,* were occasionally met with in the Al Na'im camps.

The bedouin of the south were better equipped than the northerners for hunting. They had shotguns or rifles, *saluqis* and lanner falcons *(wakri)*. Hunting was highly esteemed and valued, and it was obvious that it had earlier been an important addition to the food supply. But this it was no longer, for the reason that there was too little game.

In contrast to hunting, collecting activities were still important, and culturally highly valued, primarily when truffles were to be found after the rains in the early spring.

The gathering of firewood and shrubs for fuel was still essential., though the scarcity of both was marked in northern as compared to southern Qatar. Collecting activities had found new outlets. Flotsam, particularly timber and planks, was quite common along the seashores to the north-west among the Al Na'im. But a more and more prominent feature of the daily life of the bedouin was the collecting of discards and rubbish from the oil industry. This was also prevalent in more traditional, and apparently less 'spoilt', southern Qatar. Detonation cable was here a favourite material for use as guy ropes or lashings for saddles.

New ways of life

Throughout Qatar, oil production brought an abundance of money, which contributed decisively to changes in the traditional way of life, but I believe its immediate effect was to stabilize nomad life by making life more secure for the bedouin, both in the north and in the south. In the north, only old men, women and children were to be seen: all the others, men of working age and younger, were either employed by the oil company, Qatar Petroleum Company, or else away at one of the Qatar government's new boarding schools. The remainder received a monthly wage paid by the Shaykh of Qatar, no small sum at that. Such was not the case in the south, where each individual tent-hold was much more complete; above all, there were generally men of working age, thus securing a more traditional way of life. But even here, men went to work for the oil company, particularly as drivers, whereas boys did not attend state schools, or at least they were less noticeably absent.

These bedouin groups were closely connected to the ruler in Dohah and other Al Thani shaykhs.

Camps and tents: the Murwab camp of Al Na'im in north Qatar

The camps we visited in northern Qatar from January to March in 1959 were scattered and small, usually consisting of two to three tents, occasionally four to six. The size of the camps was presumably connected with livestock keeping and the cooperation which it entailed; it also reflected the specific conditions of that area, and the opportunities for an optimal exploitation of the grazing, made possible by the abundant and widespread occurrence of wells.[8]

The camps all lay with an east-west axis, standing freely and open in the terrain, without any form of natural protection. The protection was the tent itself, which gave the closed nature of the Al Na'im tents and others of north Qatar additional significance. The front of the tent (the side where the entrance or entrances and the projecting kitchen area lay) always faced south. The day-to-day working space was inside the tent, whereas the area in front of the tents was not incorporated into it, as was the case in south Qatar, except when working with the animals.[9]

The Al Na'im camps, as mentioned, remained on the same sites for long periods, and were not fully-functional nomad camps. In a way the Al Na'im in 1959 were 'part-time nomads', with many men and boys of working age away, while the remainder lived a subsidized life.

Camps and tents: the Al Murrah in south Qatar

These camps consisted of from two to seven tents in closely related kinship-groups, thus in type and extent resembling those of north Qatar; but they differed from the latter in being fully-functional nomad camps. Individual tent-holds were in general up to strength, with men of all ages, children and youths. No one was at boarding school, although a few of the men were away engaged in other work, for example as drivers, either in Saudi Arabia or in Qatar itself. This allowed them to maintain the intensity of labour involved in the traditional migratory life, especially in the late winter and spring, the good time of year, without any great problems with heat and water, with good grazing, an abundance of fuel and particularly of milk; and, especially prized, both truffles and the possibility of hunting. These were the considerations the bedouin stressed as attractions influencing their decisions to come to Qatar, and the reason they gave for their frequent movements.

The tents which we came to know best in south Qatar belonged particularly to Al Murrah; but we also saw a few tents of Al Awamir, Al Manasir, and Bani Hajir.

The Al Murrah tents were easy to distinguish from those of the Na'im and of the shaykhs' camps. They had no front canvas and were somewhat lower, with side walls about 1 metre high; in addition, they were generally pitched quite haphazardly. This impression was emphasized by the fact that the tent poles at the back of the tent were very irregularly placed, and even sometimes absent. This perhaps related to the frequency of movement during the spring, and the variable weather, with constant changes of wind from the prevailing northerly to a southerly direction; this provoked them simply into turning the tents, by moving the backcloth to the front, and often very shortly afterwards moving it back again.

The working area within the tent thus naturally became a part of the greater area in front of the tent, which was, as it were, a common working area for all members of the tent-hold, men, women and children, and a common area for the whole camp, for the livestock at night and for the activities of camp life during the day. This was made easier by the layout of the camp, with the tents in line or in a slight curve, all with their openings turned in the same direction, towards the south. Openness was a cardinal difference from the conditions which we had met in north Qatar and in the shaykhs' encampments.

This openness also characterized the interior of the tents during the day. In general, in daily life there was little to give the impression of any real division of the tent, if one disregards the placing of the pack-loads, which were usually piled in a heap across the long axis of the tent. And yet, the guests' and men's section was the area where women rarely worked. Nor was it equipped for the activities of women. Men, on the other hand, moved around or settled down at will in the family and women's section, and this openness applied to all the men of the camp, and in the course of time to the visiting ethnographers. Privacy could, however, be achieved and immediately established in the case, for example, of the sudden arrival of strangers; a partition wall or walls were hastily erected across the width of the tent, and stretched protectively out from the front, thus effectively screening off the guest section not only from the rest of the tent but also from the open area in front of the tent.[10]

The family section had no strict layout, unlike in north Qatar. The kitchen hearth was a hand-dug hole in the sand, with the pots and pans close by in coiled, lidded baskets with leather covers, or in a wooden box or a plaited basket.

In the tents, there was a final section in the extreme west, normally separated from the central family-section by a pile of possessions ready packed for transport. This was where the watering trough for the camels, containers for pots and pans, and the like, normally stood. It corresponds exactly with all published sketches of bedouin tents, which have the kitchen area with the hearth here,[11] although, in the camps in south Qatar, there was only one example with the kitchen here. An additional particular feature was that the extreme western section of the tent was also the sleeping place for those who wished to keep to themselves.

The Al Na'im tent in northern Qatar (see Plate 32)

The structural parts of the tent comprise:

- the velum or roof-cloth with girths underneath;
- tent poles supporting the centrally placed wooden beams and the beckets at the edges of the velum bolted to the
- guy ropes fastened to
- natural stones taking the place of the tent pegs used in less stony terrain;
- the side cloths attached with
- wooden pins or iron skewers to the edges of the underside of the velum, and held to the ground by
- stones, and finally
- dividing curtains to give privacy and protection between the sections.

A large Al Na'im tent is constructed as follows. The velum measured 3.70×15 m and consisted of six cloths sewn together, so that the reinforced edges stood up.[12] It was strengthened by five woven girths approximately 15 cm wide, crossing from one side to the other sewn on to the underside of the velum, where the tent poles were placed in rows of three, in all 21 poles.[13] The velum was of a coarse quality, the widths of cloth being woven locally or imported from Beirut, its outer edges strengthened by a rope, partly wound with cast-stitching.

The woven girths were of a type always found as an essential part of the Arab bedouin tent.[14] The girths were made locally, partly of camel hair.

In the Al Na'im tent there were small square 'cushions' of jute canvas sewn on top of the girths at the central seam of the velum; wooden sticks, 175–183 cm long, were inserted here as longitudinal ridge-beams, before the centre poles, 215–220 cm high, were raised in support of the velum.[15] Wooden beckets were sewn onto the girth and wooden beckets were furthermore sewn onto the underside of the velum in its four corners, and to a cotton rope sewn into and on the top of the centre seam at the two ends.[16] In these beckets the stay ropes were fastened and the 'forked' tent poles usually rested in the beckets, except at the ends where they rested in the special cotton rope in a hole in the velum.[17] The stay ropes were of the ordinary imported bazaar rope or locally made of plant or imported material. Tent pegs were not in use. Stones were always used to secure the tents, which was essential in a season of highly changeable weather, with many northerly storms.

The tent poles were mostly natural wooden sticks, 165–175 cm long at the rear and 170–183 cm at the front. The central poles., 215–220 cm long, were strengthened by the nailing-on of a wooden block to make a 'forked' upper end to support the ridge-beams better.[18] The side poles could be of the same type, or forked by natural branching. There were altogether 21 poles plus the extra poles for the kitchen niches.

The side cloths, three in all, were patterned in the same way, starting from the top with a narrow piece of black woven cloth, followed by one with black-and-white stripes, and then a bright white canvas cloth, followed by a greyish piece, on top of which stones were placed to stabilize the tent.

Peculiar to this tent was the way in which the kitchen openings were made by means of two extra and shorter forked poles, some 120 cm long, which held the third side cloth free of the roof cloth around the hearths.[19]

The pins used to fasten the side cloths to the underside of the velum were usually of wood or iron skewers with an eye.

To sum up, the Al Na'im tent was particularly roomy and house-like, a specific type of a very uniform construction and appearance. Variations in structure and appearance did not appear to exist.[20] Most interesting is the fact that this tent type was photographed by the German geographer Hermann Burchardt on his journey from Hufuf in al-Hasa to Dohah in 1904; it had the same kitchen niche and even such details as the guy-rope beckets.[21] The caption reads: 'Tent of bedouins, who in the winter live as nomads and in the summer by pearl-fishing'. On this photo in the catalogue of Burchardt's photos in the Museum für Völkerkunde, Berlin, it says: 'Oars placed up against the tent'.[22] This photo appears to have been taken in a settlement close to the coast with *barastîs* seen in the background, most probably in Qatar (see Plate 33).

It thus seems that this tent type is of considerable age, specific to the local Qatari bedouin, and probably also the villagers and seminomads, who traditionally spent the winter and spring season in the interior grazing with their animals.[23] To this category the shaykhly families of Qatar also belonged. In 1959 it was customary for them to establish winter camps in the desert with their animals after the winter rains had fallen. Their tents belonged functionally and structurally to the same stationary and closed type with a kitchen niche as the other tents of north Qatar. One of the tents was sixpoled and measured approximately 8 by 20 m, with 1.5 m extra in width at the kitchen niche—the biggest tent we saw in Qatar.[24]

The Al Murrah tent in southern Qatar

The south Qatari tent (see Plate 34) consists of the same main elements as the tent in North Qatar. These are:

- the velum with its fast-sewn woven transverse girths on the underside, supported by
- tentpoles in series of three across the length of the tent, the centre poles supporting two wooden beams, sewn into the velum, while the side-poles run up to loops of rope issuing from wooden beckets, which are sewn into the ends of the girths. From these loops run
- guy ropes, which end in
- iron tent-pegs driven into the sand. When these elements are established in a correct balance, the structure stands, and is completed with
- two side-cloths which are pinned together in the middle of the back of the tent and extend from that point to cover the back and ends of the tent. The side-cloths are fastened under the edges of the velum with

- eyed iron skewers, sometimes tied to each other by a cord, to prevent one of them being lost in the sand. The same cord keeps them together during camp-movement. The side-cloths consist of 3–4 widths of material in various patterns, and are weighted to the ground with
- sand. Finally there can be
- one or perhaps two woven partition curtains, normally beautifully patterned in many colours, to divide the tent up into two or three sections.[25]

From our first visit to Al Murrah camps in south Qatar, the differences between their tents and those of the Al Na'im of north Qatar were evident, as explained above. Special differences from the Al Na'im tents were

- the wooden becket in the edge of the velum was a straight stick, wound around with, and sewn fast to, the woven girth which runs under the velum;
- a short rope was fastened to the free ends of the becket, forming a loop, to which guy-ropes of old telephone or detonating cable were tied;[26]
- the guy-rope was tied to a long iron tent-peg, driven deep into the sand, while Al Na'im, as described, in their stony region normally made use of stones buried in the ground to anchor their guy-ropes;
- two relatively short parallel poles were sewn into folds in the velum as ridgebeams,[27] and that there was extra reinforcement under them where the tent-pole met them;
- some of the tents had no side-poles on the rear and at the corners, or rather they had an irregular erection of side and corner poles, where they were fastened at these points. The wall-cloths were in consequence not so high as those of Al Na'im, normally only about 1 metre;
- the girths were not sewn fast in their whole length under the velum, but only in the middle and at the edges.[28]

Such were the Al Murrah tents in the group with which we particularly associated. We also met the open tent-front among other groups of Al Murrah, a feature, moreover, which is normal among other bedouin.[29] But one Al Murrah tent-group, which had a more traditional economic basis with both flocks and camels, did not have quite such open tents. An extra side-cloth (or the end-cloth at the other end, or both) was so long that it could be brought around at the front, and screened off both the guest and the family sections. It was tied fast to the guy-ropes. In another camp we saw how the dividing curtain could be extended well out on the front side, to provide extra screening when it was needed. Both features are also found among Al Murrah just south of the Qatar frontier.[30]

In yet other features, the Al Murrah tent closely resembles other Arab bedouin tents, for example in the use of ridge-poles sewn into place and the special arrangement of the side and corner attachments. Here there is, for example, close conformity to the Kuwaiti tent at Moesgaard Museum, and to the illustrations in Dickson, who does not show, however, the use of sewn-in beams.[31] The completely open tent type is similarly a widespread Arab type, which in most places, and locally in Qatar, seems to be associated with camel-herding and frequent movement. In contrast, the situation in north Qatar seems to show that the closed tent type is associated with very limited migratory activity, and is adapted to sheep and goat-keeping in the cool season of the year. A noticeable difference was, moreover, that the south Qatari tents were in general smaller than in the north; with a single exception, they were exclusively two-poled tents, while for example three-poled tents were those we most commonly observed in north Qatar.

Among the Al Murrah in south Qatar we observed the temporary erection of tents in connection with camp movements to give shade from the sun, whereas yet other 'tents' were erected as open windbreaks (with lee to the south), consisting of a side-cloth hung upon an edge-rope supported by three to four tent-poles about

1 metre high and sloping inward, balanced by the counterweight of ropes pegged to the ground on the outer side.[32]

Use of tent-cloth windbreaks is also recorded from northern Arabia and among the Saar tribe south of the Rub al-Khali, and is in addition known among the Pashtuns in East Afghanistan.[33] It is undoubtedly a widely used practice.

Tent types in Qatar: conclusions

From the above it is clear that tents in Qatar belong to two related but distinct types. How should we interpret and explain this?

First, it can be stated that the enclosed, ridge-roofed, house-like tent is not peculiar to Al Na'im but common to people with short and especially infrequent migrations in northern Qatar, people who admittedly live in or use tents, but who are highly stationary. We have also seen such tents in use with the family of the Al Thani shaykhs, possibly also with bedouin such as the Bani Hajir in central Qatar. In the light of the photograph taken by Burchardt at the beginning of the century, we may conclude that this tent type is of considerable age in the area. The photo appears to have been taken in a settlement close to the coast, possibly at the bay of Salwa in al-Hasa or more likely further north in Qatar proper. It is precisely in these surroundings, with adaptation to short-range pastoral nomadism in the interior and to pearl fishing in the sea, that I suggest this specific tent type developed. Structurally, it is clearly an Arab bedouin tent, but with its ridge-beam arrangement and especially with its enclosed character it has points of affinity with tents within the Persian and Afghan cultural sphere. In the light of the discussion of the tent in south Qatar, we may conclude that the enclosed, or partially enclosed tent, is found particularly where sheep and goat-keeping are prominent. Similar tents are known in many areas in the Middle East where flock-keeping predominates, but also where the climate is generally cooler, as for example in both Iran and Afghanistan.[34] will not pursue this point here, as it is not the place for a general discussion of the 'black' tent.

Turning to the Al Murrah tent, it has been demonstrated that the Al Murrah tent has decisive points of similarity with, for example, the Kuwaiti and other north Arabian tents, whereas there are, as seen, decisive differences between the Al Na'im tent and the Al Murrah tent. From the available evidence it is not clear whether the Al Na'im once had another tent type (an ordinary south Arabian desert bedouin tent like the Al Murrah) or whether they have had their present tent type for a long time.

In Anie Montigny's general survey of Al Na'im nomadism, she describes an entirely traditional bedouin society, with the emphasis laid upon the prestige animals, the camel and the horse.[35] She furthermore describes how sheep and goats are kept to supply a broader economic foundation, but makes no mention of the use of donkeys or cows.[36] She emphasizes the importance of hunting, however, as a supplementary occupation. This it undoubtedly was at one time, for we know that the Al Na'im came from the south. Around 1860 they came to the Zubarah area from the southernmost part of the Qatar peninsula, where had they lived earlier in the nineteenth century and from where seasonal migrations started towards north-western Qatar. Could it be that the Al Na'im were once ordinary south Arabian desert bedouin with a tent of the type used among the Al Murrah and many others? That they acquired the tents they have today while adapting to local conditions in north Qatar and by taking over the features in common use in the more enclosed local form of tent?

I cannot answer this question. It is also possible that, before they came to Qatar, the Al Na'im already had this tent specific to the dialectical and cultural area in the Gulf littoral. Lorimer reports that they came from Trucial Oman, which supports this possibility.[37]

The material culture of the bedouin of Qatar: an overview

Material objects provide immediate information about a culture and the way it adjusts to its environment. This includes its dependence on external supplies and its technical ability.

The tools used by the bedouin primarily concern the processing of their own materials such as skins and hides, animal and plant fibres, and wood. They are few, usually not very specific, and used by both men and women. This is the case with sewing needles for clothes and thicker needles for sewing tent cloth and bags, etc., simple multi-purpose knives, an axe or axe-adze for woodwork, etc., iron awls and bodkins for leather work, special tools for weaving, such as the gazelle-horn weaving-hook. Most of the tools are purchased from the *sûq*.

Apart from metal articles and more specialized items such as saddle-bow wood, the bedouin themselves produce most of the equipment used in cattle breeding. They also make most of the leather articles, both women and men being involved in the work. The skin used was from goat, sheep, gazelle, camel and lizard. The tools were simple knives for cleaning and preparing the skins, iron bodkins, and plant fibres and leather strings for sewing. The artefacts comprise: water and churning skins; gazelle-skin bags; various skin containers or bags, mostly made of camel skin; water scoops; camel watering troughs; and leather cradles. Other items using leather include camel-riding saddles, coiled baskets and men's accoutrements.

Generally speaking, the form and production of the leather articles are very functional. Characteristically, most are for storage or transportation of everyday necessities and objects, such as water and milk products, flour, rice, coffee or clothes. All these materials adapt to the space into which they are put, so that many containers only have rather small openings or 'necks' through which they are filled and emptied. Another characteristic feature is that many containers are shaped so as to 'imitate' a whole skin, which means they have a familiar shape one was accustomed to handle. A further feature of these articles, and a variety of woven bags, is that they are provided with loops or eyes made of leather straps, rope, or detonator wire, to facilitate hanging, and to enable the articles to be easily fastened to the pack saddles for transportation.

The functional aspect is also evident in the way in which the raw material is used in the actual production process. When sheep and goats are skinned, the skins, if possible, come off in one piece, as seen in the case of water and churning skins. A cut is made on the back of the hind legs close to the hoofs so that the skin can be pulled off and parted from the carcass at the neck, thus leaving the neck and front legs intact, while the hind legs are partly or completely cut.[38] A further advantage of this method is that the skin can easily be closed at the front legs and neck and have an opening as large as the full width of the animal's body. Using a slightly different method of cutting, the skin of the hind legs (cut or plaited) may be used as handles, as in open skin bags from Abu Dhabi.[39] This illustrates well the point of keeping the skin as complete as possible. Another example of this is provided by the open bag with handles from the Al Awamir tribe in south Qatar.[40] The sides of the skin have been cut into shreds which have been plaited into loops, to which the handle has been tied or 'spliced'. A similar, functional way of making handles is found in the large camel-skin bags.[41] It seems obvious that the result of the method employed is a strong and secure handle, an important fact when it comes to transportation. Whole pieces of skin which have been cut into a circular shape are also used. The water scoops are examples of this.[42]

Ordinary tacking stitches, with one piece of skin on top of another, are always used for skin and leatherwork. In sewing the camel watering-trough a kind of 'figure' sewing has given the bottom its shape. Water and churning skins must not leak, therefore repairs are common, most commonly stitched-on round patches; a different type is when a cotton-cloth plug has been used to seal a hole. In materials from Abu Dhabi there is a more elaborate case in which, in addition to sewn-on flat patches, a ligature of pieces of wood with strips of cotton cloth has been used, so that it protrudes from the skins.[43] Yet another closing technique is when a plaited ring of plant material is tied around the teats, or around the skin of the front legs.[44]

It is a common feature that all closed containers made of whole skins which are used for storage of water or milk products have the smooth side of the skin on the outside. One reason for this is presumably that it is more practical during transportation and when handling the skins. Another reason may be that natural evaporation produces a desirable cooling effect. It is, incidentally, also a common practice to protect the skin from the ground by placing it on stones or a piece of cloth or even to provide the water bag with a canvas cover.

The smooth side of the skin is on the inside, however, in open containers such as the camel watering trough or water scoops;[45] this facilitates the flow of water and may also improve water-tightness. All other containers, whether closed containers such as skin bags for storing clothes, small carrying-bags, large open camel-skin bags or leather cradles also have the smooth side of the skin on the inside.[46] As already suggested, this may be explained in functional and practical terms. It facilitates putting things in or taking them out, whether clothes, grass-hoppers or other food items or indeed a baby, in which case the smooth surface also facilitates cleaning.

The methods employed in leather plaiting correspond to the methods used for textiles. In 1959 I checked the leatherwork of the Al Murrah in Qatar with reference to Dickson's illustrations, and concluded that only one object had fallen out of use: the large camel-skin water container used for camel transport.[47] It had been replaced by a more handy container made from the inner tube of a car tyre. Other groups used the smaller water bag made of sheep-skin or goat-skin. Camel-skin watering troughs were in use alongside a new type made of rubber tube cut into one or two pieces, stretched out with string and rope over a framework of wooden arches.[48] This recent form has been further developed, becoming heavier and much larger, and transported on pick-up trucks, as mentioned by Webster.[49] Specific was the portable leather cradle of a form used widely, from Yemen in the south, through Saudi Arabia to Kuwait.

The bedouin themselves do not braid items from palm-leaf material, but buy them in the *sûq* or (formerly) presumably from al-Hasa oasis. Braiding in which leather and yarn are used for decoration or for ropes is usually carried out by women. Coiled baskets, partly leather-covered by the bedouin themselves, were typical containers for large or small kitchen utensils among the Al Murrah. They acquired the baskets from oasis areas.

Textiles and weaving

In Qatar the following fibres were used: sheep wool, goat hair, camel hair, and palm-tree fibres, presumably from the wild dwarf fan palm as well as the cultivated date palm. All materials may be used for making rope and string.

Sheep wool was used for woven transport bags, saddle bags and blankets, bags, ornamental bands for camels and saddles, woven carpets, certain decorative trimmings, and occasionally for tent velum and formerly for clothing such as cloaks.

Goat hair was important, being the material predominantly used for the woven tent cloth, especially the roof velum. It is stronger and more weatherproof than sheep wool which, however, according to Dickson may be mixed with goat hair in the tent velum. I never noticed the use of this mixed material in Qatar. Goat hair was also used for borders in woven carpets and for ornamental bands, saddle girths and woven ropes, places where strength was appropriate.

Camel hair generally exhibits the same qualities as sheep wool but is usually softer and insulates better. It was used for needle-netted socks, udder covers and bands, saddle bags and blankets, and for panniers, often to give a decorative effect with its specific shades of beige.

Palm fibres were used for rope, for sewing in leather, for leather repairs, and as filling in, for example saddle cushions. For the making of rope, imported materials such as coir and jute were used instead.

The use of cotton is relatively old in the Gulf. In the early days it was grown in Oman. It is nowadays bought in the *sûq* as yarn and is used as warp in woven bags and for the white parts of the tent side-cloths, for braided bands, and as weft in double-twined bands. It is further bought as cotton cloth or ready-made clothing for women and men.

For weaving, the bedouin of Qatar use two types of loom: first, a plain loom or backstrap loom or, for long bands, a horizontal ground loom; secondly, a horizontal loom, mounted as a ground loom.[50]

Material culture of the nomads of Qatar: conclusion

In 1959, the dependence of Qatari bedouin in their material culture on objects and materials acquired from outside was very obvious. But these objects were just as 'bedouin' as those they made themselves. This pattern follows centuries-old traditions in the Middle East of mutual dependence between pastoral nomads, agricultural villagers, and city-dwellers.[51] Influences that came with the greater wealth and increased purchasing power brought by oil, operated within this pattern.

In 1959, modernization was particularly evident in the objects purchased in the *sûq*. These could be anything of metal, whether iron, copper, or brass, such as had also more traditionally been known and acquired from outside, ultimately from the respective smiths who formerly were often itinerant. But many traditional objects had practically disappeared. Finely crafted products in copper or brass were on the whole no longer found, and only used in the prestigious coffee-making or in women's traditional silver jewellery and men's splendidly decorated silver daggers.

Ordinary kitchen utensils, used for cooking, storing and serving, were everywhere factory-made articles of aluminium imported from India, or imported enamelware, especially for teapots, plates, dishes and bowls to eat and drink from. These imports had replaced the wooden articles of kitchen equipment and camel milking of earlier days.

Silver jewellery was all traditional in shape and workmanship and was also obtained in town *sûqs*, particularly those of Saudi Arabia. In the *sûq* of Dohah, Indian goldsmiths had become dominant. None of the earlier itinerant blacksmiths, weapon-smiths, and silversmiths were left in Qatar in 1959.

Mats and baskets typically came from areas of date-palm oases, as in al-Hasa in Saudi Arabia, or through import via Dohah.

Clothing was all, or almost all, directly or, by way of gifts from the shaykh, indirectly from the *sûq*. Qatari bedouin women's contribution consisted primarily of the actual sewing of clothing and the characteristic embroidery upon dresses.

A large category was the bedouin's own textile products, comprising items such as woven bags and sacks, camel-blankets and tent-cloth. In this category there was a notable similarity in the techniques used, and a notable difference in the repertoire of objects produced, between north and south Qatar. The materials, wool and hair, were the same in both areas, but with different emphasis, dependent upon the presence of the respective domestic animals from which they came. It is thus not surprising that camel hair was most common in south Qatar, as were knot-looped camel-hair socks, which were unique to the sandy regions of south Arabia. Darn-woven udder covers were not seen among the Al Na'im, but were normally widespread among south Arabian camel-bedouin. Ordinary tabby-weaving on a horizontal loom was known both among Al Na'im and Al Murrah, for example for tent-cloth and in various more complicated forms, where ordinary tabby-weave alternated with patterned sections. Similarly, the technique of double braiding was known in both areas, just as they had the same broad range of textile techniques, though perhaps the Al Murrah, through their wider contacts with settled societies and other bedouin tribes, possessed a greater variation than was the case with the locally-wandering Al Na'im. The bedouin also acquired woven articles from outside, such as tent-cloth and many other items in daily use. Among the southern Qatari bedouin this was seen in the adornment of their camels and their saddles, in which many different textile techniques appeared.

Wooden objects included tent-poles, manufactured either domestically from natural branches or from cut planks of imported timber (mostly among Al Murrah) or flotsam (mostly among Al Na'im). Natural wooden poles were also bent and fashioned into frames for watering-troughs, women's saddles, and holders for kitchen equipment. All these objects in use among the south Qatari bedouin were unlikely to originate from local wood. Even the woodwork in ordinary riding and pack-saddles and in litters was not manufactured in Qatar, but came from Saudi Arabia, and normally from specialists in towns or villages. The *al-hawlânî* riding saddles, on the other hand, came from Oman or Abu Dhabi.

Leather articles were few among Al Na'im in the north, while there was a profusion in the south among Al Murrah and Al Awamir. The bedouin themselves produced this leatherwork, which technically appeared well made, like objects imported from specialists in Saudi Arabia, such as water-skins, and thus belonging to the same tradition. The way in which the natural form of the animal's skin was exploited in shaping handles and apertures is worthy of mention; but in this connection it is interesting that a number of leather containers were cut and sewn as improved versions of containers made from natural whole skins. In short, it was a form considered as practical, which had attained an aesthetic and cultural value through its decorative shape.

It is important to add that all these objects were produced for transport by camel, that is, they can be said to be specialized bedouin, or perhaps more specifically South Arabian products. This is confirmed, by their identical techniques and craftsmanship. The method used by the Al Na'im woman in sewing together a skin churn or a water-skin was the same as that used for water-skins among Al Murrah and in Abu Dhabi. It is a manifestation of a common cultural tradition, overriding local differences.

The varied use of objects entirely or partly made from hides and skins recalls how much more prominent those materials once were for clothing too,[52] remnants of which can still be observed among south Arabian bedouin.[53] The materials seen in Qatar are but a faint reflection of an earlier 'leather-culture'.

During the fieldwork we experienced how various social situations found various means of expression through the material culture. This applied to dress, for both men and women, but more particularly for men when acting as representatives or appearing in public, as on formal visits or during camp-moving. Camp-moving had a ritualized and public character; the people, their camels, and in particular their belongings were on display. Especially among the Al Murrah camel-bedouin, the men wore many layers of their finest clothing, almost always finished off by the south Arabian silver-mounted curved dagger, a special leather belt with a cartridge bandolier as adornment, a rifle in a cover on the shoulder or stuck in the camel's riding-saddle, and—to round off the picture—a falcon on their sleeve-cuff. All in all, it was an imposing display of what bedouin prized most in basic masculine values, partly of a warrior character. The *saluqi,* running close to its master, has its place in this assembly of status-symbols, but is not so obviously on show; whereas the highly prized camels, colourfully adorned with woven bands and rugs, bore witness to the women's skills. Finally, the saddles, particularly the litters, coloured, decorated and hung with ribbons, could be seen and admired for miles.

These are impressions culled from the Al Murrah of south Qatar, but I believe that camp movements among Al Na'im in the north followed a similar pattern, evident, for example, in the women wearing their black *'abayahs.* But lorries and donkeys had hardly the same display value as the camel caravans of the south, though I do not doubt that the use of a lorry in itself involved a change in values, symbolizing modernity and a new aspect of wealth in addition to its practical significance. More recently still, we can see how, in Saudi Arabia among the Al Murrah, caravans and camel-trains have been completely replaced by the pick-up truck, even for transporting the camels and their foals during migration.[54]

As regards the rest of the material culture, the bedouin of north and south Qatar seemed to differ very much. Differing patterns of migration and differences in livestock composition undoubtedly lay behind this impression, but the local social context also differed. Together, these factors resulted in a definitely settled aspect among the northern bedouin, as the modern form of migration by lorry made it possible to accumulate more and more 'non-nomadic' features, such as primus-stoves, hurricane- and oil-lamps with the requisite fuel, 'buckets' made from automobile tyres, sawn-up timber as fuel, all features which brought a new dependence on the outside. Particularly space-consuming were oil-drums and water-jars in wooden stands, which required special conditions for transport.[55]

Looked at more closely, both areas proved to be in reality far advanced along the road to 'modernization'. Whatever could be easily used was incorporated into daily life. In the south, it was a question of electric cables as guy-ropes, inner tubes for water, and the rubber from the inner-tubes as lining for the camels' watering troughs, as well as sawn-up timber for tent-poles, though this was mainly used in the north. Certainly, in both north and south Qatar, all objects of aluminium and enamel proved to be merely new versions, in new materials, of articles which had always been acquired from outside. However, tinned copper cauldrons and other copper utensils, together with certain wooden objects, had gone out of use, and these traditional materials were now employed only in the form of prestigious coffee-pots. Already in the 1930s, and undoubtedly even earlier, the coffee-mortar had been found in both brass and cast-iron versions.[56] In earlier times in this area, the teapot (originally also a water-kettle) was made of tinned copper, but it never had the same prestige and status as the coffee-pot; in 1959 it had been replaced by either the aluminium kettle, imported from India, or the 'fine' new enamel teapot. Only the enamel teapot was seen in use at the shaykhs' places of reception.[57]

To summarize, in south Qatar modernization resulted in equipment adhering to a comparatively traditional way of life, whereas in north Qatar the changes were greater, and involved the introduction of articles and materials fundamentally foreign to the traditional nomadic way of life.

If we turn finally to the camps of the shaykhs, we see that their equipment included an abundance of imported articles coming from the *sûq,* actually all the conveniences of settled life. No limits were set by pecuniary or transport considerations where pick-ups and comfortable limousines were at hand, only the desires and conceptions of what was appropriate to this special version of part-time bedouin life. But behind, and on another level, lay the inherited cultural values and the traditional social order, with its triballyorganized leadership related to an earlier, more purely pastoral nomadic existence.

To place the situation in 1959 in a wider historical context, it is quite clear that we witnessed a form of nomadism which was in north Qatar in the middle, and in south Qatar on the threshold, of profound changes, settlement being the aim of government, and an aim that soon was realised. Systematic state settlements of the bedouin of Qatar began in 1960.[58] But attachment to the desert is still strong in Qatar, as can be seen in the desert picnics of 'weekend' bedouin.[59] What we saw was a final blooming of an age-old way of living.

In the light of the conditions we encountered in Qatar, and which are known from other parts of Arabia in modern times, the old question of whether nomads can live without contact with settled communities takes on a purely theoretical colouring. In 1959 and previously, these bedouin lived in quite intimate contact with their settled neighbours, and traditionally earned extra income from work in the pearl fisheries, or as watchmen in the coastal fishing towns in the summer, or by plundering.

Qatar's shaykh, or the state, have alleviated the burden of this dependence on outside contacts by introducing maintenance payments and gifts. As stated earlier, these may be regarded as a way of ensuring and temporarily stabilizing bedouin life. The bedouin might possibly be able to subsist from their animals and their products and on hunting and gathering, without outside contacts, but this has probably not been practised in the Middle East for millennia. Furthermore, such a way of life would differ significantly from the bedouin culture of both today and the past.

The bedouin's own products were predominantly connected with their traditional occupations, animal husbandry and hunting.

The nomads of Afghanistan

Nomads in Afghanistan belong, except for the Hindi-speaking Gujar, to two great cultural traditions, the Central Asian tradition of the felt-covered 'yurt' and related tent forms with self-supporting wooden frames, and the West Asian tradition of the 'black tent' or guyed tent of woven cloth with guy-rope suspension. The former is found among Turkic and Turkish influenced groups in north and north-central Afghanistan, for instance the northern Aimaqs, whereas the 'black tent' is found exclusively among peoples speaking Iranian languages, such as Pashtuns, Baluches, and Persian-speaking southern and western Aimaqs. In the following I survey the three types of guyed tents, and some other cultural phenomena encountered among the two major divisions of Pashtun pastoral nomads, and the semi-nomadic Taimani Aimaq.

The Pashtun nomads belong traditionally to the eastern, southern and south-western parts of Afghanistan. From there they moved, initially at government initiative, to north-western and northern areas of the country. In consequence, the nomads have formed a ring around the central and east Afghan highlands, where they spend the summer, with their winter camps in the surrounding steppes and low-lying mountain valleys, or in the far east beyond the Durand Line towards the valley of the Indus.[60]

Broadly speaking, the Pashtun nomads fall into two large ethnogeographic divisions: the mainly Ghilzai tribes of the east, and the Durrani and 'Durranized' tribes of the south and west. On a number of points the Ghilzai and Durrani differ culturally and socially from each other. The Durrani have generally a purer pastoral economy than have the Ghilzai, but on the other hand the settled and nomadic populations are not so sharply separated as among the Ghilzai, and semi-sedentary and semi-nomadic ways of life are common. Over the years movements from agriculture towards nomadism and vice versa are quite frequent, for example in response to climatic changes. This fluctuation is only possible because the Durrani have a double cultural heritage, comprising both agriculture and nomadic pastoralism, and within the same family one may meet both farmers and pastoral nomads; the latter thus have easier access to agricultural products such as wheat, which, in the form of bread, is the stable food of all Afghan nomads. Many settled Durrani thus own tents, and may live in them for part of the year for the sake of grazing their animals.

The Durrani have a number of cultural traits which distinguish them from the Ghilzai: for example, tent type, camel saddle, butter churn., type of felt cloak and shoes, and a more pronounced handicraft tradition (weaving of tent-cloth, rugs and carpets) which means they are more self-sufficient in regard to artisan products. Hunting also plays a somewhat more important role among them, while they have not developed the same trading activities as the Ghilzai and others in eastern Afghanistan, perhaps because in their traditional areas in the steppes to the south and west, and on their migrations to the mountains, there was little opportunity for trade.

The Ghilzai nomads are, or have over the years become, far more specialized, and their culture thrives in a context of trade. They have always migrated through areas inhabited by developed settled communities, with a distinct division of labour involving specialized craftsmen. They adapted to this network of economic relationships: from the peasants they obtain a number of essential food products, from the artisans and traders of the villages and towns they acquire goods such as wooden kitchen utensils, earthen- and ironware. They may also be served by itinerant craftsmen, for example carders and weavers, who produce their tent-cloth. In return the Ghilzai nomads can supply raw materials in the form of milk products, wool, animals for slaughter, and to a limited extent felt rugs. Besides, they themselves have often operated as traders: many of them have migrated from 'time immemorial' between the Indus country and the eastern Afghan highlands, bringing trade goods with them.

Nomadism among the Ghilzai in eastern Afghanistan falls into a number of types which can be viewed as continuum of adaptations: at one end are nomads who do occasional labour for farmers and villagers ('poor man's work'); at the other are traders; in between are true pastoral nomads who also engage in some transport work.

Not much is known of nomadism in Afghanistan in the past. For sure, before the Hazarajat in central Afghanistan was opened to them in the 1890s, eastern Afghan nomads stayed within their own area and had shorter movements. The one-humped camel has always played an important role in heavy transport, and in certain areas it is also used by villagers; the nomads used camels for long migrations, and donkeys and to some extent bullocks and cows for more restricted movements. At the beginning of this century, with the opening of the Hazarajat, the nomads increasingly adopted the camel, but with recent developments such as growing sedentarization and the passing away of the caravan trade in central Afghanistan, the eastern nomads have resumed shorter migrations with the use of donkeys and cows.

When we look at the inventory of things used by these nomads, little has changed, except for the specific equipment used. The eastern Afghan nomads are astonishingly specialized and dependent. Their most important food is bread, the flour for which (maize or wheat) must be obtained from farmers or the city bazaar. A glance round the nomad tent shows their dependence on specialised craftsmen of many kinds: the tent-cloth and some of the transport sacks are woven from the nomads' home-spun thread by itinerant Pashtun weavers, mostly of a settled background. Wooden bows for the camel-saddles, iron objects in general, camel bits, tent pegs, kitchen utensils (whether of wood, iron or other metals, or occasionally of clay), are all obtained from city bazaars or village craftsmen, as are most clothes (primarily of cotton) and ornaments.

The nomads' own products are few, some made of wild plant materials, but most connected with animal breeding. They consist of felt rugs, saddle-blankets and cloaks likewise of felt, woven materials among some, skin storage sacks (for water, clarified butter, flour) and butter churns, woollen ropes, open containers made of rope and thread. These are by and large made by women, who do most of the daily work: preparing food and milk products, sewing clothes, fetching water, pitching the tent, loading and unloading the camels. Men's work seems considerably easier: tending and (partly) milking the animals, helping the women in the heavier labour, and most important, handling all outward relations in trade or politics. This sexual division of labour and other activities is the same, with minor variations, as found among other nomads of the Middle East.

The third group are the semi-nomadic semi-sedentary Taimani Aimaqs living in Ghor, south of the Hari Rud river in south-west central Afghanistan. They combine irrigated farming and extensive dry-farming of wheat and barley with sheep breeding. From their villages they move to summer camps in the mountains, or just to nearby fallow fields where they pitch their black tents. Culturally, they have few specialized artisans but quite active domestic production of felt and woven articles, and a special type of bottle-like container (for clarified butter) made of a decoction of *eremurus* roots, whereas they usually get metalware from Qandahar or Herat.

Among the Taimani, like the Pashtun nomads of eastern and southern-western Afghanistan, the material culture of the nomads has much in common with that of the local settled population of the villages and towns. It is thus appropriate to talk of the material culture specific to an area. In several instances Durrani cultural traits match those of the Taimani Aimaq of Ghor. In others, such as tents, their distinct identity is clear.

Tent types in Afghanistan: the Durrani tent

The nomadic 'black tents' or 'guyed tents' found among the Durrani of southern and western Afghanistan and in neighbouring Baluchistan evince obvious similarities (see Plate 35). They have

- hoops at right angles to the longitudinal direction of the cloth;
- in general, merely short forked tent sticks at the narrow ends;
- a highly uniform stay system with stay fasteners and stay fastener ropes.
- Furthermore the wall-cloths are fastened on by small, unconnected wooden skewers; and
- plaited mats are used in the winter and spring tents to a considerable degree.

Within this broad region the tent sub-types form a continuum. The long-range Durrani nomads have the lightest construction with one hoop in their winter and spring tent;[61] the short-range semi-nomadic Durrani may have a double barrel-vaulted construction;[62] various short-range Baluch (and Baluch-influenced) nomads have three to seven vaults in their winter tent, and only two in their summer tent;[63] finally, barrel-vaulted, mat-covered tents or huts are structurally related to a variety of barrel-vaulted hut types made of plant materials found as far west as the sedentary, semi-sedentary and semi-nomadic groups in southern parts of the Iranian provinces of Baluchistan and Kerman.[64] The cloth tent belongs primarily among the true nomads (at least to the north), and the mat tent-hut among semi-nomads (at least in southern and western groups).

The greater the demand for mobility, the fewer vaults are found in the structure; in the tents of long-range Durrani nomads there is only a single hoop or vault, which can even be changed to a lighter T-structure, when the lower piece of the hoop is replaced by light forked sticks under the stay-fastening rope. When the top beam in the T-structure is not put up, as often happens during migration, the tent appears to be of a pointed type with a completely different structure, resembling the so-called Sistan tent, or Gafferberg's *gedan* type.[65] The Durrani tent is thus close to becoming another 'type'. I see this as a case of functional adaptation in operation in an area with a strong tradition of barrel-vaulted structures.

The eastern Afghan tent

The eastern Afghan tent has an easily recognizable form (see Plate 36), with in most cases 9 to 12 (up to 15) poles visible as peaks in the velum; the tent poles are arranged in sets of three across the tent, and in three rows along the length, with the central row being the highest and the 'centre' pole, or pair of poles, being the highest of all. Furthermore, one can recognize that, besides the velum supported by the poles, the tent normally has four sloping side-or end-cloths, fastened under its edges with iron skewers or pins connected by a woollen string. The guy-ropes, and in some cases the reinforcing bolt ropes, are usually visible under these sloping side/end-cloths, as they run from purchase-loops in the edges of the velum down to the wooden or iron tent pegs. A low mud wall may surround the tent.

The appearance thus reflects the basic structural elements of the tent: the velum or roof-cloth resting upon the tent poles and kept in balance by the guy-ropes fastened to strong loops at its edges and attached to tent pegs at the other end. The tent is thus a typical example of so-called 'black tents' within the wider group of 'guyed tents'.

In sum, the eastern Afghan nomad tent is highly uniform in structure and appearance within its area of distribution. It is also noteworthy that this tent appears to be completely unchanged since the time of the earliest photographs (1917).[66] Its age must be considerable; its range of variation is very limited. Variations are met when the tent is pitched hastily or haphazardly to make a short-lived shelter during migration, and smaller variations occur such as the sewing of the plaited loops for the guy-ropes to the top or the underside of the cloth, the sewing together of the selvedges in the central roof-cloth seam, or the use of open or closed peak-eyes in the velum. Such closure is especially a feature of very heavy tents.

It is further noteworthy that no intermediate forms have been found between the tents of eastern Afghanistan and those of the Baluch or the Durrani. These different types follow regional and tribal lines, as has been seen for the Qandahar region, with the single exception of a rather stationary group of Aka Khel weavers dwelling in multi-vaulted tents of the Baluchistan type.[67] One single trait, the use of wooden V-purchases among Taraki nomads wintering in the Qandahar region, is also common among the Durrani and the Baluch,[68] and may be an 'areal' cultural influence. In the Herat and Badghis areas of west and north-west Afghanistan, Ghilzai nomadic groups moved in towards the end of last century, adapted to dominant cultural traditions, took up the Durrani tent, and locally became 'Durranized'.[69] In northern Afghanistan, Pashtuns have adopted many local Turkistani traits, in dress for example, and the tent used there by the Durrani and 'Durranized' Ghilzais and others such as Moghols could almost be considered a Turkistani trait, whereas the Ghilzai nomads there still moving to the Hazarajat retain their eastern Afghan tent type.

It thus seems clear that in Afghanistan one should not operate with too rigid an idea of tribal and ethnic cultural traditions; regional traditions are in some respects stronger. The V-purchase just referred to I consider such a regional trait! The eastern Afghan tent type definitely belongs to a wider group of Afghan-Iranian and Arabian nomad tents using roof and side/end-cloths, but singled out by not having ridge bars (T-construction), either length-wise under the velum, as among the Taimani, Lor and other western Iranian groups, and in the Arabian tents,[70] or crosswise, as in the Durrani tent group.[71] The loops on the central velum seam appear to be peculiar to the eastern Afghan tent; their closest structural parallel seems to be in the Kurdish tents of north-western Iran, eastern Turkey and eastern Iraq—but this is not the place to go into wider comparisons.

A further characteristic of the eastern Afghan tent seems to be that it does not have the same capacity as the Durrani tent to adapt markedly in appearance or shape in response to seasonal and functional needs, apart from having bigger and smaller seasonal tents. Furthermore, to fulfil such needs, other structures and forms are substituted, as seen with the use of the *tsapar* or *kodei* winter huts. The basic structural difference between these huts and tents of the tension type is the rigid, self-supporting frame of the former, often of a barrel-vaulted construction.[72] It seems obvious that the structure of the *tsapar* has nothing to do with that of the eastern Afghan nomad tent. It is also obvious, however, that the interior arrangements of the winter hut and the tent are closely related. Many years ago I discussed in detail the relationship between barrel-vaulted hut structures and the tent types of Baluchistan and of the Durrani of south and west Afghanistan;[73] I must add here that at that time I was unaware of the existence of true barrel-vaulted *tsapar* structures in eastern Afghanistan. But at present I have no idea why the barrel-vaulted structure should have had no influence on the eastern Afghan tents, as it did on those of Baluchistan and the Durrani.

The Taimani tent

This tent is a specific type (see Plate 37). It is house-like in appearance, rectangular in form, with vertical walls and a low, gabled roof-cloth of dark brown woven goat hair. Structurally, it is a guyed tent with the velum firmly stretched over a wooden beam placed along the length of the cloth and held in balance by a becket-arrangement over seven to eight vertical tent poles at the long sides and five at the ends, and by tying the guys to wooden tent pegs in the ground. Three somewhat longer tent poles hold up the wooden beam. The tent is echoed in the simple, one-roomed, gable-roofed clay house found in the Taimani villages, which have the same internal arrangements.

When I first saw this tent it struck me as the closest one could imagine to Feilberg's hypothetical original 'black tent'.[74] Feilberg saw the gable-structure and the barrel-vault as the two basic structural principles behind the nomadic dwellings of the Middle East and Central Asia; these are, as we have seen, both found in rather close proximity within the area under consideration.

Locally the Taimani tent is called 'arabî, and it clearly has distinct structural resemblances to Arab bedouin tents, as well as to a variety of western Iranian tents (Lor, Bakhtiari and others). Functionally, this form confirms the position in Qatar and also in Baluchistan, that the enclosed and sturdy tent may be preferred by sheep- and goat-breeders with few and limited migrations.

What happens when the three Afghan tent types meet? The Durrani and the eastern Afghan tents meet in their winter area near Qandahar and in summer in the western Hazarajat, and both are found in northern Afghanistan. But these tents seem not to. mix, nor do the Durrani and the Taimani tents where they meet, further west in the Aimaq area, with a single exception.[75] Earlier I discussed the position in north-western Afghanistan, where the Ghilzai have adopted the Durrani tent. In most of northern Afghanistan the Durrani tent dominates among the Pashtuns, except where Ghilzai and other eastern nomads continue to use their traditional summer grazing lands in Hazarajat or towards Khawak in Upper Panjshir, where they meet their fellow-tribesmen coming from winter quarters in the east. Occasionally these northerners also shift over to winter in the east.

It seems to me that the tent type of the winter area is decisive in either maintaining or changing tradition. In other words the winter area can be considered culturally dominant, especially where the summer is spent in areas with other cultural traditions.

Concluding remarks

The material culture of pastoral nomads, as exemplified in this chapter, may be characterized as only partially specific to pastoral nomads as such.

1. They acquire most, or a large proportion, of their material objects from the people settled in the surrounding seasonal areas or during migration, especially from itinerant or village traders or from city bazaars and the like. To a great extent they acquire objects and materials peculiar to and in accordance with peoples of the same ethnic or tribal origin as themselves; but not exclusively so, as seen in summer areas in Afghanistan. But in general, their winter area appears to be decisive for their material equipment, tools, clothing/dress and their specific styles, foodstuffs, etc.

2. Specific to the nomads' material culture are objects connected with their economic life, particularly their animal breeding and migrations; these are primarily

   - in their dwellings: the guy-rope tent of woven goat-hair velum and ropes, bands and threads; and partially
   - in their transport gear: the riding and pack saddles, and arrangements for making objects portable through the use of ropes, strings and bands;
   - in their use, formerly extensive, of skin and leather containers and bags, and of materials woven for this purpose with threads, ropes and bands for pratical and/or decorative reasons; and finally

Plate 34 Al Murrah tent in southern Qatar (Jette Bang, 1959).

Plate 35 Durrani tent in summer area in Chaghcharan, Afghanistan, erected with one wooden hoop, seen where the side cloth is lifted up. In front a tripod for butter churning (Lennart Edelberg, 1953).

Plate 36 Eastern Afghan tents camped during the spring migration between Laghman and the Kabul area. The goats are collected for milking (Klaus Ferdinand, 1960).

Plate 37 Taimani camp with their typical house-like tents in summer camp (Klaus Ferdinand, 1960).

Plate 38 The loom on which screens are made consists of a horizontal bar on which the semi-rigid wefts are laid. Warp tension is maintained by stones. The stones also act as bobbins for storing the warp, which is unwound as work proceeds. This screen will be used as the wall of a black tent. The large number of stones used for this screen is to make the lattice pattern which, with alternating bands of reeds and willow wands, introduces a decorative element. Qala Kharawa, Kermanshahan, 1959 (courtesy of Patty-Jo Watson).

Plate 39 A *zilu* dated 1240 (1825 CE) of two-tier *saf* form (Meybod, 1984).

Plate 40 *Zilus* are woven on a large roller-beam loom, up to 20 feet wide. The weaver works standing and here has an assistant beating in the wefts (Meybod, 1984).

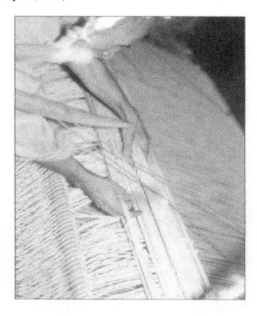

Plate 41 The pattern cords run transversely just above the weaver's head. Here he is selecting the appropriate cords for the field pattern. This is done entirely from memory.

Plate 42 Once the correct pattern cords have been chosen they are pulled forwards and held in place by two large wooden hooks. The rocker system that controls the harness for the structural warps frames the weaver's head. The heddle bars are moved by altering the position of the wooden bar behind his head. The two separate harnesses are clearly visible in Plate 14.

Plate 43 The inscription is woven 'freehand'. The weaver manipulates the 19 pattern cords as he goes along. Inscription bands (other than such motifs as repeating kufesque forms at the top of the field) always run in the warp direction. Thus the *saf* shown in Plate 39 has 16 niches side by side in two rows, a common arrangement, whereas others would have had many rows, perhaps four niches across (Meybod, 1984).

Plate 44 The key operation in drawloom weaving is making the *naqsheh,* a large-scale version of the pattern to be woven. When complete the 'warp' strings of the *naqsheh* (draw-cords or simplecords) are attached to the cross-cords on the loom, and the 'wefts' of the *naqsheh* (lashes) are pulled in sequence by the weaver's assistant, the draw-boy. The pull of the lashes is ultimately transmitted to the warpends on the loom to form the pattern shed. A *naqsheh* can take weeks to make and demands a high level of skill and concentration (Benares, 1992).

Plate 45 Three *naqshehs* attached to a loom. The vertical draw-cords are tied to the transverse cross-cords. Below the cross-cords are string heddles which control the warp ends running below and at right angles to the cross-cords. Behind the three *naqshehs* and running diagonally are three sets of draw-cords belonging to a Jacquard harness which is also being used to weave the same textile. The Jacquard punch cards are on the left (Benares, 1992).

Plate 46 Mohammed Afsari working at a design for the border of a large carpet, Kashmir, 1994.

Plate 47 Copying a *talim*. The *talim* system is efficient because it is much quicker to copy a *talim* than a cartoon (Srinagar, 1982, courtesy of Cary Wolinsky, Stock Boston).

Plate 48 Weaving from a written *talim,* in which the weaver's instruction is recorded in special notation (Srinagar, 1982, courtesy of Cary Wolinsky, Stock Boston).

Plate 49 Weaving from an electronic *talim*. The weaver's instruction is recorded elecronically on a memory chip and presented on liquid crystal displays and with coloured lights. After cutting each knot she presses a micro-switch on her knife to update the display. This system avoids the problem of weavers having to find their place every time they refer to the cartoon or *talim* (Tehran, 1993).

   – in their use of woven rugs and felts.

There is good reason to believe that pastoral nomad tent types are very stable in appearance and in structure, and this may have lasted for centuries. This I deduce from the above presentation and discussion of the Arabian and Afghan tent types, which show a marked uniformity and continuity in their distribution over both space and time. Within both regions dealt with here, the tents appear unchanged, even in detail, throughout the twentieth century, and no new types seem to have emerged.

The tent types appear to be specific both to area and to ethnic or tribal groups. The rule seems to be that the winter area of the dominant ethnic-tribal group is decisive in determining the tent type, and may decide an eventual change of tent type among other groups coming to the area.

The material culture of Middle Eastern pastoral nomads is thus another manifestation of the fact that a nomadic society does not constitute a distinct culture, and often not even a marked social unit in itself. It is a 'part-culture' and a 'part-society', with a very specific character reflecting its animal breeding and migratory life, whereas most of its other material culture is shared with its regional and ethnic-tribal surroundings.

Notes

1. See Klaus Ferdinand, *Bedouins of Qatar* (Carlsberg Foundation Nomad Research Project, Copenhagen/London and New York: Rhodos/Thames & Hudson, 1993) (based on ethnographic fieldwork in winter—spring 1959). Further references to BQ are to the figures and to the catalogue of objects in the book.
2. Bruce Ingham, 'Notes on the dialect of the Al Murra of Eastern and Southern Arabia', *BSOAS* 49 (2), 1980, p. 272.
3. Anie Montigny, 'Evolution d'un groupe bedouin dans un pays producteur de pétrole: le âl Na'im de Qatar' (These de 3e cycle, Université Paris V, 1985), pp. 51, 214.
4. BQ, Figs 6.25, 57, Cat. no. 50; H.R.P.Dickson, *The Arab of the Desert. A Glimpse into the Badawin Life in Kuwait and Sa'udi Arabia,* 2nd edn (London: Allen & Unwin, 1951), p. 85; Richard W.Bulliet, *The Camel and the Wheel* (New York: Columbia University Press, 1975; Morningside edition, 1990), pp. 87f.
5. BQ, Figs 4.8, 12, Cat.nos 52–53. Cf.Waher Dostal, *Die Beduinenin Sudarabien* (Wiener Beiträge zur Kulturgeschichte und Linguistik 16; Vienna: Horn, 1967), p. 12.
6. BQ, Fig. 7.7, Cat. no. 48a–d; cf. Figs 6.34, 36, 60. See Dostal, p. 12; Bulliet, pp. 87f.
7. BQ, Fig. 6.6, Cat. no. 47; see Figs 5.29 and 6.34.
8. J.G.Lorimer, *Gazetteer of the Persian Gulf, 'Omân and Central Arabia,* Vol. 2, Geographical and Statistical (Calcutta, 1908; repr., Farnborough: Gregg International and Shannon: Irish University Press, 1970), pp. 1516–30.
9. BQ, Figs 5.2, 6, 9, 39, 40, 42.
10. BQ, Figs 6.62, 63, 64, 67.
11. See, for example, Roger Martin Webster, 'Bedouin Settlements in Eastern Arabia' (unpublished PhD thesis, University of Exeter, 1987), p. 5, Fig. 9; Dickson, *Arab of the Desert,* pp. 67, 68, 70, 75 (with figures and plans of two-and three-poled tents); Donald Powell Cole, *Nomads of the Nomads: the Al Murrah Bedouin of the Empty Quarter* (Chicago: Aldine, 1975), p. 200; Ugo Fabietti, *Il popolo del Deserto. I Beduini Shammar del Gran Nefud Arabia Saudita* (Roma-Bari: Laterza, 1984), p. 70, Fig. 5; Sonia Gidal, *Beduinen im Negev. Eine Ausstellung der Sammlung Sonia Gidal* (München: Staatliches Museum für Völkerkunde,Wien: Museum für Völkerkunde, Mainz am Rhein: Verlag Philipp von Zabern, 1980), p. 64, Fig. 31.
12. BQ, Fig. 6.16 and others.
13. BQ, Figs 6.1–16.

14. Cf. Dickson, *Arab of the Desert,* pp. 66–107; C.G.Feilberg, *La Tente Noire. Contribution Ethnographique a l'Histoire Culturelle des Nomades* (Etnografisk række, 2, Copenhagen: Nationalmuseets skrifter, 1944), pp. 45f.; Alois Musil, *The Manners and Customs of the Rwala Bedouins* (New York: American Geographical Society, 1928), pp. 61–85; Shelagh Weir, *The Bedouin: Aspects of the Material Culture of the Bedouin of Jordan* (London: World of Islam Festival Publishing Company, 1976), pp. 1–6.

15. BQ, Fig. 6.12–13.

16. BQ, Figs 6.16, 18a, c.

17. BQ, Fig. 18b.

18. BQ, Fig.6.12.

19. BQ, Fig. 5.9.

20. Cf. photos by (and in the possession of) Peter A.Andrews from 1974 and Anie Montigny from 1978–82.

21. Exactly as depicted in BQ, Fig. 6.18b. Cf. Traugott Mann, *Der Islam einst und jetzt* (Bielefeld and Leipzig: von Velhagen und Klasing, 1914), p. 147, Fig. 159.

22. K 1591 No. 51/52. Cf. Hermann Burchardt, 'Ost-Arabien von Basra bis Maskat auf Grund eigener Reisen', *Zeitschrift der Gesellschaft für Erdkunde zu Berlin,* 1906, pp. 305–22.

23. Lorimer, Gazetteer, pp. 1305–6.

24. BQ, Figs 10.13–15a-b, 16–23.

25. BQ, Figs 5.32–4, 36–40, 42, 44, 77; 6.27, 29–31.

26. BQ, Figs 6.3, 19c.

27. BQ, Fig. 6.63, 66.

28. BQ, Fig. 6.62.

29. Cf. for example, Dickson, *Arab of the Desert,* pp. 68–70, figs;Weir, *Bedouin,* p. 2, Fig. 1, p. 14, Fig. 15; Fabietti, *Popolo,* p. 70, Fig. 5, p. 102, photo; and the survey of north Arabian tents by Ernst Rackow and Werner Caskel, *Das Beduinenzelt. Nordafrikanische und arabische Zelttypen mit besonderen Berücksichtigung des zentralalgerischen Zeltes* (Beiträge zur Völkerkunde 21, Berlin: Baessler-Archiv, 1938), pp. 170f., who classify them as a 'Windschirm' (windbreak) type.

30. BQ, Fig. 5.35; see Webster, 'Bedouin Settlements', p. 175, Fig. 9.

31. BQ, Cat. no. 187, Figs 9.159–160a-c; cf. Fig. 6.19a–c. Dickson, *Arab of the Desert,* p. 69. See also Rackow and Caskel, *Beduinenzelt,* pp. 174–5 and Tables 8–9, with photo and drawings of sewn-in beams and guy-rope beckets in tents of north Arabian *Grossnomaden,* e.g. of the 'Aneze and Shammar.

32. BQ, Figs 6.53–5.

33. Rackow and Caskel, *Beduinenzelt,* p. 180; Wilfred Thesiger, *Arabian Sands* (London: Collins, 1983, pp. 188–9.

34. See illustrations in Klaus Ferdinand, 'Ethnographical notes on Chahâr Aimâq, Hazâra and Moghôl', *Acta Orientalia* 28, 1964, pp. 175–203.

35. Montigny, 'Evolution', pp. 207f.

36. She comments that her description of animal breeding in connection with the movements within Al Na'im territory is a reconstruction based on what the Al Na'im themselves remembered and related; they never mentioned the use of cows and donkeys to her (personal communication, 30.12.1992).

37. See Lorimer, *Gazetteer,* p. 1532.

38. BQ, Cat. nos 58–61. Cf. photograph from Negev in Gidal, *Beduinen,* p. 52, Fig. 22.

39. BQ, Cat. nos 66–7.

40. BQ, Cat. no. 73.

41. BQ, Cat. nos 74–5.

42. BQ, Cat. nos 77–8.

43. As may be seen in BQ, Fig. 9.45.

44. As in BQ, see Fig. 9.43.

45. BQ, Cat. nos 76–9.

46. BQ, Cat. nos 69–71, 73, 74–5, 80–1.

47. Dickson, *Arab of the Desert,* p. 106: *thilaithi* and *minûn.*

48. BQ, Cat. no. 83; see Figs 6.37, 46, 48 and 8.6.

49. Webster, 'Bedouin Settlements', p. 127.

50. BQ, Figs 5.65–74, 9.85–90.

51. Cf. Carleton S.Coon, *Caravan: The Story of The Middle East* (revised edn; New York: Henry Holt and Company, 1968); Fredrik Barth, 'Forasien', in Johannes Nicolaisen *et al.* (eds) *Verdens Folkeslag i Vor Tid* (Copenhagen: Politikens, 1968), pp. 220–40.

52. See John Lewis Burckhardt, *Notes on the Bedouins and Wahabys, collected during his Travels in the East* (London; 1831; New York: Johnson Reprint Corporation, 1967); Charles Doughty, *Travels in Arabia Deserta* (one-volume edition complete and unabridged, London: Cape and Medici Society, 1926).

53. E.g. Wilfred Thesiger, 'The badu of southern Arabia', *Journal of the Royal Central Asian Society* 37, 1950; Dostal, *Die Beduinen*.

54. Webster, 'Bedouin Settlements', pp. 7; 174.

55. BQ, Fig. 5.10.

56. BQ, Cat. nos 8a-b, 9a-b; Dickson, *Arab of the Desert,* p. 89.

57. BQ, Cat. nos 15–16.

58. Montigny, 'Evolution', p. 130; Webster, Bedouin Settlements, p. 130.

59. John Moorehead, *In Defiance of the Elements* (London: Quartet, 1977), p. 128.

60. This refers to the situation before 1980.

61. Klaus Ferdinand, 'The Balûchistân barrel-vaulted tent and its affinities', *Folk* 1, 1959, pp. 27–50, Figs 7 and 9.

62. Ferdinand, 'The Balûchistân', Fig. 6.

63. Ferdinand, 'The Balûchistân,' Figs 1–2.

64. Ferdinand, 'The Balûchistân', Fig. 11; Klaus Ferdinand, 'The Balûchistân barrel-vaulted tent. Supplementary material from Irânian Balûchistân and Sistân', *Folk* 2,1960, pp. 33–5, Figs 7–9.

65. Ferdinand, 'Balûchistân', Figs 7a,b; 'Supplementary', Fig. 6; E.G. Gafferberg, 'Poyezdka k beludzham turkmenenii v 1958 godu,' *Sovetskaya Etnografiya,* 1960 (no. 1), pp. 112–25, Fig. 3.

66. See Oskar von Niedermayer, *Afganistan* (Leipzig: K.W.Hermann, 1924); Gorm Pedersen, *Afghan Nomads in Transition: A Century of Change among the Zala Khan Khel* (Carlsberg Foundation Nomad Research Project; Copenhagen/London and New York: Rhodos/Thames & Hudson, 1994), pp. 78 (Fig. 1.21), 200 (Fig. 5.42).

67. See photograph in Lennart Edelberg and Klaus Ferdinand, 'Arselan. Et udblik over dansk forskning i Centralasien', *Naturens Verden,* September 1958, p. 284.

68. Cf. Klaus Ferdinand, 'The Balûchistan', Figs 7b and 8b.

69. Klaus Ferdinand, 'Nomadism in Afghanistan. With an Appendix on milk products', in L.Földes (ed.) *Viehwirtschaft und Hirtenkultur. Ethnographische Studien* (Budapest: Akademiai Kiado, 1969), pp. 127–60; Nancy Tapper, 'The advent of Pashtun maldars in north-western Afghanistan', *BSOAS* 36, 1973, pp. 55–79.

70. Ferdinand, 'Ethnographical notes', pp. 192 ff.

71. Cf. Ferdinand, 'Balûchistan', Figs 6–7, 9.

72. Klaus Ferdinand, 'The nomad tent of East Afghanistan,' in P.A.Andrews (ed.) *Tent Types of The Middle East* (Beihefte zum Tübinger Atlas des Vorderen Orients B.74 part 2;Wiesbaden: Reichert, 1997); cf. Gorm Pedersen, *Afghan Nomads,* pp. 190 (Fig. 5.33), 193 (Fig. 5.36).

73. Ferdinand 'The Balûchistan' and 'Ethnographical notes', pp. 194–6.

74. Feilberg, *La Tente Noire*.

75. See Ferdinand, 'The nomad tent'.

Chapter 11
Looms, Carpets and Talims
Jon Thompson

There is a measure of agreement among scholars that weaving in both the old and new worlds developed along similar lines. Archaeological evidence shows clearly that twining preceded weaving.[1]

The screen or mat loom: warps weighted with stones

Twining differs from weaving as follows. With a twined structure, the elements which travel in the same general direction (usually the weft) interact with each other—most commonly by twisting around each other —as well as interacting with the elements that travel at right angles to them. With a woven structure, the interaction between the warp and weft elements is by interlacing. The wefts are added one at a time and adjacent wefts are independent of each other.[2]

Familiar twined structures include all kinds of basketry, bags, pouches, shoes, traps, shields, mats, hats and other small items made out of strands of flexible organic material. Twining has existed since the Mesolithic period and is found worldwide. It is most highly developed among those peoples who do not use the heddle loom.

The heddle loom made its first appearance in central Europe around 7000 BC in the form of the warp-weighted loom. Very few textiles produced on this loom have survived, but it is possible to trace its history because the warp weights are easy to recognize in an archaeological site.[3] Though once widespread in Europe, it survives today only within the Arctic circle in northern Norway, among settled Lapps who learned to weave from their Norwegian neighbours in comparatively recent times.[4]

The loom consists of a rectangular frame to which is attached a characteristic starting band. From this band the warps descend in long loops. Warp tension is maintained by tying the warps to stones which hang down in two rows.

A primitive loom which shares some of the features of the warp-weighted loom is found all over the Islamic world (see Plate 38).[5] It survives in a particularly interesting form among various nomadic groups. Almost all nomads—both the felt-tent nomads and the black tent nomads—use some kind of reed or cane screen or mat along the wall of the tent. It serves a variety of functions, is cheap to make., rolls up and is easy to transport. Its virtue is that it can be used in a flexible manner: as a temporary wind-break, to provide a measure of privacy, to reinforce the tent wall and help keep out draughts in winter, or to cut down heat glare while allowing the passage of air in summer.

The loom on which it is made consists of a horizontal beam from which the warps hang. The warps are kept under tension by two rows of stones hanging down, one on each side of the beam. The rigid wefts in the form of thin wooden wands, or the stems of reeds or grasses, are added one at a time and laid along the beam. One row of stones is then thrown across the beam to the other side and their opposite number thrown back over the beam, so that the two rows exchange places. It should be noted that the exchange is carefully done so that the warp pairs actually rotate round one another. This therefore is a form of twining, a technique more archaic than true weaving.

Some groups make patterns with the warps by moving them laterally along the beam in a regular manner during the exchange of stones. Other groups have developed screen-making into an art form by wrapping the reeds with coloured wool and then assembling the wrapped reeds into a large composition. This is highly developed among the Guran and some other Kurdish groups in western Iran and eastern Turkey. The greatest elaboration is found among the Kazakh and Kirghiz in Central Asia.[6] The Guran and other Kurds use reed screens as tent walls and not as tent dividers as is often claimed. The Kazakh and Kirghiz use them inside the wall felts so that the pattern is visible from inside the tent. The Kirghiz also have a small screen which divides off the kitchen area, and a threshold screen which is used as a door flap. This technique is not in danger of being lost. However, under communist influence, and with characteristic sensitivity to traditional culture, nomadism in Kirghizia was actively suppressed. With the virtual extinction of the traditional way of life and culture, school-children have been encouraged to find their cultural identity by learning the traditional crafts of felt-and screen-making. Since reed screens have no function in the new settled, urban environment, screen-making was 'elevated' into a politically acceptable, if somewhat self-conscious 'art form'.

Zilu weaving

In contrast, an interesting weaving technique which is in serious danger of being lost altogether is that of *zilu*-weaving. A *zilu,* as the term is now used, is a heavy, pileless, cotton floor-covering, usually blue and white, woven in weft-faced compound tabby. One side has the pattern in undyed white on indigo-dyed blue and on the reverse it reads as blue on white. Some older examples have details in red as well. Modern *zilus* are made using synthetic dyes, predominantly green, red and orange.

The age of this craft has become clearer since the discovery at Masada of archaeological textiles dating from the first century which have the same structure.[7] By the tenth century, zilu-weaving was widespread. The *Hudud al-'Alam* says that they were made in Fars, Mukan, Khurasan, Sistan, Azerbaijan, Nakhichevan and Armenia, to name some of the places mentioned.[8]

It has long been the custom in Persia to make pious donations of these floor coverings for use in religious buildings (see Plate 39). The oldest surviving *zilus* are still to be found in mosques, mausoleums and *khanaqahs* in the dry central region of Iran, especially around Yazd. None is earlier than the sixteenth century. Recently a remarkable fragment came to light in Daghestan. Its exact source has been kept secret, but there is circumstantial evidence to suggest that it may have come from the Great Mosque in Derbent. It was acquired in 1985 by the Hermitage Museum, St Petersburg. Anatoly Ivanov believes, on the basis of style and epigraphy, that it dates from the first half of the fourteenth century.[9]

Although visitors to Iran can hardly fail to see *zilus,* their weaving has been little studied.[10] As far as I can discover, *zilus* are made today only in the town of Meybod, near Yazd. They are still made to order for donors who give them to mosques. The older *zilus* have long bands of inscription which typically record the name of the donor, the mosque to which the *zilu* is being given, the date, the name of the maker, and sometimes an imprecation against anyone removing it from the mosque.

The weaving of the inscription band is a special skill, and on my last visit to Meybod in 1984 there were only five people living who could do it; one was in hospital, and another had retired. In 1993 I spoke to a weaver from Meybod who told me that currently only one person was weaving inscriptions, though three or four others knew how to do it.

The *zilu* loom is an impressive structure, of the vertical roller-beam type (see Plate 40). The beams are 12 to 18 feet long and the cloth beam is sunk into a pit. The weaver works standing up. He may have an assistant to beat in the weft, which he passes through the shed as he walks along. The fabric has two warp systems, one for the pattern and one for the structure, each with its own harness. The structural warps are controlled by a pair of heddle rods attached to a rocker system which is easily and quickly operated. The pattern warps, in contrast, are controlled by a bundle of pattern cords with string heddles stretched horizontally at head level. There may be up to 70 pattern cords for large patterns, whereas small-scale patterns require only 13.

The remarkable thing is that, even for the most difficult patterns, weavers use no cartoon or pattern guide of any kind—unless one calls the scruffy piece of paper one weaver fished out of his pocket, with the text of the inscription he was to weave, a pattern guide. The pattern cords are selected from memory and the pattern shed is held open with a large wooden hook (see Plates 41 and 42). The blue and white wefts are passed alternately; specifically, two picks of blue followed by two picks of white. Quite how the weaver succeeds in selecting the correct cords is a mystery to me. It must be a facility acquired through long practice, similar to the way string players move their fingers and bow to achieve the correct notes of a melody with a dexterity and accuracy which seems incredible to the non-musician. I came to this conclusion after watching 39-year-old Reza Sabaghi, who had been blind from the age of five. He wove *zilus* using 13 cords for the field pattern and five for the border. His work was fast and faultless and he told me he had between 70 and 80 different patterns in his head.

I was equally impressed by the way an elderly weaver selected and manipulated the 19 pattern cords required for the inscription band with only a scrap of paper to remind him of the text (see Plate 43). The formation of the letters, their spacing and the overall length of the inscription were all gauged by eye. Admittedly the lettering is sometimes piled up in an amusing way to fit the space, but overall it is an astonishing feat.

The *zilu* loom with its many archaic features is of particular historical importance in that it may be the only surviving representative of the earliest pattern loom.[11] This type of large, upright loom with two harnesses, but without any system for pre-selecting the pattern cords for the lengthways pattern repeats, was formerly quite widespread and used for making textiles much finer than the *zilus* of today. Such textiles probably included the Sassanian, Byzantine and early Islamic patterned silks woven prior to the invention, towards the end of the first millennium, of a means for automating the selection for the lengthways pattern repeats—the true drawloom mechanism. Some of these silks are up to 2.7 metres wide and variations in their lengthways repeats indicate that they were woven without the benefit of any system for the mechanical pre-selection of the pattern cords. In other words, the pattern cords were selected just as the weaver in Meybod did when he was weaving the inscription: either by eye or by copying some pre-existing design. If it is agreed that these early silks were woven on a large upright loom similar to the type surviving in Meybod, *zilu* weaving will become a focus of intense interest for textile scholars.

The drawloom

A truly momentous event in the field of textiles was the invention of a means for the accurate mechanical repetition of extremely complex patterns, used mainly for the weaving of costly silks. It is loosely called the drawloom, but strictly speaking it consists of a mechanism which is attached to a loom. Ideas on the history of this development are changing fast and some textiles formerly described as 'drawloom-woven' may have been woven by means of a much simpler system, such as that used for *zilu* weaving. Thus, in using the term drawloom, we have to define it more precisely. Here it is taken to mean a loom equipped with a device that stores the sequence of selections for the lengthwise pattern repeats, and which controls individual warp ends by means of a harness consisting of lashes (lacs) and draw cords acting on the pattern cords (cross cords). This description includes the technically advanced European drawloom, which some consider to be the *true* drawloom. However, it also applies to the recently extinct Persian drawloom and to the Indian drawloom, both of which have a mechanism that is quite different to that of the European drawloom and clearly more primitive, with features in common with the *zilu* loom. It now seems likely that the invention of the drawloom occurred later in the history of weaving than has been assumed.[12]

The drawloom mechanism is so stunningly simple in conception and so elegant in its economy and efficiency that it should be seen as one of the truly great human inventions.

Explaining how it works is not so simple, however. The pattern of drawloom-woven textiles is formed by the coming to the surface of coloured weft threads which run along invisibly in the interior or at the back of the fabric until they are required. If we imagine the textile lying face-up on the table and follow the movements of a coloured weft thread in its passage from one side of the textile to the other, then at some points it passes upwards, above the warp, to appear on the surface, and at others it disappears behind. Several hundred weft threads may be needed to complete a large pattern unit, and each one may have a different configuration in terms, whether it crosses over or under any one of the hundreds of warp threads in the width of the pattern. The task is to devise a system for raising or lowering the correct warp threads for the passage of each and every weft.

In simple fabrics, the weaver threads the weft above and below the appropriate warp ends by hand as it passes from one side to the other. Alternatively, instead of performing this same action hundreds of times, the weaver may do it once only for each pattern weft at the beginning of weaving and retain the configurations by threading a rod across the warp to mark the passage of each one. The number of pattern rods required depends on the complexity of the pattern. A third method is to place a rod above the warp and tie to it loops of fine cord (the heddles) which pass beneath the appropriate warp threads. If the rod—called a heddle rod or more correctly a pattern heddle rod—is pulled upwards, the appropriate warps are all raised at once. This system works well for small-scale repeating patterns. The *zilu* weaver uses a combination of the first method (for the inscription) with this third system, but with cords instead of rods.

For larger patterns, there is a physical limit to the number of heddle rods a loom can accommodate. The drawloom mechanism gets round this problem as follows. A pattern is drawn exactly to scale. Today it is made on squared paper, but in former times it was recorded on a sheet of micah. A specialist craftsman, the Naqshband, works out how many warp and weft threads are needed to form this pattern in the finished cloth and then produces by hand a large-scale, loosely woven version of it on a special frame, using stout cords in the place of fine threads (see Plate 44). This is extremely skilled work and requires a high level of attention.[13]

The completed scaled-up version of the design is called the *naqsheh* in Persian or *naksha* in Hindi. The free ends of its wefts are knotted together into a loop and threaded onto a string to preserve their exact sequence. The whole thing is removed from the frame and attached to the loom above the warp as follows: the warp threads of the *naqsheh* become the draw cords. They are tied at the top to a fixed point and run vertically downwards to be tied at the bottom to cross cords (equivalent to the pattern cords of the *zilu* loom). Each of the cross cords has a number of string heddles attached to it to control the warp ends on the loom, corresponding to the number of repeats in the width of the cloth. It is now possible to imagine a system in which, if you take an individual weft (lac or lash) of the *naqsheh* and pull on it, the action of this pull will be transmitted automatically to the draw cords, then to the cross cords and thence to the warps ends on the loom via the string heddles. Thus, once the skilled work of the Naqshband—making the *naqsheh* and tying it to the loom—has been done, weaving can proceed with the help of an unskilled assistant (the draw-boy) who determines the pathway of each pattern weft by pulling on successive wefts (lashes) of the *naqsheh* in the predetermined sequence.

By examining old textiles it is possible to say something about how they were woven. The size and complexity of the *naqsheh* used for some textiles is truly astonishing, and it is little appreciated what huge resources of money, technology and human skill went into making such textiles as the Safavid velvets. No wonder textiles were among the most valuable items in the Islamic world in former times.

At one time the drawloom was used widely in the Islamic world, but the development of the Jacquard mechanism in eighteenth-century France has almost completely displaced it. The Jacquard loom, incidentally, is a development of the principle of the drawloom in which the *naqsheh* is replaced by a series of punched cards. In the 1970s the drawloom was still being used in Yazd and Tehran, but I cannot confirm that it is being used anywhere in Iran or Turkey today. It still survives in Fez, in Mecca, and in India, most vigorously among the Muslims of Banares. Part of the reason for its survival there is that India is—just— still a 'textile culture', in which there is a sufficient level of awareness for people to demand the quality of work that can be achieved on the drawloom. Surprisingly, there are some manoeuvres that can be accomplished on a drawloom that the Jacquard loom cannot reproduce, and it is not uncommon in Benares to see a Jacquard mechanism and a drawloom device being used together on the same loom (see Plate 45).

In former times the Naqshbandi were very highly regarded and travelled like other great craftsmen to the courts where they were most appreciated. One Ghiyas-e Naqshband, a native of Yazd, is mentioned in the *A'in-e Akbari* as having been the maker of costly textiles which were sent as a diplomatic gift by Shah Abbas to the court of Akbar. He was reputed to be a great poet and it was said that the world had not seen a weaver like him.[14] The connection between this specialized craft and the Naqshbandi order of dervishes is clear. Mohammad Bahauddin Naqshband (1317–89) who founded the order is credited in Indian oral tradition with the invention of *naqsheh*-making. The invention is clearly older than the fourteenth century, but it may well be that the spread of the craft from Central Asia to India at that time ran parallel with the spread of Naqshbandiyeh.

Carpet weaving

If drawloom weaving is on the verge of extinction, another craft with its epicentre within the Islamic world —that of carpet making—is far from moribund.

Here it is worth noting that carpet weaving has miraculously survived the destructive effect of mechanization, in spite of the fact that in 1910 a British company, Tomkinson of Kidderminster, obtained a patent from Renard Frères of Nonancourt for a machine to produce knotted carpets on a loom based on the Jacquard principle. The Tomkinson carpet-knotting machine was not very fast and could barely compete with the acres of medium to low-quality carpets being produced early last century by the weavers of Hamadan and Isparta. Latterly it was used to make special commissions, for example a carpet with an insignia for use in a masonic hall. The last Tomkinson machine-knotted carpets were made in 1962.

Carpet weavers too have the problem of how to record and transmit designs so that weavers can reproduce them accurately. Carpet weaving is practised on many different levels, as indeed was the weaving of cloth of all kinds in former times. At the lowest technological level the weaver works from memory without a pattern guide. Alternatively, another carpet can be used as a guide and copied knot-for-knot, a method which is quite difficult and not very efficient, for there are always mistakes and distortions. In spite of this, copying has been used for centuries and is the primary means whereby court and urban designs have been disseminated to towns, villages and tents in the provinces. When a copy is used as the pattern guide for other carpets, the distortions are increased, and over a period of time the result is a sort of visual game of Chinese whispers.

In the towns and cities of Iran and its neighbouring countries the standard means of transmitting designs is by means of a squared-paper cartoon, or, more correctly, point plan. First the design is drawn on ruled paper by a skilled artist or designer (see Plate 46). This is then copied on a larger scale onto squared paper in sections by another craftsman, the cartoon maker. Here each square represents one knot and is coloured accordingly. The paper is glued onto a stiff backing and is used as a pattern-guide in this form by the weaver.

The squared-paper cartoon has the virtue of accuracy and is fairly durable. However, cartoon making is laborious and time-consuming work. Self-employed weavers who want to be sure of a sale by weaving one of the currently fashionable designs can usually buy a set of cartoons in the bazaar, but they are expensive and some skill is needed to use them. Also they can be hard to read when the light is inadequate or if the weaver has poor eyesight, and each time the weaver has to consult the cartoon it takes them a while to find their place.

Another accurate method of design transmission is used in India, Pakistan and Kashmir. The cartoon maker's skill is replaced by that of the *talim* maker. The *talim,* which in this context simply means an instruction, is a weaving program which divides the entire carpet into horizontal rows and for each row describes the sequence of knots from one side of the carpet to the other in terms of the colour and how many times it is to be repeated. In this way every knot in the carpet is exactly specified. The instruction is written in a special notation (see Plate 47).[15] The closest analogy to this system is a knitting pattern, which also employs a special notation.

The *talim* is used in one of two ways. Most commonly it is used by the weavers as their pattern-guide, in which case they must learn the notation (see Plate 48). Alternatively, in the workshop situation where several identical carpets may be being worked on simultaneously, the *ustad* reads from the *talim* and calls out the colours to the weavers in a special way which some people refer to as chanting.

The advantage of the *talim* system is that, once the *talim* maker has transferred the design from its original graphic form into a weaving program written in special notation, no special skill other than accuracy is needed to copy it out. Furthermore, it is much quicker to copy out a page of notation than to colour in thousands of little squares by hand.

In intellectual terms, the *talim* system is a definite advance on the cartoon, but the cartoon will always be popular because of its visual accessibility. Recently in Iran these two basic ideas have been taken a stage further by enterprising carpet specialists who are using what computers have to offer to find new solutions to old problems. Cartoon making has become much simpler. The drawing which is to be used as a carpet design is scanned on a flatbed scanner. The scanned image is stored in the computer as pixels, a series of rectangular spots of colour, and then fed into a computer-driven mechanical plotter, which accurately colours in the appropriate squares on a sheet of graph paper in as many colours as it is instructed. A complete section of cartoon can be coloured this way in a matter of minutes.

A second invention is a portable electrical device with a memory chip and back-up battery which is used by the weaver at the loom. The chip contains a weaving program recorded in electronic form. This information is derived from a scanned image in the same way as is done for cartoon making. It includes other information, such as the total number of knots and the number of knots of each colour, both of which are useful for calculating the cost of labour and the quantity of materials needed to produce a particular carpet. The device consists of a metal box hung in front of the weaver with a number of liquid crystal displays which give the weaver information about what they have woven and what is to be done next (see Plate 49). It tells the weaver the row number, the total number of knots to be tied, and the knot number they have reached, and it has an indicator showing the colour of the next knot (up to 30 colours). As the knot is tied, the weaver cuts it and simultaneously presses a micro-switch on the knife, which is wired into the memory chip. The signal advances the device by one knot, updates the display, and tells the weaver what to do next. There are various practical refinements. You can go backwards to review and check your work, you can set it to advance automatically at any speed you wish to suit the speed at which you work, or you can set it to weave one colour at a time in each row, which is the traditional way of working.

Some Westerners, on seeing this device, have expressed revulsion and horror, making comments to the effect that soon we will be having carpets knotted by computers. At first sight it does seem as if modern technology with all its anti-traditional ugliness is invading and threatening the innocence of the happy weaver dextrously creating her artistic masterpiece in the blissful and idyllic security of her rural home. But sentiment is one thing and reality another. There are some 1.3 million looms in Iran, and most weaving is done by women to supplement the family income under circumstances which are far from idyllic. This device alters nothing in terms of the status of the weaver and her relationship to the object she is making. Instead of straining her eyes and back while poring over the cartoon and counting the squares with the tip of her knife to find out where she is, she now has an electronic *talim* to prompt her. The weavers like it—is that so bad?

Notes

1. The evidence is summarized in E.J.W.Barber, *Prehistoric Textiles* (Princeton, NJ: Princeton University Press, 1991), pp. 124–44.
2. For a definition of twining see David W.Fraser, *A Guide to Weft Twining and Related Structures with Interacting Wefts* (Philadelphia: University of Pennsylvania Press, 1989), pp. 3–4.
3. See also Barber, pp. 92–106.
4. Marta Hoffmann, 'Manndalen revisited: traditional weaving in an Old Lappish community in transition', in Veronica Gervers (ed.) *Studies in Textile History* (Toronto: Royal Ontario Museum, 1977), pp. 149–159.
5. For a description and photos of the loom, see Patty Jo Watson, *Archaeological Ethnography in Western Iran* (Viking Fund Publications in Anthropology, no. 57, Tucson: University of Arizona Press, 1979), pp. 189–91. The author kindly supplied the photo for this article.
6. For the making and use of Kirghiz reed screens, see E.I.Makhova, 'Uzornaya Tsinovka', in S.V.Ivanov and K.I.Antipina (eds), *Narodnoe Dekatorativno-prikladnoe Iskusstvo Kirgizov* (Moscow: Akademii Nauk SSSR, 1968); and Stella Mateeva and Jon Thompson, 'Patterned reed screens of the Kirghiz in the State Historical Museum Frunze', *Oriental Rug Review* 11(6), 1991, pp. 10–15, and 12 (1), pp. 48–53.
7. Avigail Sheffer and Hero Granger-Taylor 'Textiles from Masada—a preliminary selection', in Joseph Aviram, Gideon Foerster and Ehud Netzer (eds), *Masada IV: The Yigael Yadin Excavations 1963–1965 Final Reports* (Jerusalem: 1994), pp. 212–15.
8. Listed in detail in R.B.Serjeant, *Islamic Textiles. Material for a History up to the Mongol Conquest* (Beirut: Librairie du Liban, 1972; originally published in a series of articles, 'Material for a History of Islamic Textiles up to the Mongol Conquest', in Ars *Islamica*, 1942–1951).
9. Published with colour illustration and comment in Anatoly A.Ivanov, *Masterpieces of Islamic Art in the Hermitage Museum* (Kuwait: Dar Al-Athar Al-Islamiyyah, 1990), p. 92.
10. Documentation of zilu-weaving is scarce: see May H.Beattie, 'A Note on Zilu', in Cathryn Cootner (ed.), *Flat-Woven Textiles* (Washington, DC: Textile Museum, 1981), pp. 169–74. There is a short entry in Hans E.Wulff, *The Traditional Crafts of Persia* (Cambridge, MA: MIT Press, 1966), pp. 210–11, but the information is faulty. The following two articles contain useful historical information and references: Iraj Afshar, 'Zilu', and Annette Ittig, 'A note on a zilu fragment dated 963/1556 in the Islamic Museum Cairo', *Iranian Studies* 25 (1–2), 1992, pp. 31–42.

11. This idea is put forward in Jon Thompson and Hero Granger-Taylor, 'The Persian Zilu loom of Meybod', *CIETA Bulletin* 73, 1995–96, pp. 27–53.
12. For an informed discussion of the origin of the drawloom see John Becker, *Pattern and Loom* (Copenhagen: Rhodos, 1987), pp. 253–78.
13. For an excellent description of *naqsheh-making,* see Pupul Jayakar, 'Naksha Bandhas of Banaras', *Journal of Indian Textile History* 7, 1967, pp. 21–44.
14. Abul Fazl 'Allami, *A'in-i Akbari,* trans. H.Blochmann (Calcutta: Royal Asiatic Society, 1873), p. 88 line 19. For a biographical note on Ghiyas, who was a native of Yazd, see p. 616, and Arthur Upham Pope and Phyllis Ackerman (eds), *A survey of Persian Art* (Oxford: 1938–9), pp. 2094–101, and Robert Skelton, 'Ghyas al-Din Ali-yi Naqshband and an Episode in the Life of Sadiqi Beg' in *Festschrift in Honour of B.W.Robinson* (London: I.B. Tauris, forthcoming).
15. Weaving programmes written in special notation are known to have been used in Kashmir for shawl-weaving before they were observed in carpet-weaving, and it is often assumed that shawl-weavers, driven to starvation by the collapse of the shawl industry in 1877, transferred the technology to carpet-weaving. Shawl-weaving was intensively studied in the early nineteenth century because of its commercial importance. Carpets, however, were less fashionable, and the fact that nobody studied how they were made does not exclude the possibility that carpet workshops also used *talims*.

Chapter 12
The Survival of the Bazaar Economy in Iran and the Contemporary Middle East
Keith McLachlan

Bazaar economies have distinctive characteristics which arise from both the nature of the early developing societies in which they exist and the heavily structured types of activities within the trading community itself. This chapter will analyse those aspects of the Iranian and Middle Eastern bazaars which make their operations different in style and organization from modern trading markets.

The salient principles and observations of the classical scholars offer a benchmark for establishing the economic, cultural and geographical forms of the traditional bazaars. The descriptions and analyses given in the literature are helpful, therefore, in diagnosing the direction and rate of change in the contemporary period.

There has been only modest 'modernization' of bazaar cultures in Iran in recent decades. 'Modernization' is taken in this context to imply adoption of trading practices normal in the industrial societies of the world. This situation arose partly because the course of commercial development was constrained in Iran within, first, a dualistic traditional/modern economy in the period 1960–78 and, secondly, the precepts of the Islamic revolution in subsequent years. The bazaar functioned as an integral part of the economic and political systems within the Islamic Republic, putting forward its preferred views on the flavour of the economic structure of the country and articulating political support for those who accepted the points of view current among the majority of merchants. This intimate connection between the bazaar and the body politic is not unique to Iran but found there in a more highly developed form than in other areas of Africa and Asia.

In Iran the bazaar also represents a set of religious organizations providing an alliance between Islam and commerce. In Esfahan, Tabriz and other cities there were also pockets of Armenian and Jewish traders, some with specialized activities arising from their religious affiliation. Usury and trading in liquor or other goods proscribed for Muslims were examples of this niche-trading by minority trading groups. And in other areas of North Africa, the Middle East and Asia, a more varied mixture of religious quarters was apparent.

In Iran, at the same time, traditional activities in financing internal commerce and supporting local social-religious organizations were reinforced by the bazaar's successful role in running international commodity trade. In recent years, the bazaar reabsorbed international trading and wholesaling which had been vested for some years in the 1980s in government agencies. The bazaar merchants' long-term involvement in mobilization of credits for funding property, agricultural and manufacturing activities was enhanced by this same trend and by the requirements of keeping the economy buoyant during the 1980–88 war against Iraq. In Iran, bazaar trading is still, therefore, intimately involved in most facets of national life.

This analysis looks at how and why the bazaar economy has survived and been consolidated. While much research remains to be done before definitive conclusions may be drawn, some provisional observations are worth iterating at this stage, none the less.

The theoretical framework

In so far as there is a theory relevant to the activities of traditional bazaars, it derives from the work of orientalist scholars, now perhaps misunderstood, such as Von Grunebaum, Lebon and others such as de Planhol.[1] Their premise was that there was an oriental or Islamic city of specific social structure and physical morphology, albeit varying across time and space. A model of the 'Islamic city' was constructed by social scientists from the ideas of the orientalists, although it was never the latter's intention that their concepts should be amalgamated into a formal and universal paradigm. Recent attacks on the orientalists[2] have attempted to devalue their work, though these self-same detractors have in turn been found to be crude in argument and uninformed on key cultural variables such as the role of religiously endowed properties *(ouqaf)* in Islamic urban areas, and indeed the workings of Koranic law.[3] One element of the oriental or Islamic city which has retained value, despite attacks on other aspects of the model, is the lay-out of the bazaar or mercantile zone. Here the principles involved were clear and seem to have abiding value.[4]

The major factors affecting allocation of land use were perceived to be the degree to which crafts, trades and goods were appraised in an Islamic sense as 'unclean' *(haram)* or 'clean' *(halal)* ('There was a hierarchy of respect in the crafts, ranging from work in precious metals, paper and perfume, down to such 'unclean' crafts as tanning, dyeing and butchering');[5] the functional appropriateness of goods to be sold close to the mosque or religious school *(madraseh);* the sale of valuable objects near to the main thoroughfares, with lesser trades needing more, and less costly, land pushed to the periphery; and the concentration of similar crafts in specific locations within the bazaar and perhaps within the greater construct of the city *(shahr, madina).* In some bazaars, external geographical constraints also defined the hinterland of certain marketing activities: in Mashhad, for example, in the early 1960s the geography of bazaar operations was defined externally *inter alia* by the constraints of topography, and thus the transport system of the area surrounding the city in which the bazaar lay.[6] These ground rules do not apply in all bazaars, but in many cases they are relevant in different combinations.

The allocation of land within the bazaar as outlined by the orientalists is not disputed by most contemporary social scientists, for whom the operation of economic principles can for the most part be accommodated within the notion that land rents will tend in general and over time to give prime spaces to high-profit activities.[7] Thus, there is a hierarchy of land uses, which gives primacy to book-making, gold and silver jewellery over carpet-selling and thence, through a graded scale of commodities, through metal work, ceramics, sale of agricultural goods and ultimately low-grade crafts such as tanning and dyeing. The classical theories of supply and demand, together with other factors determining location of economic activities, can adjust to these aspects of the orientalist assessment of the bazaar with little difficulty. The discord which has arisen over other facets of the orientalist view, such as the orientation of the street pattern towards Mecca, which is challenged by contemporary social scientists such as Bonine,[8] is a separate matter, where the orientalist judgement appears in many instances not necessarily to apply.

The classical theorists were also helpful in giving detailed case studies of examples of bazaars. Those field studies for Iran and the Middle East, including North Africa, are varied but immensely useful. In Iran, the database created in the period before 1940 is limited to the major sites such as Esfahan, Tabriz, Tehran and Mashhad, where there was a coalescence of interest by archaeologists, art historians and other scholars. The bazaar sections of such cities were not, however, the main attraction for these early studies, whose objects were architectural and historical, though there were exceptions. After the Second World War, there was a gradual awakening of interest in the structure of Iranian bazaars. Notable work was done in the 1960s by Iranian staff at the Institute of Social Studies and Research in Tehran, by Pakravan and others such as Darwent, Vieille and English.[9] By the end of the 1960s and the early 1970s, a flood of new work on Iranian cities became available from the agencies of state such as Plan Organization, concerned with urban development throughout the country. In particular, the market functions of towns and their bazaars became an important focus of study. The academic world also became more active, and significant works touching on Iranian bazaars were published by Bonine, Clarke, Clarke and Clark, Costello and others.[10]

The high level of official research in Iran was a direct consequence of the government's need to control and harness the trends of that period towards high economic growth into constructive paths. There was also an underlying, though never entirely dominant, desire to conserve the country's main bazaar buildings. At the same time, the continuing political and economic significance of the bazaars in national life made it necessary for planners to understand the role of the bazaar merchants, so that their activities could be taken into due account when the five-year development plans were set up. Concern for the bazaar in Iran did not save some ancient market buildings from destruction or intemperate 'modernization' in which vaulted passageways were broken open to enable new 'windows' to the sky, as at Hamadan. But overall, the Iranian bazaar, both the marketing system and its buildings, survived this period of economic turmoil.

The survival of bazaars

It is apparent from this discussion that the survival of the bazaar system calls for a theoretical explanation. Why does the bazaar in Iran flourish while in other countries this is not the case? Part of the explanation is straightforward. Historically, Iran always kept a market system only modestly controlled by the state: governments left the bazaar merchants to undertake most of their traditional trading functions. Even when, for a comparatively short period in the 1980s, the state sequestered international trade and national trading committees were set up to manage import of key commodities, the bazaar was left with all other wholesale and retail trade functions. A prolonged deprivation of the large-scale import trade might well have begun the strangulation of the bazaars in Iran on the Libyan model. In the event, the state trading agencies were dissolved after a short period in operation, and the bazaar merchants were able to reclaim this area of activity.

This seems to indicate a first principle for the survival of the bazaar, that it be left to operate a generally unrestricted trading network. The converse is also true, that the bazaar system will not survive the socialization-nationalization of trade—as the example of Tripoli, Libya, so recently proved. Tripoli's *suq* suffered greatly from the nationalization of trade under Colonel Ghadhafi's 'Green Book' programme in the 1970s, at the very time that the old city *(madina)* was being abandoned by its population for other reasons.[11] By the 1990s the *suq* was a minor area of trade even within a then slightly reviving private commercial sector.

A second principle hinges on the status of the economy. It seems that structurally immature economies are much more favourable to the bazaar than modernized economic systems. There are a number of interrelated matters involved in the preservation of the bazaar economy. First, there is a need for there to be a traditional, primary, immature third-world type of economy in which the bazaar has an established and unchallenged role. In this circumstance, the bazaar is at the apex of the commercial hierarchy in a rent-capitalist organization. Factors in the ranking of urban areas against the countryside in its various forms, as examined by English and Bonine,[12] or the intra-urban hierarchy of the rent-capitalist type defined by Ehlers,[13] are also useful analytical tools in this respect. In the Kerman case described by English, it was the capitalists of the city who organized and provided capital for the manufacture of carpets and rugs by rural peoples on an outwork basis (the system used in the early days of the industrial revolution in western Europe, whereby manufacturing, usually of textiles, was done in villages and farms using materials provided by urban merchants). Given the position of the bazaar at the top of the commercial-capitalist pyramid., it was to the bazaar that the benefits of economic activities accrued, and it was the bazaar merchants who prospered accordingly.

In traditional society, the bazaar is an important source of informal lending to both rural and urban enterprises or to individuals. In Islamic cultures the transfer of capital was organized in ways that mainly avoided direct usury. In the agricultural sector, standing crops were bought before harvest, or capital repaid by the delivery of products at harvest time. A variety of other mechanisms were used to circumvent the difficulty of the ban on taking interest from loans, so that the mobility of capital was not constrained. Indeed, some forms of lending from the bazaar were far more expensive for the user of borrowed capital than direct interest-tied credit from official sources. Non-Muslim bazaar merchants were not of course impeded by the taboo within Islam on taking interest on loans made to third parties. In Iran in the period before the 1963 land reforms, large land-owners (*'omdeh-malekin*) more generally borrowed from the Tehran bazaar merchants than from the banks to fund both their farm and private budget operations. Smaller land-owners (*khordeh-malekin*) and peasant proprietors (*ro'aya*) would tend either to borrow from the local merchants in the regional bazaars or, for short-term credits for the requirements of specific crop seasons, from Tehrani merchants and their agents.[14] Doubtless the Iranian bazaars still undertake this important function of funding agricultural investment and providing short-term farm credits.

It might be hazarded that bazaar economies thrive best where there are generally low average incomes, i.e. in the World Bank category of *low income countries* with annual per capita income at $2,500 or less. In such societies, the structure of demand is oriented towards survival, with foodstuffs, traditional clothing and textiles, together with locally manufactured material objects, in demand rather than modern-sector consumer durables. This correlation between the strong role of the bazaar and low living standards is supported by observational and statistical evidence. For example, among countries of the Middle East and North Africa where there is no heavy direct government involvement in trade and nationalization of trade has been avoided, it is Iran and Morocco that show the strongest continuity in the strength of the bazaar. Morocco possibly has the most dynamic bazaar system, reinforced by the high levels of residence within the *madinas*. Fez, Marrakesh, Tangier, Taroudant and Meknes are all prime instances of this bazaar/old town correlation, despite the effects of modernization and Westernization, felt particularly in Morocco through the provision of *villes nouvelles* by the French in the period 1912–56. Iran and Morocco both had modest average living standards, Iran with $1,940 and Morocco with $1,030 per head of population in 1993. Once states of this kind become markedly richer and undertake mass consumption of 'international' products, the role of the bazaar weakens, since it lacks the space for showrooms and the technical expertise to handle modern-sector goods where forms of high technology and after-sales service are important. Kuwait exemplifies this trend, where per capita incomes have risen to well over $24,000 per year and the old *suq* and indeed the old *madina* of Kuwait have all but vanished as institutions.

Closely collating with the matter of the structure of supply and demand noted previously, bazaars survive best when they have longstanding indigenous manufacturing industries either based within them or managed through the outwork system. The more individual and highly prized the goods manufactured, the more competitive the individual or national bazaars will be. Iran illustrates the situation rather well. Persian carpets in particular have a corner of the Iranian domestic and international markets for hand-knotted floor coverings and wall hangings. While not immune to competition from alternative sources, Iranian manufactured rugs and carpets have over several centuries had all the attributes of a first-class commodity. Their manufacture and sale have provided a strong flow of funds in both rials and foreign exchange through Iranian bazaars, permitting bazaar merchants there to fund cheaply some of their overseas purchases of goods for return to the Iranian market. A number of other products—mainly agriculturally related—have provided a similar trading strength, including pistachio nuts (*pesteh*) and dried fruits (*khoshk-bar*).

Continuity in the bazaar: the question of new entrants

A theoretical conundrum in this respect is the question of the 'open' or 'closed' nature of the bazaar from the point of view of new entrants to particular crafts. There are rather polarized theories in this area. First, it was assumed by several orientalists such as George Marçais and Louis Massignon[15] that the operation of guild *(sanf)* structures within the bazaar meant that entry to crafts was restricted. Marçais and others generally took their information from North Africa, including Egypt, and perhaps related their evidence historically to rather a restricted period of time.

A second hypothesis, more generally accepted by specialists, is that entry to crafts in the bazaar was open. Guilds, where they existed, were entirely unlike their European mediaeval counterparts, with the ability neither to enforce quality standards nor to exclude newcomers. In the Middle Eastern case, the only limitation was that the incoming leather worker, for example, could bid for space in which to ply his trade. It is argued that new entrants were generally welcomed because they tended to be dependent on established workshop owners for supplies and thus added to, rather than diminished, the volume of trade to share within that particular craft group.

> The openness of the bazaar leads to the proliferation of businesses and saturation in the marketplace, according to culturalist thinking. To survive, the sellers trade with each other rather than compete against each other. Economic anthropologists have found that the number of transactions between traders exceeds the number of transactions with customers. There is no separation between the wholesale and the retail market.[16]

Case studies of the departures and entries of owners and renters of workshops in traditional bazaars are few in number; recent examples in North Africa indicate a general freedom to enter bazaar crafts. In Taroudant in Morocco, where recent fieldwork was done by London University, there was no guild system in operation. Newcomers qualified by their financial resources and their trading abilities rather than through membership of a trade association. Rentals for shops and workshops were not expensive by local standards, and by and large shopkeepers in the *suq* made little special provision for tourists, so that competition on this account was limited. Experience at Taroudant suggested, therefore, that the 'open entry' model was operative in Morocco.

There are some obvious limits to entry. In the Iranian case, makers of rough sandals *(giveh)* required little in the way of raw materials and tools and only a small area in which to manufacture and display their goods. Newcomers in that trade simply crowded into an already densely packed congregation of sandal-makers, in Mashhad in the same street as all others in the craft.[17] For the carpet seller, however, the situation was different. Large amounts of capital or equivalent credit were needed to provide safe store and display-rooms in the central part of the bazaar. Competition for space was often strong and entry thus expensive. Carpet sellers also need reliable suppliers of new carpets, arising from established family contacts in one or more specific carpet-making regions, not to mention credits to fund manufacture and long-term stocking costs. Entry into the larger Iranian bazaars under these conditions was not easy. It would be done, where feasible, through alliances and partnerships with others, possibly relatives, already in the trade.[18] To suggest that entry was 'open' in such conditions would be misleading.

Similarly, merchants dealing in basic imported goods needed symbols of creditworthiness, established contacts overseas, and agency agreements with foreign traders, which in most circumstances precluded newcomers from setting up as instant competition for the existing merchants in the bazaar.

Allied to openness of entry to the bazaar was the activity of peripatetic vendors: itinerant sellers of goods from trays, small carts or shoulders. The bazaar in this sense acted as a mobilizer of the underemployed:

'The crowded field of retail trade, with its itinerant hawkers and pedlars, makes up another large portion… Characteristic of all these occupations is that the labour input is low and insufficient.'[19] Trading of this kind gave an added dimension to the freedom of individuals to enter the bazaar community. The bazaar thrived generally on cheap labour. The porterage of goods through narrow and crowded streets absorbed a great deal of casual labour, as did the use of youths as apprentices *(shagerd)* in the handicraft industries and men as general hands in the heavy trades such as tanning and dyeing. Payment to skilled artisans who were not shop owners in their own right was a more complex matter. In large and sophisticated bazaars in Iran, qualified craftsmen would often set up their own workshops, with or without a shop outlet, so that a skilled labour market existed in only limited form. In effect, therefore, rates of return to labour, even skilled labour, were low throughout the bazaar system.

The return to capital was altogether better than that to labour. The large merchants in Iran who possessed both rial and foreign exchange accounts of substance could exploit traditional low-cost production systems by providing credit, storage and transport within the wholesale and retailing markets. To what extent the merchants formed sales cartels, price fixing rings and monopsonies is unclear. The frequent claims by governments in the recent past that merchants as a whole (not simply in the bazaar) are 'hoarding' and 'profiteering' suggest that an element of management of trade to the benefit of merchants does go on. Rates of return on capital invoked through Islamic mechanisms rather than usury by giving credits to individuals— in practice a useful equivalent of interest rates and expected returns on capital—have been put at more than 300 per cent.[20] This rate of return is perhaps a useful indicator of the kinds of profits expected by owners of capital within the bazaar system.

Underdevelopment and the bazaar

That bazaars flourish in countries where development and modernization are at low levels is perhaps a key correlation in explaining the survival of the system in some countries and its demise in others. Two considerations arise in this respect. First is the power of merchants to maximize their profits through the bargaining procedures that prevail within the traditional bazaar, against fixed prices or even discounted prices elsewhere. Second, and more important, is the ability of bazaar merchants to continue to provide commercial and financial services where other provision either does not exist or is poorly developed.

An enduring characteristic of bazaars is their use of pricing through bargaining for every transaction, however large or small. Bargaining has evinced rather polarized views from economists. One analysis represents bargaining as a function of the efficiency of the bazaar.[21] Each business transaction, it is argued, is done with the finest of margins, so that prices are very sensitive.

Contrary opinions are not lacking which maintain that, far from being efficient, bazaar transactions maximize profits for the seller per article sold rather than optimizing potential total profit flows. Bazaars thus act as a brake on the expansion of commerce as a whole. They also rely on the ability of the seller to exploit the absence of quality controls, trade-mark conventions and other types of consumer protection. In these situations, the seller treats each transaction as an opportunity to cheat the customer. Under this analysis, bazaars are places where the buyer must be doubly wary, since short measure, adulteration of goods and falsification of provenance of goods for the benefit of the seller are normal. The evidence frequently quoted for this is a famous case in the town of Fez in Morocco, where merchants argued in court that it was normal for substances to be adulterated and that, in their case, they were merely conforming to the standard everyone expected![22] By definition, this system can operate only in countries with minimal regulatory regimes and where consumer information is unorganized; mainly, therefore, in the third world.

Lack of commercial modernization limits the competition faced by the bazaar. Poorly constructed domestic capital markets outside the bazaar force borrowers in a single direction: towards the merchants. Highly bureaucratic and inefficient formal banking systems have the same effect, with would-be clients faced with obstruction and delay. Similarly, chronic shortages of foreign exchange, or badly articulated exchange rates within the formal banking system, will assist the informal sector, likely to be based ultimately within the bazaar. This was the case, for example, for many years in the Kabul bazaar, where the bazaar merchants acted as the country's principal clearing house for foreign exchange transactions in the private sector. In the 1960s and early 1970s, personal cheques drawn on Western European banks could be encashed in the bazaar. Merchants protected themselves by liaising with foreign embassies on the likely creditworthiness of their nationals.[23]

Other areas of weakness within the formal financial structures of developing countries were also made good by the bazaar. Poor or non-existent stock markets meant that entrepreneurs, whether rural or urban, were often pleased to turn to the informal sector for raising money or disposing of assets within their activities. In Kuwait there was an irony in the recent past where a free-market stock exchange thrived—until its catastrophic collapse—in an abandoned bazaar: Suq Al-Manakh. Perhaps more widely felt was the matter of the inadequate articulation of state or formal financial agencies into the provincial areas and the rural areas at large. In Iran, where a fair regional-branch banking network has been constructed, the difficulty is one of shortage of overall financial resources.

Naturally, relatively modest standards of literacy[24] and limited economic sophistication make using modern, formal-sector banking facilities a formidable task for many people. For their small-scale or familiar needs, unless offered friendly and comprehensible banking services by the formal sector, they will tend to turn to their longestablished channels for raising credit: local shopkeepers or a known bazaar merchant.[25]

Low-grade economic information systems assist the above process. The lack of regular and reliable data on the costs of borrowing from different sources and the way in which to do business with the formal banking sector inevitably makes the informal system seem, quite often wrongly, more understandable and approachable to farmers and other groups.

In addition to the lack of competition for the bazaar arising in the formal sector, bazaars thrive best where there is only a feebly developed 'new' trading middle class, operating physically outside the ambit of the bazaar, sometimes working in the same fields as the traditional merchants. In Iran there was a perceptible expansion of the trading community outside the aegis of the bazaar in the period 1965–78, though especially in the years 1973–78. This change was expressed in the opening of modern departmental stores, supermarkets, cooperative stores and individual shops in central and northern Tehran, and on a smaller scale in other cities. The new middle class owed little to the trading traditions of the bazaar and made its money in a wide range of activities, from civil engineering and other contracting, construction, and above all acting as agencies for modern consumer goods. It catered for changing tastes in a much augmenting urban market with a rapidly rising standard of living. Iran's population grew from 26 million in 1966 to 33 million by 1976, with a rise in the proportion living in cities from 38 per cent in 1966 to 47 per cent in 1976. Income per head in the years 1965–78 rose in real terms from $450 to $2,450.

The discontinuity occasioned by the revolution of 1979 deeply influenced the activities of the new middle class. A change in commercial and social ethos took place in Iran after 1978. The flight of population and private capital, affecting as many as 1.5 to 2.0 million Iranians, comprised large échelons of what had been the new middle class. With few exceptions, it appears that the external competition to the bazaar merchants was much diminished by the events surrounding the revolution and the succeeding Iran-Iraq war.[26]

Thus, in explaining the survival of the powerful bazaar system in Iran, in contrast for example with other oil-exporting economies of the region, the impacts of the revolution and the war with Iraq play a major role.

This conclusion applies not simply to the problem of the arrested development of the new middle class but to other variables such as the curtailment of growth in personal incomes and the rejection of 'Westernization' in merchant culture. These factors and others directly assisted the survival of the Iranian bazaar system by changing the country from a rapidly growing market for foreign goods and services provided increasingly by recently arrived traders, to one where traditional consumption patterns were dramatically restored. The statistical pattern makes the case. Population numbers continued to grow, if anything more rapidly after the revolution than before, with the total rising to approximately 63 million by 1995. The rate of urbanization also persisted, so that more than half the Iranian population lived in urban areas by 1990. But per capita incomes fell dramatically at constant prices, from $2,450 in 1978 to $750 by 1993. In effect, from the point of view of consumption patterns, Iran resumed its place as one where basic demand for food, clothing and shelter dominated household budgets. This favoured the bazaar, in any case much strengthened by the widespread withdrawal of its *nouveau-riche* competitors.

Anti-Westernism served also as a general cloak for the exclusion from the Iranian market of foreign trading companies, notably the multinationals based in the industrialized countries. With few exceptions, the large multinationals as independent concerns were absent from Iran. The capital, managerial skills, manufacturing facilities and marketing networks of these organizations were systematically kept out of much of the Iranian economic system for political reasons. The economic effects of this option chosen by the government were to restrict market competition by foreign interests to the benefit of the bazaar merchants. The latter indeed had a strong vested interest in the maintenance of this *de facto* embargo on the activities of the multinationals.

Temporary economic factors reinforced this position. In the period 1990–94 the Iranian government suffered from a declining oil income and in consequence a fall in the value of imports of non-essential goods. The bazaar merchants, with accumulated capital overseas,[27] and a ready flow of funds from exports of traditional products such as carpets and pistachio nuts, were able to fund direct and informal imports on their own account, where other traders were unable to raise official support through letters of credit. Secondly, the bazaar merchants, through their unrivalled access to trade and foreign exchange, were able to strengthen their relative position in the domestic economy by benefiting from the declining value of the Iranian rial against foreign currencies during this period (a fall from approximately 1,600=$1 in 1992 to 3,000=$1 in mid-1995). Inevitably too, the bazaar, with stocks of, in effect, index-linked merchantable commodities, was comparatively better placed than other Iranian groups to survive during this period of high domestic price inflation, estimated by observers at more than 50 per cent per annum in the years 1992–94.[28]

The oil sector also ceased to be so powerful an engine of economic growth after the revolution, much reducing its damaging effects on the rest of the economy, the problem of so-called 'Dutch disease'— the cliché devised to describe a range of negative impacts on countries which became foreign-exchange wealthy as a result of exporting oil or natural gas; the debilitating impact of oil wealth undermined existing, mainly physiocratic, elements of the economy, such as agriculture, by pushing up wage rates and altering economic expectations. Quite apart from the determination of the Islamic Republic in 1979–80 to limit oil exports by volume to less than 3 mn b/d, Iran met deep difficulties in keeping up even low-volume exports after the start of the Iran-Iraq war, as a consequence of hostile Iraqi activities such as bombing oil facilities.[29] Global demand for crude oil stabilized, with total consumption growing meagrely from 57.83 mn b/d in 1982 to 63.2 mn b/d by 1988, at an annual rate of less than one per cent each year.[30] The unit price for crude oil on the international market also fell markedly in the period, from $31.80 per barrel for spot Arabian light/Dubai in 1982 to $13.22 per barrel in 1988. The combined effects of these adverse factors was that Iranian oil production fell over that same period from 2.41 mn b/d to 2.265 mn b/d. Oil revenues dropped from more than $20 bn to less than $13 bn a year over the period, without taking into account the deteriorating Iranian purchasing power in overseas markets.

The rapid rate of growth of the economy which characterized the years 1965–78 faded away and, other than a slight rise in the value of national output in 1983, real national income fell throughout the period. All the forces working towards 'modernization' or 'Westernization' of the Iranian economy in the period of rapid growth were eliminated or much reduced, thereby leaving the bazaar to operate in a restored traditional society and economy. The fortunes of the Iranian bazaars were thus separated from those of most other oil-exporting states during the 1980s. While traditional *suqs* were made redundant elsewhere in the oil-rich states of the Persian Gulf and North Africa, Iranian bazaars enjoyed a form of restored prosperity.

Conclusion

Bazaars survive and thrive only where certain given conditions apply. It is suggested here that three principles are at stake. First, that international, domestic wholesale and domestic retail trading activities are left in the private sector. Where interventions by governments occur in these areas, the bazaar seems to suffer. In the observed case of Tripoli, Libya, total nationalization of trade meant total loss of the country's principal *suq*. Second, bazaars appear to thrive best in third-world economic conditions, where modernization and Westernization of sales and consumption patterns have not advanced and modern financial services are poorly represented. It is an interesting fact that rich oil-exporters other than Iran have all but lost their bazaar systems. Third, that the existing bazaars have a self-generating economic drive within their own structure in the form of the manufacture of handicrafts or the control of agricultural products and other items in international or local demand. Carpets from Tehran, gold jewellery from Damascus, and morocco leather from Marrakesh are examples of this.

It might also be concluded that, economic factors aside, those societies which still have a vibrant bazaar culture, with all its human colour, noise and bustle, are far richer than those who have, in the process of 'modernization', lost their traditional central markets.[31] Iran would not have the same attraction if the vigorous trade of the bazaars were to be extinguished.

Notes

1. Gustav E.Von Grunebaum, *Islam: Essays in the Nature and Growth of a Cultural Tradition* (2nd edn, London: Routledge & Kegan Paul, 1955), and *Islam and Medieval Hellenism: Social and Cultural Perspectives* (London: Variorum Reprints, 1976); J.H.G.Lebon, 'The Islamic city in the Near East', *Town Planning Review* 41 (2), 1970, pp. 179–194; Xavier de Planhol, *The World of Islam* (Ithaca: Cornell University Press, 1959).

2. Cf. *inter alia* the writings of J.Abu-Lughod, an assailant of the orientalists and others, whose class-based synthesis questioned whether the Islamic city was different in any dimension of principle from other cities. She concluded that the very concept of the Islamic city was created in the colonialist countries, principally France, as a means of demeaning peoples of the Muslim world. See her 'What is Islamic about a city? Some comparative reflections', *Proceedings of the International Conference on Urbanism in Islam* (Tokyo, mimeo, 1989), Vol. 1, pp. 194–217. An apparent retraction of her original views appears to flavour her most comprehensive critique ('The Islamic city: historic myth, Islamic essence and contemporary relevance', *IJMES* 19, 1987, pp. 155–76). Others have not been slow to attack the orientalists, often in the caricature rather than the philosophical substance; see e.g. D.F. Eickelman, 'Is there an Islamic city? The making of a quarter in a Moroccan town', *IJMES* 5, 1974, pp. 274–94, and *The Middle East: An Anthropological Approach* (2nd edn, Englewood Cliffs: Prentice-Hall, 1989), pp. 100ff.

3. Cf. E.Ehlers, 'The city of the Islamic Middle East', in E.Ehlers (ed.) *Modelling the City—Cross-Cultural Perspectives* (Colloquium Geographicum 22, Bonn: Ferd. Dummlers Verlag, 1992), pp. 89–107; B.S.Hakim, *Arabic-Islamic Cities: Building and Planning Principles* (London: KPI, 1986), esp. Chapter 1, pp. 15–54.

4. See essays in L.C.Brown (ed.), *From Madina to Metropolis* (Princeton, NJ: Darwin Press, 1973).

5. A.Hourani, *A History of the Arab Peoples* (London: Faber & Faber, 1991), p. 113.

6. Darwent, for example, described how poor road access across wadi systems limited the movement of melons to market in Mashhad: D.Darwent, 'Urban Growth in Relation to Socio-Economic Development and Westernization: a Case Study of the City of Mashed', unpublished PhD thesis, University of Durham, 1966.

7. M.E.Bonine, 'Bazaar', *Encyclopaedia Iranica* 4, 1990, pp. 21–5.

8. Bonine, 'Bazaar'.

9. E.Pakravan, *Vieux Teheran* (Tehran: Private, 1962); Darwent, Urban Growth; *P.Vielle, Abadan:Tissue urbain, attitudes et valeurs* (Tehran: Institute for Social Studies and Research, 1965); P.W.English, *Kerman: City and Village in Iran* (Madison: University of Wisconsin Press, 1966).

10. M.E.Bonine, *Yazd and its Hinterland: A Central Place System of Dominance in the Central Iranian Plateau* (Marburger Geographische Schriften No. 82, Marburg/Lahn: Universität Marburg, 1980); J.I.Clarke, *The Iranian City of Shiraz* (Durham: University of Durham, 1963); J.I.Clarke and B.D.Clark, *Kermanshah: An Iranian Provincial City* (Durham: University of Durham, 1969); V.F.Costello, *Urbanisation in the Middle East* (Cambridge; Cambridge University Press, 1977).

11. See K.S.McLachlan, 'Tripoli and Tripolitania: conflict and cohesion during the period of the Barbary corsairs', in *Settlement and Conflict in the Mediterranean World, Journal of the Institute of British Geographers* 3(3), 1978, pp.285–94, and 'Tripoli—city, oasis and hinterland: reflections on the old city 1551 to the present', *Libyan Studies* (Ninth Annual Report of the British Institute for Libyan Studies, London), 1978, pp. 53–4.

12. English, *Kerman;* Bonine, *Yazd.*

13. E.Ehlers, 'Rentkapitalismus und Stadtentwicklung im islamischen Orient, Beispiel: Iran', *Erdkunde* 32, 1978, pp. 124–42.

14. J.Rajai, 'The Merchants of the Tehran Bazaar', DPhil. thesis, Oxford University, 1978.

15. G.Marçais, 'La conception des villes dans l'Islam', *Revue d'Alger* 2, 1945, pp. 517–33, and 'L'Islamisme et la vie urbaine', *Comptes Rendus* (Paris: l'Académie des Inscriptions et Belles Lettres, 1928), pp. 86–100; L. Massignon, 'Les Corps de Métiers et la Cité Islamique', *Revue Internationale de Sociologie* 28, 1920, pp. 473–89.

16. F.S.Fanselow, 'Bizarre economies', *Geographical Magazine,* May 1992, p. 16.

17. See Darwent, 'Urban Growth'.

18. Fanselow, 'Bizarre economies', p. 19.

19. G.Myrdal, *Asian Drama* (Harmondsworth: Penguin, 1972), pp. 240–1.

20. Figure derived from studies of returns to capital in Iran on loans to farmers in the period 1963–78. It reinforces similar figures given by land-owners who borrowed money in the Tehran bazaar at that time.

21. The matter is looked at in some detail by Fanselow, 'Bizarre economies', p. 16.

22. Fanselow, 'Bizarre economies', p. 16.

23. In 1964, for example, when shopping in the Kabul bazaar, I frequented one particular merchant who acted as changing house for the British.

24. The World Bank suggested an adult illiteracy rate of 46 per cent in 1990 (*World Development Report 1993,* Oxford University Press, p. 239).

25. A.K.S.Lambton, *The Persian Land Reform, 1962–66* (Oxford: Clarendon Press, 1969), pp. 291–2.

26. There is little field research available in this area. Any discussion of the issue here must therefore be extremely tentative. The judgement implicit in the analysis is based on the nature of the expatriate Iranian population rather than on observation of the far larger residual community now in Iran. Serious conclusions in this matter will have to await sociological and economic field research in the future.

27. One official of the Central Bank of Iran, interviewed by the author in June 1994, suggested that the bazaar merchants held upwards of $40 bn in assets abroad.

28. Economist Intelligence Unit, *Iran: Country Profile* (London, 1994).

29. E.G.H.Joffé and K.S.McLachlan, *The Iran-Iraq War* (London: Economist Publications, 1985).

30. *BP Statistical Review of World Energy* (London: British Petroleum plc, 1993), p. 8.

31. St John Gould notes the problem of loss of urban identity and character in contemporary Marrakesh: 'Marrakesh, a modern city?' in J.-F.Troin (ed.) *Urban Research in the Middle East: Comparative Approaches by German, British and French Geographers* (Tours: URBAMA, 1993), pp. 17–33.

Chapter 13
The Political Significance of the Bazaar in Iran
Mahmoud Abdullahzadeh

Among the institutions which form the foundation of Islamic civilization is the bazaar. The study of the bazaar in the Muslim world is highly rewarding and brings to light the interesting story that elucidates how people of different beliefs and divergent views of trade and commerce came closer to create a social environment in which bazaars became centres not only of trade but also of culture. In the world of Islam, the bazaar is marked by historical continuity, resilience and inner dynamism, and has played and continues to play, though on a diminished scale in some places, a significant role.

The expansion of bazaars came with the growth of urbanization in the Islamic world, and it can be said that the bazaar became a necessary but distinct quarter of the Islamic city. The famous cities of Khorasan, Bokhara, Samarqand, Isfahan and others attained international fame for their flourishing and splendid bazaars.

Perhaps as a unique institution in the world of Islam, the bazaar reflects an interesting Islamic ethos which admits of no disjunction between religious and secular pursuits. The bazaar has served a multiplicity of functions such as economic, social, cultural and religious. In addition to these, the bazaar has also served literary, academic, and in the particular case of Iran, political functions. The economic function of the bazaar hardly needs elaboration. In many parts of the Islamic world bazaars still operate as the nerve centre of the economy while providing employment for a large section of the population.

The main social function of the bazaar has been the interaction not only among the different sections of the urban population but also between peasants and pastoralists and townsmen. The bazaar has also served as an effective vehicle for communication and social mobilization. The Prophet at times utilized the bazaar to disseminate Islamic teachings. The Iranian bazaar was the most important outlet for the propagation of Imam Khomeini's religious and revolutionary ideas in the recent past. The bazaar has retained its religious function in many parts of the Islamic world where it is a source of income for the maintenance of mosques, religious schools and charitable organizations. The cultural function of the bazaar can be best seen in India, where the bazaar served as an important mechanism for the formation and dissemination of a composite cultural heritage.[1] Bazaars of the medieval period, like the bazaar of Ukaz, provided an exciting opportunity to poets and genealogists, among others, to demonstrate their literary, oratorical and other skills. Calligraphers, scribes and copiers, as well as book-sellers and binders, had their respectable place in the bazaar.

By comparison with the other functions, however, the political function of the bazaar in many parts of the Muslim world has been minimal except in Iran, where the bazaar has had a distinctive place in socio-political movements.

The bazaar in Iran

It is hard to think of a time when bazaars were not a part of the urban civilization of Iran. Yet, some of the major Iranian cities either did not exist before the advent of Islam or were comparatively small. There were fortified points on caravan routes, which had walled areas with some few thousand inhabitants, but it would not be realistic to call them cities.

After the Arab invasion of the seventh century, true cities began to appear around these fortified points in many parts of Iran. The growth of these cities marked the beginning of substantial commercial activity. Therefore, the expansion of small centres of trade into major bazaars took place in the process of urbanization. According to the medieval Arab geographers, mosques and major government buildings as well as bazaars appeared in the outskirts of major cities like Ray, Nishapur and Isfahan. But this pattern cannot be generalized, as it also appears that some other famous bazaars evolved within city walls such as those at Tehran, Tabriz, Isfahan.[2]

In the Safavid period the bazaar, embodying the totality of merchants and guilds, along with the ulama, gradually became a source of power. The relationship between commercial life and the ulama, which continues in Iran up to the present day, could be traced to the late tenth century when a fundamental change in status took place for at least some of the ulama. They left their workbenches and established themselves in the bazaars as merchants or brokers. Trade began to blossom and hence the ulama gained power and status. Most probably the ulama's desire to travel in search of religious knowledge also equipped them with the knowledge and contacts to go into commercial activities in a substantial manner. The burgeoning of ulama-related merchant activity in Iran at the end of the fourth Islamic century had no parallel in the Arab lands.

The political role of the bazaar: the Tobacco Rebellion

Socio-economic changes in urban life in Iran, which had begun in the late nineteenth century, had a crucial impact on the bazaar. With the rapid growth of Iranian foreign trade, and the increasing influence of foreigners in commercial activities, the need to create a new apparatus to protect the interests of merchants became apparent.

During the reign of Naser ad-Din Shah, his Prime Minister, Moshir ad-Douleh, formed a new Ministry of Commerce and Agriculture in 1872. The task of this newly created organ was to protect merchants against encroachment on their rights by government officials, and also to facilitate trade in the country. In practice, this ministry turned out to be a corrupt body, extracting funds from merchants.[3]

Abbas Mirza Molk-Ara, the Shah's brother, who became Minister of Commerce and Agriculture, wrote in his memoirs that the lack of interest among government officials in dealing with the problem of commerce prompted merchants to complain to the Shah about the new ministry.[4] Subsequently the Shah dismissed the Minister and issued a decree establishing the Assembly of Merchants' Deputies (*Majles-e Vokala-ye Tojjar*) in 1883. Tehran merchants were quick to prepare a constitution for the assembly.[5]

Such an assembly, with the rights and powers demanded by the merchants, would have been a nuisance to the government, who succeeded in turning it into another tool of the authorities. Once again, merchants found themselves on the losing side and began to strengthen their alliance with the traditional forces, the ulama.

The first popular movement resulting from the alliance between the bazaar and the ulama was the Tobacco Rebellion of 1891–92. In 1890 Naser ad-Din Shah granted a 50-year tobacco concession to Major Talbot, a British subject. According to this concession, the production and sale of tobacco in all parts of the country became Talbot's monopoly. Merchants suddenly realized that they had become semi-employees of a foreign company, and that they would receive wages for selling its products.[6] By resorting to the ulama, the merchants succeeded in turning their economic conflict with the concession-hunting foreigners into a confrontation between Muslims and infidels.

Having received the merchants' demand, Ayatollah Mirza Hasan Shirazi issued a religious edict *(fatwa)*. It was short but effective: 'Smoking tobacco is the war against the Hidden Imam'. Interestingly enough, it was reported that the Shah's wives and his entourage also stopped smoking in order to show their religious duty to obey the fatwa.[7] The nationwide protest, mobilized by the ulama and merchants, culminated in the cancellation of the concession.[8] The merchants' defeat of the concession and eventually the government restrengthened the alliance between the bazaar and religious hierarchy.

The Shi'a religious establishment has always received financial support in the form of a voluntary tax called *sahm-e emam* (the Imam's share) paid by wealthy merchants. This system of financing has made the establishment independent of rulers and governments, but highly dependent on the bazaar. As an illustration of this, Ayatollah Motahhari writes that when Ayatollah Haj Sheikh 'Abd al-Karim Ha'eri, founder of *Houzeh-ye 'Elmiyeh-ye Qom* (Qom Religious Schools), decided that his students should learn foreign languages, a delegation of merchants from Tehran Bazaar went to Qom to tell him that they paid *sahm-e emam* to him as their religious duty but not to be spent on teaching the religious students the languages of the infidels. The merchants warned that if he carried on with his plan they would stop paying their religious dues. Implementing his scheme, the Ayatollah realized, would put the merchants' financial support in jeopardy. He therefore conceded their demands.[9]

The bazaar in the twentieth century

A decade later the bazaar played an even more significant role during the Constitutional Revolution of 1905–6. The bazaaris once again allied with the ulama in opposing Qajar governments which had limited their economic and political power for the benefit of concession-hunting foreigners. At last, Mozaffar ad-Din Shah was forced to grant the demands of the people to establish first a 'House of Justice' and finally the Constitution of 1906.

Threatened by social changes inside Iran and foreign economic competition, the bazaar did not stop opposing secular governments. It is claimed that the bazaar opposed Reza Khan's republican movement in 1921 apparently because the ulama-bazaar alliance feared that he would abolish the constitution and establish a dictatorship.

During the oil nationalization campaign in the 1950s, the bazaar, through Majma'-e Mosalmanan-e Mojahed, a group close to Ayatollah Kashani and led by Shams Qanatabadi, supported Mosaddeq's government. To show their solidarity with the government, the bazaaris bought National Loan Bills and almost doubled exports (from 4,390 to 8,425 billion rials) between 1951 and 1953, during the two years that Iranian oil was boycotted. Later, Kashani fell out with Mosaddeq and a large section of the bazaar subsequently deserted him too. After the coup of 1953, Qanatabadi changed side and joined the Shah's camp.

Feeling psychologically and economically insecure in the years after the coup, the bazaar once more tried to regain respect. In 1963, Ashura, the tenth day of the Arabic lunar month of Moharram (commemorating the martyrdom of Imam Hosein some fourteen centuries earlier), fell on 15th Khordad of the Persian calendar (5 June). The bazaar chose that day to launch a severe counterattack on the Shah's regime. Five months earlier in the holy city of Qom, the Shah had strongly criticized the ulama and the bazaaris. Referring to a demonstration which had taken place in the Tehran Bazaar a few days earlier, after Ayatollah Khomeini's declaration of support for the bazaar against the formation of cooperatives, the Shah said: 'they (the ulama) were the same persons who sent a small ridiculous group, a handful of stupid bearded bazaaris into the streets to make a noise'.[10]

After two days of rioting in Tehran, the ulama-bazaar alliance failed to topple the regime, perhaps because of a lack of adequate political organization. Ayatollah Khomeini was sent into exile in Iraq, but his supporters, bazaaris in particular, began regrouping in small secret societies which eventually coalesced under the name of *Jam'iyat-e hei'at-ha-ye mo'talefeh-ye Eslami*. This politically motivated religious organization, formed in 1960 to topple the Shah's regime by armed struggle, was charged with carrying out the movement. In 1964 a number of prominent leaders of the group were arrested and executed following the assassination of Prime Minister Hasan 'Ali Mansur by a young activist, Bokhara'i.[11]

As the 1960s gave way to the 1970s, pressure on the bazaaris increased. Government policies had further alienated the ulama and bazaaris, who felt that the triumph of an Islamic Revolution would restore their status. They were proved right. During the Islamic Revolution of 1978–79, the bazaar stepped up its campaign against the Shah's regime, and generously financed the Revolution. Meanwhile, Imam Khomeini's leadership assured the bazaaris that under an Islamic system they would regain their economic prosperity and cultural identity.[12]

To establish their hegemony in post-revolutionary Iran, the bazaari members of the *Jam'iyat,* together with clerics of the Islamic-Republic Party, campaigned against the liberals under the then president Abol-Hasan Bani Sadr. When other Islamic segments of the bazaar, such as the pro-Mojahedin 'Traders Touhidi Guild' and the liberal 'Society of Islamic Association' joined the Bani Sadr camp, *Jam'iyat's* fears of losing to the other side increased. On 8 March 1981 the clerics, allied with the *Jam'iyat,* called for a closure of the bazaar in protest at Bani Sadr's attack on the Islamic Republic Party at Tehran University a few days earlier. Bani Sadr, in return, asked his bazaari camp to remain open. A chaotic situation prevailed, some shops were shut while others remained open. Neither side could claim victory. Meanwhile Imam Khomeini, who was witnessing these developments, felt that he might lose his grip over the bazaar by allowing the situation to continue, as he believed that the call for closure of the bazaar could only be decreed by the *Marja'-e taqlid,* in this case only himself. To end this 'calamity', as he branded the conflict, on 21 June 1981 Imam Khomeini dismissed President Bani Sadr, because he could not afford to alienate the other camp —the clerics and the *Jam'iyat.* Immediately after the President's dismissal, bazaaris who had supported him and the Mojahidin were executed for counter-revolutionary activity.

By the end of June 1981, the *Jam'iyat* and its clerical allies had established their authority in the bazaar. But they had greater designs for the future.

Summary

Social changes and urban developments, especially in big cities and particularly in Tehran, have undoubtedly altered the traditional characteristics of the bazaar, but its cultural totality still remains relatively intact. Today the bazaaris do not feel threatened by the spread of shops and superstores outside the bazaar, a complaint of their predecessors under the Shah's regime. A highly influential member of the bazaar writes: 'The bazaar and bazaaris are now on the side of the government, and have the same importance and fundamental role. Should they turn against the government and begin hostility, it will become apparent that they are more powerful than in the past.'[13]

Notes

1. Tara Chand, *Influence of Islam on Indian Culture* (Allahabad: Indian Press, 1936).

2. Michael E.Bonine, 'Bazaar', in *Encydopedia* Iranica, Vol. 4, p. 21.

3. Ahmad Ashraf, *Mavane'-e Tarikhi-ye Roshd-e Sarmayadari dar Iran, Doureh-ye Qajariyeh* (Tehran: Zamineh, 1359/1981), p. 107.

4. 'Abbas Mirza Molk-Ara, *Sharh-e Hal-e 'Abbas Mirza Molk-Ara,* (ed.) A.H. Nava'i (Tehran: Babak, 1361/1982) pp. 167–9.

5. Fereydun Adamiyat and Homa Nateq, *Afkar-e Ejtema 'i va Siyasi va Eqtesadi dar Asar-e Montasher Nashodeh-ye Douran-e Qajar* (Tehran: Agah, 1356/1977), pp. 312–20.

6. Firuz Kazemzadeh, *Rus va Inglis dar Iran* (Tehran: Ketabha-ye Jibi, 1354/1975), p. 232.

7. Sheikh Hasan Karbala'i, *Qarardad-e Rezhi-ye 1890 M, ya Tarikh-e Enhesar-e Dokhaniyat dar Sal-e 1309 HQ* (2nd edn; Tehran: Mobarezan, n.d.), p. 70.

8. Ervand Abrahamian, *Iran Between Two Revolutions* (Princeton, NJ: Princeton University Press, 1982), p. 73.

9. Mortaza Motahhari, *Moshkel-e Asasi dar Sazman-e Rouhaniyat* (n.pl.: n.pub., n.d.), pp. 187–8.

10. *Kayhan,* 24 January 1963. B.Afrasiyabi, *Iran va Tarikh* (Tehran: Zarrin, 1364/1985), pp. 324–40.

11. A.Badamchian *et al., Hei'at-ha-ye Mo'talefeh-ye Eslami* (Tehran: Ouj, 1362/1983). The monthly organ of this organization, called *Enteqam* (Revenge), was circulated among the bazaaris, students, and clergymen. Its other publications were in the form of leaflets which were collected after members had read them. The group liaised with Ayatollah Khomeini in exile through Ayatollah Mortaza Motahhari, Ayatollah Beheshti (both murdered after the Islamic Revolution), and 'Ali Golkadeh Ghafuri. Mohammad Javad Bahonar, who became Prime Minister in the early years of the Revolution and was later killed in a bomb attack, had been the co-ordinator of the group while Sheikh 'Ali Akbar Hashemi Rafsanjani, later President, acted as the speaker of the *Jam'iyat.*

12. Misagh Parsa, *Social Origins of the Iranian Revolution* (New Brunswick: Rutgers University Press, 1989), pp. 260–75.

13. A.Badamchian, 'Tarikh-e siyasi va ejtema'i-ye douran-e akher va bazaar' ('The political and social history of recent times and the bazaar'), paper presented for the Bazaar Colloquium, Tabriz, September, 1993.

Chapter 14
The Impact of Oil Wealth on Traditional Technologies in Rural Oman
Roderic W.Dutton

Rural Oman before oil

Oman is a Muslim and Arab country at the eastern extremity of the Arabian Peninsula. In an area the size of Britain, Oman has a population of approximately 1.5 million people (according to the census of December 1993). Separated from Saudi Arabia by the forbiddingly arid Empty Quarter, Oman borders the Indian Ocean and has many cultural links derived from the Indian sub-continent and from East Africa. Along the east-facing coastline there are communities involved in fishing and sea-faring. Inland there are widely scattered villages, whose agricultural economy was traditionally based on the date palm, and large areas of plains and deserts sparsely occupied by pastoralists. All of the above have made their contributions to Oman's traditional technologies and artisanal heritage.

Until recent decades Oman's rural communities remained fairly isolated from material and social changes in the rest of the world. Oman was a very poor country, and its leader, Sultan Sa'id bin Taimur, preferred to balance the books rather than modernize the nation through extensive overseas borrowing. It was also very difficult for foreigners even to visit the country, and if its citizens migrated overseas for work or to take up opportunities for higher education they were banned from re-entry. Thus the country did not modernize its health or education services, nor did it develop any aspect of a modern twentieth-century system of communications. Outside Muscat there were no schools (apart from village Koranic schools) or hospitals or surfaced roads, and only a few vehicles. Very few material goods were imported, apart from basic foodstuffs such as rice and coffee, cotton yarn and cotton cloth.[1] People had a simple and repetitive diet (based on rice, wheat, dates and fish), life expectancy was low and infant mortality high. Thus life in rural Oman was harsh. People lived only where they could gain local access to scarce water supplies, which were themselves dependent on a local rainfall that was low and highly unpredictable.

On the other hand, rural communities in Oman had qualities whose virtues are increasingly appreciated in those parts of the world where they are long gone. There were deeply held cultural traditions combined with great tolerance towards different customs and beliefs held by visitors to the country. The sense of family was very strong, and people were almost totally honest in their dealings with each other and in their respect for other people's property.

Internationally, in recent years, it has become fashionable to talk of concepts such as 'conservation of the environment' and 'sustainable development'. Rural Oman practised these concepts to the full. The village and pastoral communities followed a way of life which had changed but little over a very long period of time, and therefore had proved itself to be sustainable. The members of the communities were highly interdependent and, as a corollary, had a high level of independence from the outside world. Responsibility for maintaining the community was thrown on to its members. A high proportion of food and other material requirements was grown or manufactured by members of the community, making full use of local resources and developing the necessary technical skills to undertake the work involved. Also, the communities took responsibility for their own education and training and their spiritual well-being.

The role of village technologies

The skills employed in the processing of basic resources resulted in the practice of a wide range of village technologies. Collectively the products played a central role in the rural economy and domestic life and drew upon a great variety of raw materials, both local and imported. Of local origin, date palms, livestock and clay were of particular significance, but imported metals and fabrics were essential as well. Some of the work was undertaken by full-time specialists, including weavers, silversmiths and potters, but a large number of people practised other skills on a part-time basis. The latter skills included spinning, the manufacture of palm-frond products and the processing of milk. Some skills were practised by specialists and non-specialists alike. Weaving and the tanning and sewing of leather are good examples—the larger villages had weavers and a tanner *(shammar),* but also members of most pastoralist households knew how to tan leather and sew milk churns, and many women in the households knew how to weave.[2]

As a source of materials the date palm was of particular interest, as most parts of the palm were used to make a wide range of basic goods. Apart from dates, the palm yielded fronds with a long, straight midrib, a butt, long, tough leaflets and sheets of fibre. The fronds were primarily tied side-by-side to make sheets of *barusti* for constructing the walls and roofs of houses. They were also tied together to form the hull and deck of a very versatile float-boat *(shasha),* peculiar to Oman and very important as a small fishing boat on Oman's Batina coast. Rope made from palm fibre was used to bind together the fronds which formed the hull of the float-boat. The same rope was also used in the manufacture of *barusti* sheets, and in many other ways. From the palm leaflets were plaited endless braids which were subsequently sewn edge-to-edge to make a very wide range of mats, baskets and bags. The palm trunks themselves were skilfully split to provide timbers for house construction and, in the Rostaq region., lengths of trunk were hollowed out to form beehives.

Omanis have always kept livestock, either in small numbers in the village houses or in large numbers on the plains or mountains. Apart from meat, livestock of course yield skins, wool, hair and milk, all of which have formed the raw materials of other craft skills. Skins have long been tanned according to complex and locally evolved techniques using the pods of the *garata* tree, *Acacia nilotica,* as a source of tannin. The *shammar* not only tanned the skins but also, for the farming community, fashioned them into huge leather buckets *(dellu)* used for raising irrigation water. The *shammar* or individual householders also sewed other skins into milk churns for owners of cows, and leather water containers for pastoralists. For more general usage, sheepskin rugs, sandals and belts were also manufactured. As for the wool and hair, this has long been spun by both men and women into a wide range of products including tents, rugs, bags and donkey and camel trappings and harness. Milk was treated and churned in many households to produce both *leben* and butter.

Other Omani village technologies are related to Oman's use of the sea. All types of craft, from large ocean-going trading ships to the float-boats mentioned above, were made in various coastal villages. Additionally, traditional and modern forms of fishing traps are (or were) made, and fish was preserved by skilled drying and salting.

Local natural resources formed the material basis of other technologies. Regional potteries made a very wide variety of vessels, including beakers, water-cooling jars, large water-storage jars up to a metre high, and pots for storing dates. Carpenters in most villages were skilled at using the indigenous trees in the manufacture of doors, window frames, ox ploughs, well heads and the framework of the plank boats. Other artisans were skilled in such crafts as making gypsum cement and in making and using paints from local ores. Teams of builders made *barusti* houses on the coast, and mudbrick or stone houses in the interior plains and on the mountains.

Finally, other village technologists were dependent on imported raw materials, notably the weavers of cotton cloth, who used imported Indian yarn, and the metal smiths who made copper vessels and silver and gold jewellery. Village blacksmiths working with old car springs and other scrap metal were responsible for the manufacture of tools used by the farmers, including ploughshares, sickles, hoes, diggers and palm-trimming knives.

The products of the village technologists were almost all essentially functional in character. The exceptions to this rule were a few products of the silversmiths, notably the decoration of the ceremonial knives *(khanjar),* which were valued more for their aesthetic appeal than their practical value. Normally the village technologists provided the range of basic tools, equipment and goods which were of key importance for the primary producers and for domestic life.

However, the practice of these technologies also had a more profound set of economic, social and environmental values to the community. The local manufacture and usage of goods, from available natural raw materials and from the produce of agriculture and fisheries, created those multiple linkages in the social networks which are one of the basic elements of community structure. The practitioners of float-boat making, for example, linked the farmers with the fishermen, in mutual dependence, by using the date-palm fronds grown by the farmers to make the basic fishing vessel on which the fishermen depended. Similarly, the makers of *barusti* sheets, the framework of houses, beehives from hollowed palm logs, and baskets, bags and mats, linked the farmers with householders, beekeepers and the general village population by making so many products essential to their daily lives. The village skills which permitted the manufacture of leather products as diverse as huge leather *dellu,* milk churns and sandals, made farmers, milk processors and the general public inter-dependent with the pastoralists for much more than meat. And the fact that the population as a whole was completely dependent on its natural resources for mud-bricks and plaster, gypsum cement and paint, storage pots and utensils and many products manufactured from indigenous trees, made the people naturally aware from childhood of the need for conservation and protection of their environment.

Thus the village technologies were practised by a large number of skilled and mutually respected people who were essential to the survival of their community. The artisans also created a sense of inter-dependence and self-reliance. They therefore played an important role in maintaining social cohesion and in protecting the community from unnecessary types and levels of dependence on the outside world. Additionally they minimized the need for imports by fully utilizing local materials, while at the same time creating some exports. Furthermore, they provided skilled work for the old and infirm, thereby giving them an active role within the community.

The special case of the *aflaj*

In many parts of the world, technologies have been devised for digging near-horizontal galleries into hillsides down to the water table, so that the water then drains by gravity to the surface, where it is used for all village requirements including crop irrigation. The water flows continuously, 24 hours a day, and its distribution between the farms as well as the maintenance and repair of the gallery demand a sophisticated system of organization. In Oman the whole system of construction, operation and maintenance is known as *a falaj* (pl. aflaj). The *aflaj* supply water to a community, not to an individual, and therefore intricate and complex systems for sharing the responsibility for water distribution and of *falaj* upkeep have evolved on a community basis. Thousands of these communal water-supply systems have been built at different periods of Oman's history,[3] and in the early 1980s it was estimated that they delivered to the surface some 75 per cent of the groundwater consumed in the country. The *aflaj* had (and still retain) many strengths. The water was generally of very good (or good) and near constant chemical quality. There was no possibility of endangering the water table,[4] in contrast with wells which are easily deepened. Water is brought to the ground surface by gravity, and therefore without any pumping costs. Village falaj land is long nurtured and of good quality. Villages are a model of crop water use prioritization: when water is in short supply it is, in order, cut from seasonal, annual and perennial horticultural and field crops, so preserving at least some water for the date palms. The *aflaj* management system is also the best example of cooperative water management in Oman. It is a model of self-funding and self-help and could form the basis of future local water management organizations.[5]

Impact of oil on rural Omani traditional technologies

Oil began to affect rural Oman some three decades before it was first discovered in commercial quantities in Oman itself. The discovery of oil in Bahrain in 1934 led to a partial replacement of its rural labour force by Omanis who came to work in the date gardens. Later other Omanis found work in Saudi Arabia, and during the 1960s they migrated in much larger numbers into Abu Dhabi and the Emirates when oil was exported from there. Surveys undertaken during the early 1970s revealed that a high proportion of the most active age group of men was employed outside their villages, often outside Oman in the Gulf States. Only rarely did they use their inherited village technology skills, and in consequence skilled and experienced rural producers were being turned into a raw and largely unskilled labour force. Any new skills they learned, in the army or police force or the oil industry, were mostly irrelevant to increasing the productive capacity of their villages. An ever-higher percentage of village wealth was being created in the form of salaries earned elsewhere.

A growing proportion of the new remittance income was spent on goods manufactured overseas. Items like pump-sets showed a willingness to invest in the future of agriculture and therefore a continuing commitment to village life. Other major items of agricultural or fishing equipment, such as tractors or aluminium and fibreglass fishing boats, were often provided by the government, heavily subsidized, with the aim of modernizing the industry and stimulating production. But all this capital equipment directly or indirectly replaced equivalent equipment which had previously been manufactured locally. Thus, on the Batina coast, the pump-sets replaced the *zajira* as the means of lifting water from the shallow water table for irrigation. But the *zajira,* of which there was at least one on every small farm, were a product of many complementary technologies: carpentry to make the frame and wheels, leather workers to make the *dellu* water bucket, and rope makers to twist the date-palm fibre into the various ropes that linked the bull to the *dellu*. Skilled artisans had devoted their lives to perfecting these technologies, but within the space of a few years all of them were rendered unemployed unless they left their homes and their villages and joined the ranks of unskilled labour in the armed forces or in the Gulf.

Tractors, provided through the new extension services, were very heavily subsidized. They therefore acted in direct and completely unfair competition with the traditional ox-ploughs. Thus the plough makers, the blacksmith who made the share and the ploughman who trained his bulls to the plough (and the bulls themselves) all became de-skilled and unemployed within a few years, and this in spite of the fact that their operation was much more cost effective than the tractors in the restricted fields in which they worked.

Similarly the many highly-skilled people who had made the great range of boats, from the simple float-boat mentioned above to the plank-built fishing boats and the large ocean-going *beden,* were deskilled. Oil wealth led to such a rapid, all-embracing and profound change in rural Oman that the traditional industries had no time to adapt to changing circumstances—they were simply swept aside, together with the people who practised them. It is paradoxical that the government efforts to assist the agriculture and fishing industries led to the demise of many of the village technologies. While the government at least thought about the needs of farmers and fishermen, the needs of the village technologists always seemed to escape their notice.

Many other new imports directly replaced goods that had previously been produced locally. The list of new purchases included plastic sandals, woollen rugs, cement for concrete blocks, timber, plywood, brushes, buckets, rope, beakers, water pots and storage jars and a range of small agricultural and fishing implements. These kinds of imports undermined the village technologies and therefore wasted local raw materials, ended the interdependence and mutual self-reliance of members of the community, and made the community as a whole unnecessarily dependent on a very uncertain outside world. In the case of things like rope and mat making, they reduced the opportunities for the old and disabled to be active and self-sufficient members of the village. Furthermore, because the villagers were much less dependent than previously on the natural resources of their own environment they rapidly lost their inherited commitment to conserve them and use them in a sustainable manner.

Oil and the *aflaj*

Much has been spoken and written about the *aflaj* in recent years. It is generally believed that a system of water management that has stood the test of time for 2,000 years must be good and will therefore continue into the indefinite future. It is assumed that the *falaj* serves the needs of the whole community in a reasonably efficient and equitable manner. But it must be remembered that when the *aflaj* were constructed, the falaj communities had only one possible source of water, so the people were constrained to act as a community even though the community was strongly hierarchical. Also, the community was largely self-reliant with a low demand for material goods and an acceptance of a simple diet. Under these conditions the *aflaj* thrived and sufficient money was earned by the system to pay for maintenance, repairs and extensions of the system, which were undertaken by skilled, specialist *falaj* technologists, the *awamir*.[6] However, since the advent of oil wealth and the opening up of the economy to the outside world which took place in 1970 when Sultan Qaboos came to power, the social, economic and technological context in which the *aflaj* have had to operate has radically altered, in the following ways. Diesel and electric pumps have provided an alternative means for raising relatively large volumes of water. The *falaj* communities are no longer self-reliant— the demand for varied foods and material goods has far outstripped the potential of the *falaj* village to provide. A very high proportion of village money is remitted from workplaces elsewhere, which means that people are no longer constrained to work together for the common good, so those low in the hierarchy (but with new remittance wealth) have broken free from the constraints of the *falaj* system and sunk their own private wells. Also, the *awamir,* unable to force up their fees for *falaj* work because of cheap imported labour, have taken to other occupations.

These changes have taken place so rapidly that there has been no time, immediate incentive, or opportunity to learn new knowledge to modify the system in order to take advantage of new technologies and crop demands and so keep the *aflaj* socially and economically viable. Thus the traditional *falaj* system has been severely undermined. A key technical question is the traditional eight-day cycle of water to each farm.[7] Water delivered at this interval was suitable for winter wheat, alfalfa (with its very deep roots) and date palms. Wheat is no longer grown, however, thanks to cheap Australian imports, date palms are uneconomic, and alfalfa is a very costly way of using water if one considers that the ultimate demand is food for human consumption. An on-demand system of water distribution is required for a whole new range of horticultural and other crops that are now eaten in Oman and are of high value. The technical changes needed are relatively simple (though they would create some problematic social issues needing resolution), but the necessary combination of time, knowledge and incentive to make the changes, as mentioned above, has not in practice been present. Therefore the *aflaj* throughout Oman are in rapid decline.

Does the demise of village technologies matter?

Perhaps the most important loss resulting from the demise of so many of the village technologies has been the loss of the whole notion that it is possible and respectable for Omani villagers to be highly-skilled artisans. The oil changes came so rapidly that there was no time or obvious motivation to modify or modernize traditional expertise, or to graft new skills on to old ones. Yet Oman, apart from its relatively short-lived oil resources, is a poor country, and, in the not-too-distant future, rural technological skills will be essential to rural survival. Their loss is also important because it has broken the link between the people and their environment. The value of environmental resources is no longer understood, and so the resources are no longer respected. For example, indigenous trees are cut and uprooted because they are now deemed irrelevant to present-day living.

The decline of the *aflaj* system matters for many inter-related reasons, particularly now that water in Oman is becoming a scarce commodity relative to the size of the population, which is rapidly growing, and to its greatly increased consumption per head of population thanks to the widespread use of pumps for irrigation and piped water in the towns. In Oman there is a need to use water with ever-increasing efficiency. Instead, in the falaj villages, the opposite is the case and an opportunity for change is being missed. Falaj water is normally of very good quality, but it is mainly being used to irrigate either uneconomic date palms, which will tolerate very poor water, or alfalfa, which is a very water-costly means of ultimately providing protein for people. The good-quality *falaj* water should be used to grow a wide range of high-value crops which demand good-quality water. If the crops provide an economic return, this will restore interest in, and provide money for, maintaining the system and introducing further beneficial change. Also, new technologies will have been introduced into the village repertoire which create more skilled employment and also the social bonds of inter-dependence mentioned above. Furthermore, a revitalized *falaj* system will also breath new life into the falaj committees and give them a new role, in partnership with the Ministry of Water Resources, for the long-term management of water, Oman's most precious resource.

In conclusion, the dominance of oil in the Omani economy, and the rapidity with which oil wealth permeated every facet of rural life after exports began in 1967, have led to the near-complete elimination of a great variety of traditional village technologies, and have severely impaired the *falaj* system. Many actions by the government to support the fishing and agricultural industries simply ignored the village technologies. New, and often unsuitable, technologies were introduced with heavy subsidies which competed unfairly with the old technologies and prevented any realistic possibility of their being updated to fit into the new economic circumstances. Thus the government has played a major though unwitting role in the decline of rural artisanal skills, which will be a real disadvantage as oil wealth and related opportunities for automatic government employment in the civil service and armed forces decline. The loss of most village technologies cannot now be reversed, but it is still not too late to update the falaj system,[8] though each year's delay is making the task more difficult.

Notes

1. R.W.Dutton, 'Interdependence, independence and rural development in Oman: the experience of the Khabura development project', *J. Oman Studies* 6 (2), 1983, pp. 317–27.

2. R.W.Dutton, 'Handicrafts in Oman and their role in rural community development', *Geoforum* 14 (3), 1983, pp. 341–52.

3. J.Wilkinson, *Water and Tribal Settlement in South-East Arabia* (Oxford Research Studies in Geography, Oxford: Clarendon Press, 1977), p. 276.

4. Y.P.Parks and P.J.Smith, 'Factors affecting the flow of aflaj in Oman: a modelling study', *J. Hydrology* 65, 1983, pp. 293–312.

5. *National Water Resources Master Plan: Volume 2—Main Report,* prepared for MWR by Mott MacDonald International Ltd in association with Watson Hawksley, December 1991.

6. J.S.Birks and S.E.Letts, 'The 'Awamir: specialist well and falaj diggers in northern interior Oman,' *J. Oman Studies* 2, 1976, pp. 93–100.

7. H.Bowen-Jones and R.W.Dutton (eds), *Research and Development Surveys in Northern Oman: Final Report Vol. IVa, Agriculture* (1982), p. 290.

8. R.W.Dutton, 'Towards a secure future for the aflaj in Oman', in The *Sukanate of Oman International Conference on Water Resources Management ind Arid Countries* (MWR, UNESCO, 1995), Vol. 1, pp. 16–24.

Index

Please note that illustrations are indicated by page numbers in italic print